Lyndall Gordon was born and grew up in Cape Town in the 1940s and 1950s. She studied at the University of Cape Town and Columbia University, and then taught in Oxford where she is now Senior Research Fellow at St Hilda's College. Her biographies include *Virginia Woolf: A Writer's Life* (winner of the James Tait Black Memorial Prize for Biography), *Charlotte Brontë: A Passionate Life* (winner of the Cheltenham Prize), *T. S. Eliot: An Imperfect Life* (winner of the British Academy's Rose Mary Crawshaw Prize), and *A Private Life of Henry James: Two Women and His Art*. A new, two-generational biography of Mary Wollstonecraft and her heirs is published by Little, Brown.

Also by Lyndall Gordon

T. S. ELIOT: AN IMPERFECT LIFE

VIRGINIA WOOLF: A WRITER'S LIFE

CHARLOTTE BRONTË: A PASSIONATE LIFE

HENRY JAMES: TWO WOMEN AND HIS ART

MARY WOLLSTONECRAFT: A NEW GENUS

Shared Lives

LYNDALL GORDON

Virago

A *Virago* Book

This edition published in Great Britain by Virago Press 2005
Reprinted 2005

First published in Great Britain by Bloomsbury Publishing Ltd 1992
Published in Great Britain by Vintage 1994

A CIP catalogue record for this book
is available from the British Library.

ISBN 1 84408 143 5

Typeset in Bembo by M Rules
Printed and bound in Great Britain
by Clays Ltd, St Ives plc

Virago Press
An imprint of
Time Warner Book Group UK
Brettenham House
Lancaster Place
London WC2E 7EN

www.virago.co.uk

For Anna and Olivia

List of illustrations

Page 1   'Ellie looked you in the eye, intent, as though what
          you said was of vital importance.' With Romy (right)
          in the summer 1966–7

Page 9   Annie Hoffman (seated) with her sisters, Betsie,
          Minnie, and Gertie, in 1910

Page 34   Standard 8, Good Hope Seminary, 1956. Front row:
          first left, Lyndall; second from the right, Flora; far
          right, Rosie

Page 66   Philip and Annie Press at Klawer in about 1920 in
          front of Klawer Hotel

Page 93   'Phillippa had no part in the gruesome.' Varsity Rag,
          1959 (with Robert in the background)

Page 126 Flora at her graduation from the University of Cape
          Town, in December 1961

Page 159 Romy as a bridesmaid, 1968

Page 203 Romy and Lyndall in January 1969 when Romy
          debated the question of marriage

Page 234 Rose as the vulnerable Dodo in *Sport of My Mad
          Mother*, a university production in 1961

Page 257 Winston and Romy on a visit to Cape Town, under
          the fig tree with Elizabeth Gevers in January 1976

Page 284 Ellie braving her illness, 1984

Page 326 Rosie Kunene and Romy looking alike a month
          before Romy died

Contents

	Preface	ix
1	Friends *(1954–76)*	1
2	Families *(1880s–1950s)*	9
3	School-days *(1954–58)*	34
4	Pasts *(1957, 1920s, 1894–1910)*	66
5	Experiments *(1958–59)*	93
6	Changes *(1959–62)*	126
7	Partners *(1963–68)*	159
8	Futures: I *(1968–69)*	203
9	Futures: II *(1969–72)*	234
10	Moves *(1973–76)*	257
11	Memories *(1976–89)*	284
12	Words *(January–April 1990)*	326

Preface

This revised memoir was written to recover three school friends who died young, and come to know what their friendship had meant and how the fifties had shaped us as women. By the end, their voices did feel close, but what I didn't foresee was the impossibility of sustaining those voices in quite the way they existed while writing this book. The loss that followed was more final because this memoir was no longer in the making.

It would be untrue to say that I never thought of publication, but it seemed at the time unlikely since the feelings of people who had loved these women might forbid it. I feared too that the doings of insignificant girls in so remote a place might be off the map. As it happened, it was accepted at once by Mary Cunnane at Norton, Liz Calder at Bloomsbury, and David Philip in Cape Town. With their understanding of Africa, David and Marie Philip were the perfect publishers to initiate this book, and I was honoured to be on the list of this pair who had carried on oppositional publishing through dark and dangerous years of apartheid. When I met them in December 1991, there had been a break-in at their publishing house. 'A little nothing,' said Marie. 'Damage? Theft? What's that compared with raids of the Special Branch who destroy whole runs of books?' As she and David took us round their garden, they pointed to where they discussed risky undertakings, since their home was bugged. Apartheid was still in place, but Mandela had been released and a new South Africa was about to be.

That was the political moment when this memoir was written, a time of transition, so that the situation in 1988 when I began had changed dramatically by the time it was completed in 1991. 'The

Struggle', the inescapable topic of South African writing from the 1940s to the 1990s, would soon end – local readers were already sighing at its predictability – which meant that different kinds of writing had to come into being. As apartheid ended, South Africans would have to start seeing themselves in relation to the rest of a world that had undergone a women's revolution in the seventies and eighties. This revolution had not penetrated the barriers that cut off our country for several decades, reinforced by a mentality of distance which, strangely, persists even now. To go from America or Europe to visit family in Cape Town was like going back to another age. South African men still behaved as in the fifties.

So it was that what I had conceived initially as an experiment in applying the methods of biography to the lives of the obscure, turned into an expatriate perspective on forms of female life produced in the fifties in that most twisted and rigid of societies. How should biography approach girls whose gifts for friendship had no public importance?

This memoir opened up new friendships with readers; in particular the writer Joan Smith all of whose feminist detective novels I had already enjoyed; Mary Dyson who had lived in Ethiopia and was then with the World Bank; Nicola Beauman who was to found Persephone Press; and the political activist Hilda Bernstein who had founded the first multiracial women's organization in our racist society, the Federation of South African Women, and told her own story of women's defiance as prisoners of the apartheid regime. Each of the readers who made contact had some story to share. A letter came from an Englishwoman, Anne Maxwell, who had left for Canada as a war bride before her husband could join her. She wrote vividly of her lone journey across a country that she had to make her own. Then there were letters from South African contemporaries like Sue MacGregor, and various men (one a London barrister filling me in about two of the characters) who had points of contact with the story I had to tell. Curiously, readers from very different places like the north of England or

New Zealand also conveyed a sense of kinship, even if younger or older. It has intrigued me that what we experienced as Jewish girls in the fifties embedded in the mindset of a colonial town could speak to other times, other places.

Many people who are part of this story helped to reconstruct it through their memories and photographs. I must thank Winston Rosenberg and Ronald Klein in particular, and also Shirley Gelcer for new details: an extraordinary dream she heard from Ellie and a letter from our friend Phillippa who was with Romy when she died. Some names were changed, and some elements fictionalized, but two central contributions can be identified: one by food writer Phillippa Cheifitz whose eye and artistry have helped make Cape Town as distinctive in spirit as in natural beauty, and the other by Sindiwe Magona whose novel *For My Children's Children*, set in the Cape Town of our divided generation, gripped me while writing this book. I heard the confiding voice of her survivor as sister to Romy's dauntlessness. Both told woman-to-woman stories of domestic and sexual disaster, and both had the vivacity to give these a comic twist.

I am grateful to Lennie Goodings at Virago for taking this on, and to editor Sarah Rustin for handling revisions in so friendly a way.

It remains to thank Siamon Gordon who participated in all drafts and gave, as ever, transforming advice. Finally, a special thanks for the enthusiasm of our daughters, Anna and Olivia, to whom this book is dedicated.

Lyndall Gordon
Oxford, 2004

The best present I can give you are my friends

Romy Gevint

That mysterious being, the ordinary man or woman . . .

Anthony Storr, *Solitude*

The question now inevitably asks itself, whether the lives of great men only should be recorded. Is not anyone who has lived a life, and left a record of that life, worthy of biography – the failures as well as the successes, the humble as well as the illustrious? And what is greatness? And what is smallness?

Virginia Woolf, 'The Art of Biography'

1

Friends

That we had to leave an indefensible way of life became clear when Flora and I were students in Cape Town. In March 1960 came the Sharpeville massacre, when police opened fire on demonstrators against apartheid in a black township. I went to America; Flora to many places. She died in Paris in 1976. This book is her biography, as exact as if she had public importance on the stage of history. It is also the story of our origins and friendships, shared lives which go on in memory, though now I see these were sharings of women in a particular place and time: South Africa in the late '50s.

We were the last virgins, growing up in an increasingly fantastic colonial tribe. Dimly, we knew this at our girls' state school: our lessons seemed hopelessly distanced, at the bottom of Africa, from the great world, six thousand miles away from thoughts that mattered, from cogent opinion, political and otherwise, from education itself. Once, Flora, Rosie and I lay stubbornly at the bottom of the grounds after the bell had gone, saying 'It's pointless to go in'. We were sixteen, in our matric year, 1958. The bell seemed to fill the whole jar of space around us, resounding like the boom of the speech teacher, like the insistent, half-heard clamour of what we must grow up to be. We lay on the farthest verges of the school grass, not rebels without a cause, but held − for a space − intact by the sun, in its circle of heat.

Miss Potts, in her white lab coat, bore down. I can see her, a white speck, growing larger as she strode down the dried lawn, looming over our heads, blocking out the fierce African light. 'Now, gals' (she had a Cockney accent), 'lazing? Inside. Quick march.' Inside, we took down notes on the digestion of the fish. In English, Miss Tyfield, in what Flora called her 'iron' hairnet (against the tearing south-easter), dictated a character-sketch of Heathcliff. In maths, flecks of foam appeared at the corners of Miss Johns' mouth as she strove to explain a theorem to girls who could feel their breasts pushing against the buttons of their green uniforms. Those buttons were always straining, for the uniform had been designed by British teachers who had come out to Africa in droves after the first world war and had in mind bony girls who played hockey in the rain. Here on the scorching beaches our bodies ripened early to the pulse of the climbing waves as their crests broke over the rocks.

'God, make me normal,' I prayed at assembly that last year at school. 'Don't leave me plain; take away my freckles.' The word 'normal' called up my sporting father at cocktail parties, winking, surrounded by blondes with painted claws and beaming, wide-open lips who giggled easily at his jokes.

It occurred to me to offer God a bargain: 'If You make me normal, I'd be willing to fail maths.'

As we sang through the many verses of 'All Things Bright and Beautiful', I looked down the line at Flora, who was coaxing her lips into the inviting pout of Brigitte Bardot. The pout had been designed to hide her slightly crossed front teeth; its success prompted further efforts: her plumpness was redistributed by a powerful Merry Widow whose emphatic outline managed to defy the severity of the uniform, and her wild red crop was growing into the vivid mane that was to make her a beauty. At this time her work began to lapse (except for maths, where irrepressible aptitude showed itself in quick flares of comprehension). A psychological idea occurred to the speech teacher, Mrs Grazinsky: the lapse might be explained by Flora's dismay at the angle of the offending tooth. So, after assembly, Flora was summoned to the Head's office where Miss Tyfield, like a small hawk in her black suit, fixed her with a hard eye.

'Open your mouth,' she ordered without ado.

Astonished, as Flora reported later, her jaw dropped automatically.

Putting on her glasses, Miss Tyfield peered into the cavern. 'Nonsense,' she said crossly. 'Go back to your classroom.'

In the classroom the overtrained voice of Grazinsky, articulating every syllable of Tennyson with exaggerated distinctness, reverberated from the walls into every crease of our skulls. 'Stand up, class,' she boomed. 'All together now.'

'Break – break – break –' she conducted with heavy pauses – 'On thy cold grey stones, O Sea!' It was easy to overdo the agony as we stood to attention, perspiring a little under our arms, in that still, dust-laden heat of the afternoon under the crest of Lion's Head.

My mother used to say that the name Flora Gevint sounded like a girl in a story but this, I repeat, is life, not fiction. It will be an authentic record of a group of women who met in 1954 at the age of twelve at a girls' school. I should not be writing it if three of this group had not died prematurely in their thirties and forties, but primarily it is about the most vital member of the group, Flora, or as she called herself variously, Florian, F'lora, and (finally) Romy. There were, then, different Floras. There was the exuberant redhead who bounced from the slums into a classroom full of girls who knew one another, and unabashed, in a poor-white gabble we could hardly follow, demanded of twenty-five girls in succession to know our names. There was the Flora who took up Xhosa at the University of Cape Town, and who taught maths in Jo'burg in the '60s and loved Mark, the intellectual; there was the glamorous Romy who mingled in fashionable circles, smoking and dieting; there was the member of the Black Sash who opposed the regime, and the Romy who left South Africa and settled in Paris. Whatever milieu she entered, she took on its colouring so completely – through quick sympathy – that it took to her as one of its own.

Flora was not, in fact, her name, any more than the names she later adopted. Her parents, who had fled Europe at the last poss-ible moment to avoid the extinction that befell other Jews during the second world war, had given her a Yiddish name: Fruma. This is what she was called at home, but when she went to school she was given the more acceptable name of Flora, which stuck through her teens. The old-fashioned propriety of 'Flora' was incongruous: she was a raw, untamed girl who seemed to belong neither to her bowed and struggling parents nor to suburban Cape Town, which retained in the '40s and '50s the exaggerated Englishness of a colony. Girls at school talked of England as 'home': Flora called them dismissively 'Rosemary-Anns'.

Later on, when she returned to South Africa after her first stint abroad, she came back as 'Romy'. We agreed to call her that though, privately, I thought it a movie star sort of name. But by the mid-'60s, when she was at the height of her beauty, she was no longer quite the wild creature of our school-days – though she retained something of her freedom always. By then, she did not look much like a Fruma or a Flora, with her long, straightened hair cut in provocative chunks around high cheekbones and her strong, slimmed-down body in the tight miniskirts of the time. She argued that 'Romy' was closer to 'Fruma' than either name to 'Flora', but the real reason for change was to cast off finally and for ever her outlived identities as child of vulnerable immigrants or undesired fat girl. The stunning Romy would replace these according to the standard female dream of transformation. I, alas, remained plain, and perhaps for this reason more attached than any in our group to the Flora with whom I once shared a phase of freedom. For plainness has this advantage: it can free women from the distorting temptations of conformity. For a space in our teens we gave rein to authenticity, and this was formative, for later we both rebelled against certain norms of womanhood in more serious ways. Flora's rebellion took the form of a protracted refusal to marry, which she sustained in the face of pressure from suitors and, more difficult, from her distraught parents.

Plainness, if nothing else, absolved me early from the struggle to look right, but Flora and others, Rosie and Ellie, took up the business with ironic dedication. As we had known one another in what Flora called our 'gruesome' stage, there was always the understanding that rightness was contrivance – and it was with glee as well as reproof that Flora continued to call me 'Gruesome' at the time when she and the others embraced fashion. All were daughters of immigrants and, as such, were compelled to take on a society in which their parents remained aliens. They took on its shallow glamour, its visual opulence, the lavish make-up and body culture of women whose undemanding lives were propped by servants. Savagely, at sixteen, Flora nipped her waist to set off stiff petticoats and forced her sturdy toes into the narrow points of 'winkle-pickers'; her spontaneity was transformed into the gushing warmth that was the mark of womanly responsiveness. And yet she and Ellie, the most determined image-makers, were the two to hold out against marriage.

They were helped in this by their attractions. The plainest girls married first. Beauties could afford to wait. Looks were so important because, in that time and place, women could express almost nothing else. You could not hope for discernment from the run of South African males. They were virile bodies on the beaches, saying to schoolgirls with thrilling condescension: 'Phone me in five years' time.' You had to speak to those bodies or be left out. I knew already at fourteen I was to be left out when Phillippa, her strap slightly stylishly off one shoulder as we strolled along the promenade at Muizenberg, asked if I were a member of the 'WHS'.

'I've never heard of it.'

'It's the Wandering Hand Society,' she explained in the low, secretive voice of an initiate. She was projecting an image of sophistication, not confessing any infringement of our code of virginity. The sign of Phillippa's superiority was that she had been chosen to be put to the test.

A boy might put his arm around you or lay a ducktailed head in your lap or stand face to face holding your hands, but you were known – by virtue of your family – to be destined to be a 'nice' girl. When I went abroad for the first time, at seventeen, I was shocked by the lunges of a man in a taxi. Unprotected by family, you were prey. But at home, the price of protection was another sort of trap: the assumption that the nicest girls would be engaged by twenty-one to a boy from a comparably nice family.

It is impossible for any outsider to understand fully the rites that governed our lives, their anthropological rigidity, all the more primitive for the fact that they were, for the most part, unstated – imprinted in preverbal habits of mind, deeper than language, and therefore unquestioned. The obsession with group-identity in South Africa extended far beyond the racial divides that excited international attention: each group closed off from others, and none more exclusive than Jews who, anyway, looked upon themselves as a Chosen People. In this they were mirrored by Afrikaners, who had seen their Great Trek into the interior in terms of an exodus to a promised land, and imagined themselves, too, the People of the Book. So the ghetto mentality of eastern Europe fitted rather well in the remoter rural areas of southern Africa, where Afrikaners farmed and where many of the immigrants tended at first to settle. Within this group nothing could have been stricter than the rites to do with women and marriage. It was these that Flora was to refuse through her twenties, and Ellie to invite and evade to the end of her life; and to these Rose succumbed.

None left any record apart from letters. What, we might ask, shaped these lives in the shadow of possibility that lurked between the certitudes of conformity and those of liberation? Were there forms of sharing as yet unrecorded in the years before women emerged as political 'sisters'? What unrealized possibilities lie unnoticed behind the silence of women's lives in the outback of history, biography, and memoir, the standard records of the past? I shall approach this through my own past in South Africa, through diaries, letters, and memories, my own and those of my contemporaries who were, most of them, forced into exile and scattered widely in England, America, Israel, Canada and Australia.

Inevitably, the obscure reaches of Flora's life, and the lives of Ellie and Rosie, took on the peculiarity of white women in South Africa. Their potentialities struggled within the framework of a white tribe in which mental habits of categorization – of gender no less than race – verged on the grotesque. Though Flora, Rosie and Ellie grew up amongst liberals who repudiated apartheid – a milieu that found it easy to distance itself mentally from the country in which it lived – no woman in the '50s in this society could be impervious to the norms of gender. These women, coming to adulthood in the late '50s and early '60s, belonged to the last generation to have no political awareness of their fate as women, and yet each contrived to resist, in different ways, the models which they did also absorb.

To look back in this way is to attempt to recover what Henry James called 'the visitable past', which in any generation is still within reach of memory: a doomed way of life, like that of the American South, at its apogee in the late '50s, just before the Sharpeville massacre that could be said to mark the beginning of the inevitable end of white minority rule. This will be an attempt to convey both the rot and residual vitality of individual life in a terminally sick political context, now outlived and passing away: a particular generation of the white middle classes whose way of life, as they were intermittently aware, was on the edge of eventual extinction. It has to be a form of history, going on below the platform of public fact and usually lost to record. Acts of memory will dredge up four or five motes in creation as they pass swiftly in the current of time, moving steadily towards oblivion.

I have thought of this book all through middle age, from 1976 to 1988, through my mid-thirties to mid-forties, but only at forty-six did I see in perspective that Flora's death at the end of youth, in 1976, foretold a first lapse of energy twelve years later, marking the imminence of the moment when our generation will move into the past. The time has come, then, to record the end of a way of life and, more elusive, the truncated lives of women who were shaped by a warped society yet who were, all the same, portents of the future.

2

Families

'Isn't it pointless,' I said, on a cloudless summer day in December 1954 as Flora and I were making the low-tide trek from the deep sea to the beach at Muizenberg.

Pointless. Flora 'tasted' that word, she said later. It was not one that her parents could afford: Mr Gevint toiling in his crowded furniture shop – called a 'business' in imitation of men who were not 'greeners' [immigrants] – in the run-down thoroughfare of Salt River; Mrs Gevint opening her modest dress shop on the edge of District Six where coloured families then lived. There, she sold local copies of styles from overseas, sleeveless versions of the new A-line, in pinks and yellows that stood up to the African glare.

The Gevints lived in the adjoining white area of Woodstock, which was almost as poor and violent as District Six but in its way more marginal: predominantly, in those days, Portuguese and poor white. Such were the advantages of simply being white that to sink to Woodstock was to fail. This, of course, did not apply to the community of hard-working immigrants like the Gevints for whom Woodstock was a way-station to security. When, eventually, I met the Gevints they seemed shy, muttering their welcome in broken English, only to duck away. Ten years after the Holocaust, they were still survivors, for their families were gone, and like all such survivors were excessively anxious for their children's health.

'*Es, es, mein kind*' ['Eat, eat, my child'], Mrs Gevint urged Flora, who grew steadily plumper. Flora and her two brothers were tall, almost twice the size of their frail parents, who, I imagined, had been undernourished during terrible Russian winters when they were fleeing as refugees during the first world war. They never spoke of past sufferings; they preferred to forget them – or perhaps they did speak within the knowing circle of the *Landschaft* Society. This was a society for immigrants from the town of Ponevez in Lithuania. When Mr Gevint arrived at the Cape in 1927, the society numbered forty to fifty; by the '80s it had dwindled to nine or ten and Mr Gevint was still a member. There was a certain gap between the Gevints and their robust, noisy South African children, who could reach them only through an almost protective affection. Years later, I saw Flora collect the Gevints from the airport as though she were the parent, they the children, as they struggled for words, intimidated by petty officialdom.

Survival was the Gevints' real business, and it shaped their attitudes, as it had shaped refugees before them. As the flourish of 'pointless' would have been, for them, an unthinkable luxury, so too were the indulgences of romantic love. Clara, as an unmarried girl, had arrived in Cape Town when legally it was too late: rising anti-Semitism backed D F Malan's Quota Act which became law in 1933; the last ship with immigrants arrived in '36. The only pretext for Clara's visa was to visit her elder sister. To have returned to Europe after this visit would have meant almost certain death, so (the story went) the only way that she could stay was, very quickly, within three months, to find a husband. She found Itzhak Gevint. There was an outing to the bioscope, and the decision was made. She knew at once that this was a man she respected. I can't see that warmer feelings, at this point, came into it, for they remained vastly different: Mrs Gevint was a pretty woman, with rosy colour and tight-curled hair, but a shy and abject manner obscured her prettiness. She behaved apologetically in her own house; so she greeted me as a mere schoolgirl, not knowing how much I responded to her maternal style of unconditional love.

She and her sister, orphaned early, had been farmed out to various members of their family with whom they had spent their childhood in the position of unwanted dependants. Clara always retained her diffidence, backing away from the affection she aroused, so that, to her daughter's friends, she conveyed welcome through remote gesture as she retreated in the direction of the kitchen.

Though her husband, too, appeared shy to strangers, he was a forceful character with a straight-faced vein of Jewish humour.

'Daddy, how's business?' asked Flora, throwing herself at him as he came through the door.

'Quiet in the morning but [pause] dead in the afternoon.'

He was not demonstrative, but she was confident of his love and almost defiantly proud of him. She told me repeatedly that he was a great reader, in Yiddish and Russian, and enjoyed keen arguments with his cronies. Mrs Gevint, simple-hearted and self-effacing, was not of his mental world, and yet they made a marriage of it and gave life to three strong children. And even if survival had not been the immediate issue it was, they came from a society which did not go in for overt expressions of feeling between man and woman. Weddings in the Old Country were arranged, and with a prime concern for dowry and family position. Passion and tenderness were for relations with children: those emotions were recognized, talked of, intense.

As a child, Mr Gevint had been the *ben yachad,* the cherished only son. His parents, he said, had 'carried me on their hands'. They never punished him, reproached him, or required anything of him beyond a creditable performance at school. He might have become a little monster of helplessness; instead, he became resilient. As an immigrant on his own, his independence was a matter of pride.

'Don't cry for yourself,' he told Flora. 'You got ten fingers and your brain. Use the ten fingers and the brain, and God helps you.'

It was a matter of principle to ask help from no one, least of all 'the high and mighty', by which he meant established Jews of English or German origin. 'I used to solve my own problems,' he said. 'I always had my own opinion.' There was something impervious, a deliberate withholding of the self, in this independence that became his proudest value over the slow, hard years of adaptation. He preserved a determined reserve which sustained him through domestic turmoil – the savage fighting of Flora and Reggie, these huge, fierce children who were trying to throw each other out of the window. He did not expect to be disturbed after his day at work. 'I don't want to hear,' he said, shutting his door, retrieving his book.

He was born in 1907 in the town of Poshtor in Lithuania. 'We were not rich,' he said, 'but we were well-to-do, with two shops and four assistants: Jewish girls, hard workers and honest.'* The *babushka*, his grandmother, took care of the house, while his mother ran the shops. She came home at night as 'a welcome guest'. The father was bookish – there were 'shelves and shelves' of books – and devoted himself to a Zionist organization that was forbidden under the Tsar. He was imprisoned briefly, and his son was allowed to bring him kosher food if he gave the guard five roubles.

---

*Details of Mr Gevint's history are from an interview he did in July 1983, at the age of seventy-six, for the Oral History Collection: South African Jewry, Kaplan Centre for Jewish Studies and Research, University of Cape Town. I am grateful to the director, Sally Frankental, for providing a copy.

Mr Gevint recalled how, in 1915, when the Russian army retreated, 'they made a pogrom in the *shtetl* and every Jew hid himself. The Cossacks lined Jews up against the wall and they wanted to shoot them but – I don't know where from – came a Russian officer [who] asked "What is wrong here?" and the people started crying and explaining what is it. He told the soldiers to scram, and he took out his revolver and threatened to shoot them: a miracle.'

The family then fled into Russia and there they remained at Pogtavna until the Revolution. When they returned to Poshtor everything they had owned had been burnt: 'We did not recognize the street.' They settled in Ponevez and again they opened a shop, but this time did not prosper. For all who returned 'the pockets was empty. It was very depressed. Rich weddings, we could not afford them: a little bit of brandy, a little bit of cake.' Still, the community was strong: 'The door was open, the windows was open, everything was open – "just come in" – everybody was welcome.'

His older sister left for Palestine, but when the time came for him to follow her, the British, then in control, refused him entry. 'I decided to come to South Africa. America was closed. No country wanted Jews. The only country with still a small door open was South Africa.'

In 1927 Itzhak found himself, at the age of twenty, on board a ship bound for the Cape. For the first time since the war, food was plentiful and the thirty emigrants 'used to eat and eat – and still always hungry'. In Cape Town a shoemaker from Ponevez 'signed' for him and gave him shelter for a year while he worked as a dental mechanic. He earned five pounds a week: from this he spent a fraction on bus-fare, ten shillings on cigarettes, and absolutely nothing else. Every month he sent ten pounds to his family in Lithuania – half his salary. For entertainment, he walked the streets and window-shopped. He told himself that he could afford no films, no theatre, and no time for women. Poor and without prospects, he would not have appeared eligible to

Jewish families, and he would not risk falling in love with a non-Jew.

After a year, he became a furniture salesman who went to private homes. The human aspect of the job delighted the lonely boy: 'Contact with people, white people, Indian people, African people, it came easy to me, as if I was born to it. I liked the people, liked to talk to them, listen to their grievances, tell them my grievances.'

After two and a half years, he opened his own furniture shop on the wide, squalid Main Road in Salt River, and extended the network of his clientèle: 'I dealt with a mother, then a daughter, then a grandchild: three generations.' He lived wholly for his customers, partly from a determination to succeed, partly from this absorption in the relationships he was forging with coloureds who lived in Salt River and with the poorest Afrikaners and English-speakers who lived in the adjoining areas of Woodstock and Observatory. The English pronunciation he had learnt at school did not prove intelligible, so he took lessons with a private teacher and tried to read with the help of a dictionary. 'It did not take me long.'

When Itzhak was thirty, a friend invited him to meet Clara. Here he was reticent. 'She wanted to get married or she would have to go back,' was all he would say. There was no money for much of a wedding: 'I was poor and she was poorer.' They invited ten to fifteen people, and Itzhak 'had to scratch my head to pay for it'. He was taken aback to get an account for the twenty pounds that Clara spent on bridal clothes.

'Did you have a honeymoon?'

'In the shop.'

After two years in a flat in Observatory, the Gevints moved to Woodstock. Reginald was born in 1940, Fruma in 1942, and David in 1945. There were five Jewish families on one side of the street and two on the other, and they renewed the community habits of Lithuania. 'When a neighbour moved in, we all used to come over and meet him. I went to our *shul* and there everybody

knows everybody else, like one family. We never had any distinction between rich and poor; we never had such a thing as high
society. We were born plain people and we lived plain lives.'

A consolation for plainness was the increasing brilliance of special occasions. These were lavish in the extreme as though to
make up for the privations of the Old Country. 'A bar mitzvah
was like a wedding, and a wedding like a feast. Everybody was
inviting each other. When a family had a wedding, two, three
hundred people used to come. We used to bring a carload of
presents – by the hundreds.'

The community closed in on itself with the rise of Nazism
amongst Afrikaners. 'Most of my customers were Afrikaner, and
when I came into their houses, I saw the swastika . . . As soon as
Hitler came in, all the hatred came out: what is hidden in your
character for a long time must come out.' Mr Gevint was increasingly taciturn and, at the same time, bound to his group. When
Flora was growing up he would tell her, 'I found that you could
not be out of the crowd, against the stream. You must swim with
the crowd.' In the '50s, in the thriving economy of expanding
white privilege, the crowd was swimming in the direction of
better living, moving from Woodstock to the pine-clad mountain
suburb of Oranjezicht, and from Oranjezicht to the gregarious
beach-front suburb of Sea Point, and from Sea Point to the ver-
dant, exclusive estates of Kenilworth and Constantia.

The Gevints took their first step away from Woodstock when
they sent Flora to Good Hope Seminary, perhaps for its proxim-
ity to Oranjezicht. But by the time Flora and I met at Good
Hope the whole area had run down. My mother, who had
attended the school during the bracing influx of British teachers,
imagined it had remained unchanged. She and her school chum,
Jessie, resolved to send their daughters, in turn, to Good Hope. In
fact, as Myra and I soon discovered, the school had deteriorated
with the neighbourhood. The teachers were for the most part
bored, and found it easiest to underline textbooks and dictate old
notes, which the girls were to learn by heart. At no stage was it

expected that a thought would pass through your mind, and if that did happen, you knew better than to inject it in your work. So, propelled by our mothers' blithe nostalgia, we made the long, daily journeys from Sea Point – Myra by chauffeur, I by bus – to undergo a systematic process of stupefaction.

In 1957 the Gevints moved to Sea Point, to a barely furnished house that was, to me, refreshingly different from the showpiece houses of the area with their claw-and-ball tables, display cabinets, and heavy brocade curtains. The smugly secure of Sea Point tended to wad their nests with a clutter of ugly ornaments: as a child, I particularly disliked silver sweet-dishes, toast-racks, gold-rimmed plates and figurines that had been wedding presents (bought on the cheap from wholesalers) and displayed on long trestle-tables as the indispensable cement of a marriage. This clutter, cleaned scrupulously every single morning by two servants, closed us off from any immediate awareness of child mortality, starvation, and murder in the unsanitary, smelly black townships, Langa and Windermere, on the edge of Cape Town. The perfumed lotus-people, golden with sunshine, reclined beside the sea and echoed the usual lamentations of distant racial wrong,

> Like a tale of little meaning though the words are strong;
> Chanted from an ill-used race of men that cleave the soil . . .

In this, the wadded homes of a suburb which considered itself responsibly anti-government actually reinforced the ultimate perversion of apartheid, which was to separate not only races, but mental awareness: the perversion, in short, was to instil mental habits of oblivion. It was impossible, growing up in Sea Point, wholly to escape this insidious comfort, despite its lip-service to political enlightenment. The children of Sea Point, gravitating from the card-tables of the smoking, idle mothers of the '40s to the living centre of the kitchen, occasionally broke through the illusion of security, for in the kitchen the 'maids' received their visitors, and we overheard bits of their stories, stories quite

different from our mothers' old books, like *That Girl* by Ethel
Turner or *The Jolliest Term on Record* by Angela Brazil, which lined
the shelves of our frilly bedrooms. The kitchen stories were of
drunken brawls – 'and he knifed her in the tummy . . .' – and of
babies who should not have been born because there was no one
to care for them – '. . . and the Meddum wouldn't give her off' –
and so the babies had accidents and died. And shooting through
these juicy stories, related with a certain dramatic pride, there
came now and again the thrill of fear, the fear of women who had
no control over lives spent in service to white 'madams' who
doled out the occasional ten-shilling note or extra food in lieu of
asking to hear the whole impossible truth.

Though the Gevints moved, inevitably, to Sea Point, they never
went in for the useless clutter and the oblivion that went with it –
not because they were high-minded but simply because they could
not dissociate themselves, in their new prosperity, from the
ingrained habits that in time became the comforts of triumphant
struggle, and they still went every day to work in Salt River. And
if Mrs Gevint did happen to be at home, she would not be sitting
in high heels pouring tea, like other mothers, from a tray prepared
and brought in by the maid. I felt easy with her precisely because
she had no notion of being gracious but was awkward, loving,
spontaneous. Endearingly, she thought me an 'angel', as Flora,
hooting over her mother's innocence reported: 'angel', she
taunted, putting on her mother's greener accent. Yet her mother's
feelings, transplanted in the stark Africa which she could not
comprehend, touched Flora with the pathos of the lost ghetto, in
which extravagant maternal tenderness had a special weight
recalled in plaintive melodies. Where my toes curled at the sob-
bing violins of Jewish song which played so blatantly on the
heart-strings, Flora, closer to the lost world, had the measure of
her mother's unconditional love. For this there were no words;
only deeds: she gave, she spent, she reverenced and spoilt her
children, and said 'come in, come in' to their friends.

Flora, in turn, was fascinated by my family, who was as strange to her experience as hers to mine. She was drawn, oddly enough, to the two most dutiful: my grandmother Annie, and my Aunt Berjulie. Most women have looks that fluctuate according to morale; these two had the steady good looks of unshakeable confidence. Berjulie had sparkling, dark-blue eyes and dark hair, cut in the glossy Italian Boy style of the mid-'50s. Granny's hair was the kind of gold that is just touched with auburn, a colour not allowed to fade until her last illness in her ninetieth year. All her life Granny fought the tendency to freckle that went with that colouring – she used Metamorphosa cream, which bleached the skin as well as the freckles, and she was never without her large hat or parasol, beneath which she forged ahead with determined readiness, expecting to know people and be known. The joy of her life was placing antecedents, particularly if she could trace links with her family; she was an encyclopaedia of names and connections. She judged by appearance alone: you were not really acceptable if your hair was not freshly set, if you wore no make-up, or last season's fashion. What drew Flora was the certainty of Granny and Berjulie, the *bella figura* of women who knew exactly what they wished to be – which was what all women should be. For a daughter of immigrants they had the attraction of social authorities, who were prepared to take a flattering interest in an unkempt girl who showed herself willing to be formed by their rules.

Berjulie had married Granny's youngest son, Hubert, and they had settled at 'Willow Stream' in one of the outlying areas of Johannesburg. She had been brought up by two formidable aunts called Bertha and Julie in Lusaka, in what was then Northern Rhodesia. 'Berjulie's aunts' were family watchwords for the punctilious performance of duty. When Berjulie delivered her ultimatum to Hubert – an effective proposal to a cautious bachelor – her reputation for attentiveness to her exacting aunts was welcomed by the family as a sign that she would make an admirable wife. And so it proved when Hubert's fads asserted themselves, politely but firmly. They centred on a delicate stomach. Berjulie was by nature brisk, busy, and not given to fuss, yet

Flora, meeting them on a visit to the Cape, was struck by the patience with which Berjulie peeled and de-pipped each grape before Hubert consented to eat it.

When my aunt travelled, she forged ahead of my uncle, with tickets and cases (all matching and packed with tissue paper in every fold to prevent creases). Her case contained shirtwaist dresses with crisp stripes and small, neat tucks and, for shopping in Town, she had Swiss Hanro suits with toning Italian shoes and matching bags. In the '50s, a hat and the best leather gloves completed the outfit in which, in those days, the worldly from Jo'burg made their appearance in windy, provincial Cape Town: they would dress up to 'arrive' after the dusty, thousand-mile train journey (two nights and a day across the highveld and the empty, baking stretches of the Karoo). My mother deplored 'getting and spending' yet, out of loyalty to family, she did defer to the arbiters of appearance, and I remember being compelled, at fourteen, to wear a particularly silly white hat and white gloves to meet my aunt and uncle when they arrived with Granny for the summer season at Muizenberg.

That summer of 1955–6, the girls of our age graduated from the family beaches at the breezy far end of the promenade to the central Snake Pit, as it was called, an airless triangle of coarse sand enclosed on two sides by the promenade and pavilion, and on the third (sea) side by a line of bathing boxes. There, teenagers baked for hours, oiling their limbs as they turned with languid movements from back to front so as to brown evenly. Their bodies lay tight-packed, exposed, and churning slightly as they eyed one another. Popular boys like my cousin Leonard chaffed the more grown-up girls all day at the Snake Pit.

I asked Leonard: 'Who's your favourite girl?'

'Marilyn Monroe,' was the prompt and, I vaguely felt, crushing reply.

One day, while Leonard was at the beach, Flora and I went through his bag. All we found of interest was a novel that began: 'Dames are my trouble – blondes, brunettes, redheads, and in-betweens.'

When Flora and I made our way to the Snake Pit, we wore our neckerchiefs like brave flags, but kept our distance. We preferred to sit on the balustrade of the promenade, looking down, envious and doubtful, rather than make the descent to the Pit itself. Berjulie thought me prim. Noting my mother's unworldly absorption in matters of faith, she drew me into her bedroom, and shut the door.

'Do you or don't you want to grow up like others?' she demanded. She put it to me that I was absurdly backward. 'It's time you wore stockings and lipstick,' she said in her quick, decisive way. 'Someone has to tell you that it's not a crime for a man to have a few drinks, and it's nothing to kiss a boy. Don't you be a prude.'

Two weeks later, the chance came to prove my normality. My ballet school was to perform at a gigantic New Year's party at a vineyard estate at Somerset West, about thirty miles from Cape Town. In costume, with stage make-up and hot-black on my lashes, I looked more than fourteen. After the performance, when we joined the party under the starry sky, a grown-up man asked, 'Will you marry me? If not, let's dance.'

He fitted exactly one of my mother's two images of the colonial Englishman. He was not the 'stiff' administrator, typified by the Governor-General or the Commander-in-Chief for the South Atlantic who used to appear in the classier pages of the *Cape Times*, flanked by an angular wife with the correct brooch pinned to the left of a lifeless bosom. John was the other, hedonistic kind, who drank heavily to overcome inhibitions my mother had explained. He had slack lips which hung wetly open.

'Kiss me,' John murmured, thick with alcohol, as the clock struck twelve and the band played 'Auld Lang Syne'.

Mindful of Berjulie's injunctions, I braved the fumes. The kiss was, fortunately, quite brief and friendly. I was proud of this act of normality, and still more pleased when the car broke down at 2 a.m. It took ages to change the wheel and by 4 the dancers, all older than I, were ready for another round of drinks. We pressed on to a pseudo-Bohemian flat, all divans and floor cushions, belonging to a not-very-good dancer called André. It was 6 a.m. when another dancer – who looked, I thought, as noble as the Scarlet Pimpernel – drove me home.

This solitary escapade failed to convince Berjulie of my normality. When she heard of my love for tragic arias from *La Traviata* and *Rigoletto*, she sent Flora and me to hear Johnny Ray sing 'Cry'. His trademark was to sob as he sang – accompanied by sympathetic cries from his audience. 'The Nabob of Sob', said the posters, 'The Prince of Wails'. He shook and wept, a wimp with his hand over his hearing-aid as he sang:

> When your s[sob]WEETheart sends a letter of
>   good(aah)-BYYEE,
> It'd be (aah)better if you(wah) sat right down and
>   c-ah-ah-CRY-YEE . . .

The floodgates opened. Everything in the theatre was soaked in seconds. I was obliged to tell Berjulie that I had enjoyed it, to cover the shame of not being able to 'Cry' along with the others.

Flora was more genuinely appreciative, and it occurred to Berjulie that she was more promising material. When my grandmother, never tactful, rebuked Flora for coming untidy and unironed to the beach – 'you can let go *after* you're married,' she said – Flora was not resentful; she was amused and conciliatory.

'You're right, Mrs Press,' she said warmly, 'and I'll always remember that.'

Her extravagant warmth was not quite a sham: it was designed to egg on elders to make those revealing pronouncements about women's fate which she would repeat as 'stories'. She could take the faintest hints to convert into 'stories'. We laughed all the time, as girls are always laughing, doubled over, at fourteen. In a forthright voice, Flora would repeat Berjulie's warning, 'Don't go *too* far' when, eventually, we went on dates. 'There's no going back.' Her prudential advice leapt several steps ahead of our intentions.

Who would fondle weedy, immature Ernie and Bernie, or 'Slimy Hymie', or any other 'pathetic' (our current adjective) boy of fifteen? So much was made of the boys of the beaches, the potential husbands, that they behaved with the careless indifference of lords. And yet most of them were callow, with thick belly hairs underpinned by the knobs of tight tangerine bikinis. I never dared voice my resistance to sitting out what I called in my diary 'the awful clashing boredom' of the Vic Davis band at the pavilion in the silent, eyes-front company of Ernie and Bernie.

In a few years, our contemporaries – to our amazement – would be engaged to slightly older but no less unappealing versions of Ernie and Bernie. To Granny and Berjulie, this would have been entirely acceptable, given the fact that they came from the right sort of families – those with means. Our advisers presented a model of assured women, untroubled by the darker places of the imagination, for whom the life of a woman was simple if one followed the rules. The prime rule was to respect men as providers and protectors – and, of course, the richer the man, the better he could provide. Some years later, when Flora broke off an engagement, after months of doubt, my grandmother, tripping along like the Queen of Muizenberg under her yellow parasol, asked with her usual directness:

'Why didn't you marry him?'

'You see, Mrs Press,' Flora lowered her voice with teasing confidentiality, 'he wouldn't give me a great big diamond ring.'

Granny thought this over very carefully.

'Well,' she said after some time, 'it's not *the* most important thing.'

My grandmother was unusual in her generation for having known no other world than South Africa: the very predictability of her world gave her a confidence that was attractive to a girl like Flora whose parents went burdened by the cruelties of history. Granny would tut respectfully over the Jewish Problem while she planned her next party. Mindful of the most distant relations, she left out none, but to accommodate so large a group she gave her parties in relays, over three days. On the first day she had the rich, important relations to a lavish tea; on the second day the middling rich had the left-overs; and on the third day the poor and distant relations were given a tea of reconstituted remnants. They appeared humbly grateful to be part of Granny's indefatigable network of connections.

One of my cousins used to tell his children Bible stories which always ended 'and the Jewish people lived happily ever after'. This witticism was, as it happened, applicable in its straight sense to Granny's family. For generations they had lived, free of trouble, in the town of Shillel in Lithuania, where a great river ran through a dense forest. Granny's great-great-grandfather and some of his friends had obtained permission from the local baron to clear the edge of the forest for settlement. His son built a watermill and married three times, on each occasion the daughter of a learned man.

Though marriages were arranged by the *shadchan*, the love-match was not unknown. In 1863 Granny's grandmother, Gute Milner, at the age of eighteen, became engaged to a man she loved, Isaac Hoffman, but at that time had the misfortune to lose her mother. Her father, determined to remarry, withdrew her dowry in the form of a *kest*: this was a promise of board and lodging for ten years, as well as clothing for children to come. Isaac, who had recently completed his Talmudic studies, wished to become a rabbi, but to do this he did need the support of a *kest*.

'Under such conditions,' said Granny, 'an engagement would have ended, but Isaac and Gute were determined to go ahead and trust in the Lord.'

In the event Isaac did not fulfil his religious bent, nor did he succeed in secular enterprise: a dairy farm failed; a school lasted only a year, for he talked above the children's heads; matzah-baking (for the Jewish festival of Passover), in demand only for ten weeks a year, proved too seasonal for profit. For some time the family's supporter was really Gute, who grew groats which were exported to Germany. Then, unexpectedly, Isaac came into his own when he organized the building of a synagogue. He became an assistant to the mayor and soon mayor himself.

None of the sons was caught by the dreaded twenty-five-year draft of the Tsar, though recruiting officers, on duty in the area, actually stayed in the mayor's house. The pogroms of 1881 passed them by. The intelligent eldest son, designated for the rabbinate by Gute's wish, turned to mathematics and chemistry. The second son, Jacob, was different: he left school at the age of twelve; at fifteen he wished to emigrate. His parents restrained him until the age of seventeen. In that year, 1883, he left for Wisconsin. Four years later he returned to Shillel to persuade his parents to return with him, but they held out for two more years while Jacob took up logging on the river. In the meantime, in 1886, gold was discovered on the great reef beyond the Vaal River, and it occurred to Jacob to go there instead. In the summer of 1889 he left with his father and elder brother. His father died soon after their arrival in Johannesburg: one of the first graves in the Jewish burial ground.

The handsomely-bearded Jacob had the resilience of the unimaginative. He was a *bon viveur*, an urban character and, unlike most immigrants, never did a stint in remote parts 'up-country'. In those early Johannesburg years he ran a hotel and imported woollens from England. In due course he sent for a bride from the Old Country. So Rebecca made the arduous journey from the huddled, ingrown *shtetl* under leaden skies to the wide, blazing veld as the coach jolted its dusty way from the end of the railway at Kimberley, another few hundred miles north to the half-remembered bridegroom in Johannesburg. She bore him six children; Annie, born in 1892, was the eldest. During the 1890s, England was promoting *uitlander* grievances to provide an excuse for invading the gold-rich Republic. By 1896 there were 44,000 *uitlanders*, who probably outnumbered the Boers. Annie's first memory was of the family's flight at the outbreak of the Anglo-Boer War in 1899; they managed to board the last train for the Cape. Jacob left everything except some notes which Rebecca sewed into her corset. They were searched on the train, but not thoroughly. Jacob's English connections gave him the credit to begin again, and the firm of Rabkin and Hoffman took shape in a room in the new home in Cape Town. And then, said Granny, as the main wave of immigrants rolled forward, Rebecca would go down to the docks to meet the ships, and Norman House in Maynard Street became a welcome point for greeners.

Amongst the arrivals there came, every so often, a governess for Rebecca's children. Jewish women were scarce. After a term of service, the governess would marry and Rebecca would send for the next. To bring about a marriage was an act of religious benevolence, a *mitzvah*. Because of the scarcity of women, some men ordered brides from the Old Country.

'When a ship docked at the old pier, my father went with the husband-to-be, to support him. They were nervous, you see. What's a photograph? One man, when he saw his bride coming down the gangplank, so ugly, he fainted.'

'What happened to them?' Flora asked.

'Oh, he married her, of course. My father said he must – persuaded him it would be right, after bringing her so far. And he'd *paid* her passage,' Granny added. 'It cost a lot of money. You wouldn't throw it away when you're a man with your way to make.'

'But did it *work*?' Flora urged. Her thoughts, like mine, flew to the ugly bride. To provoke recoil, and still to marry, to go to bed with a stranger who would do his duty, as Jacob in the Bible had been compelled to take on Leah, unwanted Leah who tried to please him. Reuben, she called her first-born, which meant in Hebrew: 'Look! A son.' But however many sons she produced, Jacob could not love her – though impregnate her he did, again and again.

'They were married,' was Granny's laconic reply. She was not to be drawn about feelings. She retained the Old Country view that right conduct, backed by security, took precedence over taste. To her mind there would be, in fact, no discrepancy, for a good woman would wish, above all, to preserve the community: good connections, good homes, good children, who perpetuated what was proudly called 'tradition'. This was exactly what Mr Gevint meant when he advised Flora to 'swim with the crowd, not against the stream'.

The unusual fortune of Granny's family in the grim context of Jewish history had produced cheery characters with an infectious enjoyment of food, eiderdowns, afternoon rests, morning bathes in the sea, and songs at the piano. They respected people in their own image: energetic men who were providers; spruce women who were skilled housewives. None of them ever read a book except for daily prayers, and though none was accomplished in any artistic sense, they all played the piano in an easy, light-hearted way, songs like 'I Do Like To Be Beside the Seaside' and 'K-K-K-Katie', with many introductory chords and trilling embellishments, followed by happy clapping.

There is a photograph of my grandmother in 1910. She is seated in a white blouse and skirt, dark stockings, and well-polished black shoes with a strap across the instep. Eighteen in that year, she holds a posy in her lap and her golden hair is up, in contrast with the flowing hair of her younger sisters who stand grouped about her: Minnie, Gertie, and the youngest, Betsie, a child of nine in dirty white buttoned boots, one hand behind her back as though she were holding something out of sight, and refusing to look at the camera. Betsie was to be the rebellious one, fractious with Annie who ruled her siblings with a determined will.

'Papa was strict,' mused Granny. 'When he came into the room he tapped his heel for attention, and we stopped talking as he went across to the fire and stood there, flapping his coat-tails. He used to tell off his sons for looking up at the female gallery in *shul*, but he'd do it himself. After my mother died, he used to take a woman to tea at the Waldorf every Saturday afternoon, and he'd present her with a posy of violets.'

Soon after her mother's death, when Annie was twenty-two, she married Philip Press. Her choice of husband was the only unusual act of her life. Philip, coming from up-country to order goods, saw a young woman seated on a stool. She was doing the accounts, her back to him. Her gold hair glowed against her black dress. Later, when her father had Philip to dine, she sat at the piano, in white, and sang 'Cherry Ripe'. Coming to this from the rough veld, he saw a vision of all that was beautiful, and he fell in love at once – in the way of a bookish man, with little knowledge of women, who seizes on a lovely ornament without thinking what it will be like to live every day with a trivializing mind.

Annie's acceptance was more surprising in that Philip had no looks or riches to commend him and had the seriousness, behind his glasses, of a thinker. At the age of thirty-six, he had yet to establish himself at Klaver (later Klawer), on the Namaqualand border, a place that was in 1914 nothing more than the end of the railway to the north-western Cape. A more improbable setting for Annie, twirling her fashionable parasols, could not be imagined. Nor, given her optimistic, unreflective temperament, would she have visualized in advance the stunted thorn bushes stretching to the horizon, broken only by the slow-moving expanse of the Olifants [Elephants] River.

How did Annie discern Philip's character? For she did, she said, recognize his superiority though he was a man who had been a *smous* [pedlar], wearing *verweelbroek* [corduroy trousers] like a Boer, and sleeping under his cart, pulled by two mules called Plaatjie and Donkerbok. At the time that he started to roam the veld in 1894, Annie had been a child of two. Twenty years later, he still could not support a wife in the comfort of Norman House. He had, moreover, this intellectual bent, having studied the Scriptures in the Old Country, and continued to mull over the Bible which was always on the table in the *voorkamer* [front room] of the farflung farms of the Afrikaners, who had been, for years, Philip's only and intermittent company.

Flora's questions drew from Granny details I had not heard before. When she related her courtship story of the day they walked on the old pier, and the day he came to the door with flowers behind his back, and what she wore – her brown silk with beige lace insets, and a frilled beige parasol – Flora interrupted:

'But, Mrs Press, you haven't told us about the proposal itself. How did he do it? What *exactly* did he say?'

'It was difficult for him, you see, because of his position. I knew he wanted to speak, but he had to wait and be patient, not like you girls of today, rushing to phone boys, inviting them into your room, showing yourself on the beach. I'd be ashamed . . .'

'But, Mrs Press,' Flora diverted her back to the past, 'what did he *say*?'

'He couldn't say anything, of course, until he had spoken to my father. I knew what it meant when he came to the door and asked for Papa, and I waited above the bend of the stairs. And then they called me, and my sisters stayed peeping round the stairs, and I said yes, I would marry Philip.'

'And then,' persisted Flora, 'when you were alone?'

'We sat on the sofa, and he said, "Would you take down your hair?", and I didn't know what to do because, you see, I wore a hairpiece. My hair *was* lovely – tinted now, and not the same – but it was always a bit thin.' Granny's voice took on the confidential note for womanly matters – the really important matters of appearance. 'It had to be padded out to look right.'

'Did you tell him?' Flora pressed her.

'Tell him! Go on! Of course not. You girls have to tell everything, but it's not necessary. They don't want to know.'

'So what did you do?'

'As I unpinned my hair,' said Granny triumphantly, 'I felt for the hairpiece and dropped it behind the sofa. He never realized. He thought I was beautiful.'

'Tell us, Mrs Press, tell us, *please*,' Flora urged, 'about the wedding night.'

'We went to Caledon. It was *the* place to go because of the natural springs. Visitors took the waters for their health. And when we were alone in our room, my husband said to me, "Now we'll enjoy the fruits of our love."'

Granny was teased by the family for inviting her sister, Minnie, to join her on the honeymoon. Minnie, who was accustomed to share a bed, had not been willing to sleep alone. So it happened that Philip was displaced from the marital bed, by common consent of the sisters, and made to sleep behind a screen.

'Didn't he mind?' asked Flora.

'He knew, you see, that Minnie was missing our mother the most. And one day, while we were playing croquet, he said to me: "This place would do poor Minnie good. I have a plan." So we telegraphed Minnie to say that Philip was called away, and I was left alone, and could she come and keep me company. Minnie wouldn't have come, otherwise. And, anyway, what I couldn't tell,' again her voice became confidential, 'I had my period. According to Jewish law, a husband must leave the bed until it is over, so, you see, it had to be, and Minnie had the benefit of a holiday. He was always kind to my family, that way, thinking of others, not himself. He was a generous man, and that's why I, why everyone, respected him.'

It proved a happy marriage of the sort in which little was expected of a woman but to be seen and adored. Philip indulged his ornamental wife. He did not expect her to share the heat and privations of the country, where he stayed on his own during the worst months.

'You must go to Town now, darling,' he would say when summer began. And so the green, domed trunk was packed with Annie's many necessities – her kosher china, her hand-embroidered tray cloths, her freckle-cream, her wide hats (one to match each outfit) – and she, and the four children, would board the overnight train for Cape Town and the ease of her father's house. Every summer, from December to February, they took a place at Muizenberg, and Annie would preside in her pale silks, and invite her great network of connections to her relay teas.

So Annie, we discerned, remained for a large part in Town, running her father's home and managing, with benevolent intent but insensitive practice, her brothers and sisters. Those who were subject to Annie all confirm that in the years when she had the backing of an indulgent husband, her power had been awesome. With the buffer of a generation between, we saw Granny, for the most part, in a different light. What gave Flora fierce delight was her frankness about the body. The Gevint parents were too busy, and too inarticulate, to talk of the body; while my mother relied exclusively on the Scriptures. At weddings she would observe: 'The bridegroom rejoiceth in the bride.'

'What', Flora asked when we were alone, 'if the bride did *not* rejoice in the bridegroom?'

The Scriptures offered no help on that vital question. To console ourselves, we read and reread the beach scene in *The Lying Days* by a new South African writer, Nadine Gordimer:

> We went to the beach in the morning on our own . . . We had walked a long way, past the rocks where no one but Ludi himself came to fish, and he had unfastened the halter of my wet bathing-suit and peeled it down from my breasts. Neither he, nor anyone else, had ever touched or seen me before . . . Round the nipples tiny fragments of shell and pebble, worn membrane-thin by the water, stuck, shiny, pinkish-pearly to the skin. I lay so still I might have been waiting for a dagger. But Ludi, with a tone of delight that astonished me, smiled, 'Look, the sea has been here . . . You're all gritty.'*

We read this on the ledge outside the upper windows of Flora's house on the High Level Road, while we munched hard-boiled egg on Provita (as part of a diet), saying to the sky with extravagant passion: 'I want, I want, but I don't know what I want.'

What we wanted was too much for simple solutions. The boys of the beaches with their scrawny or podgy bodies, their self-

---

* From Chapter 8. First published by Gollancz in 1953.

satisfied, blank eyes, and whining 'Jo'burg accents', were too 'pathetic' to contemplate. They paled to insignificance beside Mr Rochester, whose inward authority set Jane free to explore the unknown frontiers of her nature. Could Mr Rochester, could Mr Darcy, men who might offer an equal discernment of women, come into being? We doubted it – and continued to live in our impossible dreams.

All this was as far as possible from Granny, who read only *The Jewish Chronicle* on Fridays and a set passage from her prayerbook before she turned out the light, and who dictated an ethic of deference to a man's 'position'. Yet Granny and Berjulie compelled us with their clear articulation of what we must bring ourselves to face. They spoke as acknowledged arbiters of social rituals, weddings and funerals, rituals that obscured what we called the 'gory details' of sex and death. Jewish society was obsessed with the minutiae of a set of customs that, as practised then in South Africa, seemed to deaden feeling. The rituals of joy and grief had become so ornate, in our affluent society, as to verge on decadence. The prayers that were chanted ritualistically, and translated in the prayerbook into pseudo-lofty English, came to us drained of the spiritual meaning inherent in the Hebrew. So the bridegroom had to be seen to rejoice in the bride; the bride to play the game of radiant surrender even if, in fact, both were rather fraught by battling family claims, guest lists, bridesmaids' frocks, and a sulking mother-in-law whose wish for the prominence of a favoured uncle at the top table had been overlooked.

Granny and Berjulie were a relief because they insisted on no pretence. Berjulie readily owned that marriage had its disappointments as she laid out its duties in no uncertain terms. 'Duty' had for her the attractions of heroic sacrifice, as in 'England expects every man to do his duty'. Yet, with disarming honesty, she did acknowledge the imprisoning aspect of duty for women who were constrained to visit themselves at the oddest hours.

Granny described to Flora and me how ignorant brides of her generation would urinate after intercourse in a vain attempt at contraception. She did not shrink from 'gory details', and did not mince words as she counselled, like Berjulie, obedience to custom. Their realism was a bracing antithesis to our ineffable dreams: it had the fascination of glimpsed truth. Both were pre-pared to state what women actually experienced, as they spelt out the compromises we were to make for the benefit of sharing the male 'position'. They told us what to expect in blunt terms, and our natural dismay at the prospect of a 'difficult' man and the acknowledged 'agony' of childbirth – Granny told us how she would tear the sheets tied to the foot of the bed – was tempered, at least in their company, by the brisk resilience of their manner. They were too sane, too matter-of-fact, too conditioned to the norms of custom to approach our horror. Weddings brought custom to an elaborate climax. This was to rivet Flora as some-thing she could not bring herself to face; a ritual tinged with comedy but, yes, a special kind of horror that was to play so large a part in her story.

Years later, in 1988, I was having my hair cut in Cape Town when I overheard a conversation between two middle-aged women. 'Mrs Gelb is *desperate*,' said one in a low voice.

Desperate? I leaned closer.

'You see,' the voice went on, 'she's got a bar mitzvah in only a week, and she still hasn't got her dress. It's got to be *under*stated.'

This, then, was the reaction against the lavishness of the '50s and '60s. One was desperate for understatement while racial oppression slowly destroyed the country; while protesters of the mildest kind could be whisked into detention, without trial, many tortured, for six months at a time; while Dr Asvat was mysteri-ously gunned down in his surgery, a tireless worker who was dearly needed and loved in his Soweto community.

I relayed Mrs Gelb's plight to Phillippa over lunch at Freda's Restaurant in Tamboerskloof. Now a successful journalist, she was elegant as ever in her khaki skirt and black jacket, her straight, chin-length hair cut in a classic line, her sun-glasses pushed back on her head, and unbelievably cool in the midday glare. She was writing a photographic article on new white lifestyles.

'The new young Afrikaner', she said in her slow, faintly caustic way, 'lives in a converted Old Dutch homestead in Stellenbosch, and serves *lovely* food, a simple quiche and bread and fruit – all very casually. The Jewish architect and his wife live in Sea Point, and their taste is *perfect*, with wonderful works of art. But it's competitive, all the same,' she added. 'The food was too carefully presented.' With a little rueful smile, she owned that this perfectionism had been so insistent that she simply *hadn't* been able to tell them that the article was sponsored by an inferior wine, photographs of which would accompany the contrived chic of the Sea Point lifestyle at every point.

We went on to wonder if such material perfectionism was the ultimate debasement of the moral fervour of the Hebrew Bible, the intensity and will of the old Prophets, the detailed strenuousness of the old Law. And then we touched on Flora – and, as ever, words faded. I had returned to visit my mother, but also to bring back Flora and Ellie and Rosie, sharers of a past that still hovered intact in the silence that bound Phil and me. All the summers since their deaths, and there they were. And behind us loomed the unchanging rocks of Lion's Head and below us the steep, humped streets going down to Good Hope Seminary where we came together in Miss Smit's class on the first day of high school in January 1954.

3

School-days

Lemumba, Myra's chauffeur, drove us to school, his white-gloved hands turning the wheel full right and left, as the car swung round the lower slopes of Lion's Head on a road that edged the precipice of the gorge below. We sat on the back seat like miniature ladies, wearing white hats curled up at the back, with the school colours, green and blue, around the brim.

We sat quietly in mild apprehension. For Myra it was not easy to leave the plush haven of her home and the protective routines of her close-knit family. Excessive shelter made her shy: she was unprepared, she knew, for a government school in decaying Hope Street. Myra's unbroken shell seemed to tempt fate. I imagined that some cataclysmic awakening lay in wait, but this banal story was not to be. For, of all who made their way to Good Hope on 20 January 1954 – Phillippa and Ellie from peeling white houses with purple splashes of bougainvillaea in Oranjezicht; Flora from the tough back-streets of Woodstock; and the boarders on nights-long train journeys from Rhodesia, Namaqualand, or even the Belgian Congo – Myra, in her gleaming black car with her history of protection against her, was to suffer least, to doubt not at all, to want nothing but marriage, and to have the good fortune to fall in love once and for all with just the older man to love her with experienced devotion.

I was quiet in the car because I had begged that lift and felt out of place behind a chauffeur, being only twelve, and covered in freckles, disfigured further by the panama hat, and dreading the moment when I would be called upon in class to declare my awful name. If only it had been Linda or Sandra or Shirley or any of the acceptable names of the '50s. My mother, who had affinities for Olive Schreiner, for that writer's solitary years on the beloved veld, had called me after the heroine of *The Story of an African Farm*. Later, Hubert, who shared her nostalgia for the veld, gave me a first edition of the novel, published in 1883 with the writer's pseudonym, Ralph Iron. Inside, there was a faded inscription: 'Henry Redhead Yorke, in remembrance of our trip to S. Africa, from Edith Lytton (Simon's Bay, 1892).' My uncle wrote:

> 'Willow Stream',
> Coronation Road,
> Johannesburg.
> 4 November 1962

> It is twenty-one years since I sat on your mother's bed at 'Rhodean' and we thought of the name, Lyndall, because of our strong feeling for her in the *African Farm*. The significance of 1892 is that it was the year of your grandmother's birth.
>
> Very affectionately,
> Uncle Hubert

The fictional Lyndall was a creature of delicate beauty, with tiny, perfectly formed hands and feet. She was also a bold feminist who chose to die for the Cause rather than marry the cad who had fathered her child. This woman, with her strange nobility of soul, was invariably unknown to teachers in the government schools of the 1950s, who would ask me to 'stand up please, and spell the name slowly' as they wrote it into the register.

The first page of my diary records that day in Standard Six: between the first two periods, Flora perched rather clumsily on the lid of her desk and demanded instant introductions to every one of us. I wrote: 'She has cropped red hair and a fierce spirit. The other girl who attracted me was Phillippa who was so efficient and spoke so nicely.' (I used 'nice' with the indiscriminateness of Jane Austen's ignorant Catherine Morland, but can remember that it meant, in Phillippa's case, verbal grace.) I wrote with some detachment; not expecting to be friends with girls of such obvious attractions. I was resigned to be, to some degree, an outsider, a position that was not without its compensations. I was an avid reader of historical novels, and lived almost entirely in extravagant dreams. As I played out the tragic death of Violetta to the strains of the last act of *La Traviata* behind the closed door of my room, I feared discovery, as once my chortling coloured nanny had surprised me lying bloody on the railway track, in ballet costume and stage make-up, whispering to a distraught husband and a confounded impresario: 'Take off the red shoes.'

From an early age, I took cover with normal girls who played Authors, Happy Families, and Monopoly, which were enjoyable enough on winter afternoons when the foghorn boomed from Mouille Point, and ice-green breakers flung their spray against miles of rocks reaching far out into the heaving seas of the South Atlantic. Such days recalled the fact that nothing but those seas stood between the Cape and the southern polar region. I liked to ask, 'May I have Miss Smut, the Sweep's daughter?' with storm-scenes rather pleasurably in mind, frail ships toiling through deep troughs, the broken sails of Bartholomew Diaz or Vasco da Gama, who struggled to round the Cape of Storms in the late fifteenth century when men were forging the sea-route to the East.

Though I saw Flora or Phillippa at the Snake Pit, swam with Flora and took in Phil's nubile grace as we strolled along the promenade, I did not expect their interest. Socially, I was undeveloped and had nothing to offer, but each in her way – Flora with unselective exuberance, Phillippa with grown-up *ennui* – bore with my hovering. During the first three years in high school, my real friend was a less arresting girl called Linn Lorriman.

My diary notes Linn's 'sweetness' (another word, like 'nice', that Jane Austen despised: Elinor Dashwood knows that 'the sweetest girls in the world' are to be found in every drawing-room). But again, sweetness had a special meaning beyond my vocabulary. What Linn had was natural goodness. The finer this quality, the less it asserts itself, and Linn was seen to be simply an agreeable, well-mannered girl who could be relied on to do the right thing. Mothers liked her, which wasn't particularly to her advantage. She had curly chestnut hair and round pink cheeks, and wore home-made dresses of pale-pink cotton. Her hair was brushed and clean; her dress freshly ironed; her nails unbitten; her smile ready and kind. For all this, Linn had a strength which was to show itself in her mid-twenties in a public ordeal. In the meantime, she had a rare blend of astuteness and humility. She could judge character, though did so with maximum charity, and if charity were not possible, she would fall silent – oh, I remember the gravity of her silence. But it was Linn's humility that drew and baffled me, for with all her insight she seemed content to befriend the dullards in school, as later she was content to go out with very ordinary boys and worse, the 'drips' with whom Flora 'wouldn't be seen dead'. Linn makes me think, now, of the lovely, selfless wife of plain, bungling Amos Barton: a Victorian sort of heroine, making no claims and finding fulfilment in service to others.

Our friendship, for me, had the attraction of opposites for, on the Day of Atonement, my mother, who knew best, used to place her finger on a particular word in the prayerbook during the *Kol Nidre* service: the sin her finger underlined, year after year, was 'stiff-necked'. Yes, indeed, I was stubborn, resentful, and even when forced to say sorry, sometimes did not mean it. For this reason, I admired, and envied, Linn's goodness.

Her fibre was put to the test when she was twenty-four. She had married beneath her, not socially, but morally. Herman, her husband, was a weak boaster and, also, unappealing with a large thin nose through which he snuffled and snorted. He was what we called 'a social misfit'. Few girls had been prepared to go out with him, and he was accustomed to take solace in 'cheap tarts' and predatory pounces. My diary describes one such incident when a group (not including Linn) spent a vacation working on a farm: we belonged to youth group, connected with Israel's kibbutz movement, and the work was meant to be a discovery of the Dignity of Labour.

Klapmuts, Cape.
25 July 1958

The work was shovelling dung and digging it into the ground. It is not so bad to work when it is a combined effort. There were no lavatories and we had to go behind bushes. There were no showers so we had to swim in the dam. (Disadvantages: it is mid-winter and we shared the dam with cows.) We cooked all our food over a fire and slept, boys and girls together, on the floor of a barn. We lay in the dark telling stories and jokes. One night I woke at about 4 a.m. to find Herman lying practically on top of me and snorting down my neck. I roused a friend and asked her to come for a walk. I was shivering with revulsion.

This sort of harmless incident – for Herman would have liked to have been more of a threat than he was – provided him with material for his boasts. He was a compulsive liar, possibly because it assuaged his inferiority to diddle his listeners, possibly for the sheer pleasure of invention. It was his way, like Iago, to disseminate malicious innuendo, but in this seemed more pathetic than wicked, though a reputation for unspeakable and important evils would have tickled him.

Linn never explained why she went out with Herman, but I assumed her predilection for lame ducks, and friends would remind themselves, in moments of incredulity, that Herman was a clever anti-apartheid lawyer with a connoisseur's taste in opera. We wondered if Linn, coming from a mild, book-free home, was over-impressed by Herman's flirtation with Communism and not inconsiderable air of culture.

When they had been married three years, in 1966, Herman was charged under the Immorality Act. This Act, together with racial classification of every single person in the country, racial Identity Cards, and the Pass Laws that controlled the movement of blacks, was central to the social engineering of apartheid, under D F Malan and the Dutch-born Nazi sympathizer, Hendrik Verwoerd, between the early '50s and mid-'60s. The Immorality Act made it illegal for whites and blacks to sleep together – which of course was happening all the time as it always had. By night, the police would prowl along the line of cars parked beside the sea, and a couple locked in an oblivious kiss would be startled and humiliated by a sudden flood of searchlights. The police were not interested in sex itself but in faces: the precise colour of lovers' skins. This surveillance was all the more ridiculous because colour classification was, in many cases, impossible. Seven to fourteen per cent of Afrikaner genes are non-European. Even without statistics, it was a common observation that the most rabid racists often had skins that were darker – a consequence of three centuries of (unacknowledged) mixing – than some people formally classified coloured and, as such, subject to all the current, tortuous forms of social disruption and indignity: having to watch their homes knocked down or being required to stand in buses when there were empty seats reserved for whites.

Herman's trial blazed across the front page of the papers. To a society rife with the semi-discreet adultery of the idler whites, the headlines conveyed the delicious shock of sexual crime, while the liberal papers rejoiced in the opportunity for public outcry against the state's definition of 'immorality'.

To Herman's astonishment, Linn divorced him. For her, it was not an issue of publicity. What mattered was that trust was gone, for though Herman was acquitted, the trial had compelled him to admit both that he had visited the woman and that he maintained a flat in Sea Point for what he called 'private purposes'.

With a lawyer's eloquence, Herman expected to persuade Linn that the whole incident was a ploy of the Security Police. Given her charitable nature, she would forgive. But Linn was cool, decisive: she did not wish to see him again. In the months that followed, he would intercept her en route to the school where she taught, and there would be dramatic scenes: operatic protestations of undying love. For Herman was as in love with Linn as he could be, and in self-defence told her, and perhaps (as consummate liar) actually believed, that he had been a victim of a cruel law and that his acquittal had been a significant moral and political victory. Sooner or later, he would prove this to Linn, and she would relent. Linn, he was sure, was conventional; she would abide by the sentimental norm of all the ages by which a wife shared a husband's disgrace – or triumph, as Herman chose to see it. But Linn remained firm. At the core of her sweetness was this strength. When she saw through to the rot, she had the pluck to rescue her life.

Herman's went downhill. He left South Africa on an exit permit; taught Roman-Dutch Law at a polytechnic in London; married a dark showpiece from Tangier, but she too left. Once, in our thirties, we met at an exiles' dinner in London. He asked eagerly after Linn, said 'she should have trusted me'. A few years later, he committed suicide – pathetic Herman who had surprised me asleep, at sixteen, in a typically ham-handed bid for the role of Prince Charming in his own perverted form of fairy-tale, in which the sleeper was not a beauty and the intentions of the prince strictly dishonourable.

Linn married a second time, and was happy. Though she had been a born teacher, she accepted almost thankfully the care of a businessman. To her supportive role as wife she brought unself-conscious goodness, her fine instinct to do right. Her husband suspected me of feminism. This had to be tested whenever we met. But Morgan adored and supported Linn in turn, and was clearly a kind and more considerate partner.

In the later classes, I shifted into closer friendships with those girls whose centrality I had contemplated, as it were, from afar: Flora, Rosie, and eventually Ellie. One way that they differed from Myra and Linn was that all three were daughters of immigrants, and this applied too to Phillippa's gentle father. This fact did not strike me at the time but, in retrospect, I see that it underlay a compelling quality which they had in common: their conspicuous command of words. They were all intensely artic-ulate, as though to compensate for parents who would never speak English properly. Flora's speech was dashingly fast: almost a gabble when she arrived in Standard Six, she revealed, as her accent changed, a racing, irrepressible stream of observation. She used words with abandon, like the life-giving jet from a hose turned from one dry bed to another, the dry beds being our lessons.

Phillippa was articulate in a different way: each word was selected, stylish, enunciated with care. Where Flora's desire was communication – she lived for 'empathy' – Phillippa, already at twelve, had taste. This had an overlay of conscious sophistication that was not without its charm. She played up her similarity to Audrey Hepburn, the wide smile, the brown doe eyes, and slim, upright figure – but it was the poise of her speech that I noted in my diary on the first day of school.

Ellie, different again, had incisiveness, a penetrating intelligence that was to be fulfilled in her eventual career in clinical psychology. She had large, widely spaced blue eyes that looked you in the eye, curious, intent, as though what you said was of vital importance.

Her gift was to listen for the unspoken: to this you felt a response both gentle and intense. Where many girls modelled themselves on film-stars, she had a distinctive look of her own, with that inward attentiveness that had its focus in her light eyes, in brilliant contrast with her cream-brown skin, pale lips and immaculate sprayed head. She wore sleek, couture clothes and turned heads as she walked. With men she had a vein of soft baby-talk when she called them endearing animal names. Then she would change, be indecisive and distant. She foresaw encroachments on her freedom. Her understanding also made her vehement. Men were charmed by the attentive tilt of her pointed chin but, sadly, those who would have been her equal were conditioned, in those days, to respond to submission. Ellie's vehemence, which expressed her integrity, unnerved the male of her generation: she was too opinionated to be womanly. Accomplished as she was with patients, her relations with men were almost an extension of psychotherapy in that she would attract lamed specimens: mothers' boys who liked her strength, or the rejects of failed marriages who craved her trained concern for replay dramas.

Rosie was quieter, low-voiced, with a meditative rhythm that paced itself to long walks about the grounds. We thought in unison, as we ventured on the language of judgement or silence or wit. Rosie wished to become a writer: her model was Dorothy Parker. I wondered at this choice, given her range of talent, but see now that she was drawn to the element of contrivance in self-creation: the comic voice of Parker, the sexpot image of Monroe. For Rosie, like Monroe, sexiness was a comic contrivance that mocked its own display and, sometimes, when the image did not hold, she was vulnerable. Like Sylvia Plath, part of her was deathly serious, part drawn by popular norms. Out of school, she modelled her image on Monroe, peroxided her wavy, pale-brown hair, wore tight pastel sweaters to set off large breasts, and rolled her eyes comically as a dimwit Little Me. She had an oddly vague look when she shunned her glasses. To avoid seeming to peer, she assumed an expression of one who passed in a dream. In school she was another person: observant, astute, and rather sarcastic in her detachment. In some ways I thought us alike (though never said so, for fear of offending): insignificant, pale, too freckled for cuteness, too serious for comfort. Rosie was a prodigious reader who went her own way. Once, we had to write an essay on 'My Favourite Author'.

'Whom did you choose?' I nudged her as we put our essays on Miss Tyfield's desk.

'Joseph Conrad,' she said carelessly. Despite the inexplicable determination of her Monroe ambitions, she was searching, quirky, adventurous: this was superior to what the English call 'clever' (with that subtle nuance to which the flat colonial ear slowly becomes attuned; in Oxford, in 1974, when Helen Gardner said 'clever' it was revealed a word of contempt). In my diary on Sunday, 29 April 1956, I noted the growth of our friendship in banal words which used 'clever' as straight compliment: 'I often go off with Rosie and we have such interesting conversations. She is certainly the cleverest of my friends, cleverer than I as well.'

Rosie revolutionized drama. When she joined the class, we were working in pairs, devising scenes in which shock was to be conveyed. Most of us took the shock, whatever it was, with stunned gestures or a graceful collapse to the floor. But Rosie, low-murmuring, tremulous, exploded into a new voice with loud, raw sobs. They shook the school stage literally and figuratively. Soon, we were practised sobbers, aiming at a crashing end to inhibition.

Ostensibly, these girls cultivated dramatic manners and appearance, but what drew me, apart from words, was a sense of latent strength – something other than conventional forms of power for which there are no easy phrases of the kind that define such cared-for women as Linn and Myra. Absorbed by the lives of the obscure, George Eliot was alert to 'that roar which lies on the other side of silence'. To hear that roar of the inward lives of each of these women requires a freedom to push biography beyond its

standard form. It could be easy to piece together the usual narrative of dates, events, and facts, leading to affecting scenes of tragic
finality. But the stories of these women cannot be told with the
linear simplicity of the dessert-course romances of Myra and Linn.
For the lives of Flora, Rosie, and Ellie were more buried, more
disturbed by talent, and rooted in aspects of womanhood that
remain, as yet, undefined. They need more time, more delicate
sifting of fact, more searching of what remains unknown in
women's lives: the fluid adjustments of character (often mistaken
for female capriciousness); the almost bodily need for the language
of response (often mistaken for female vanity); and, strangest of all,
the close-guarded, comic fixity of the stale roles that girls of the
'50s chose to play – games of compliance that carried, already,
some element of amused, spectatorial detachment. In what mysterious ways did their half-known gifts and half-played games
propel each towards an abrupt curtailment of her unfolding life?
The need to make sense of lives co-exists with futility, for there is
no end to knowing a life, and its distilled essence is but another
fiction.

Admittedly, I know too little about the childhoods of Flora and
Rosie, beyond the fact that, their parents being immigrants, they
had more than the usual incentive to become adroit at games of
social acceptance. These games took a grotesque form for pam-
pered white women who, under the extravagant privilege of
apartheid, lounged on wide white beaches, and threw huge parties at a word to servants, and placed themselves in new-built
ornamental palaces, poised precariously on mountain slopes that
rose sheer out of the sea. Women of that time lived idly like
members of an *ancien régime*, but without the intellectual salons
that gave a genuine social function to certain leisured women of
pre-revolutionary France.

This context will have to serve for what I do not know about
the childhoods of Rosie and Flora: the scenes and models that
ranged themselves before the wondering eyes of immigrant house-
holds. What I do know was the formative phase of adolescence, in

which the ambience of school was decisive. To arrive at Good Hope, at twelve – with puberty at its most secret sproutings beneath one's buttoned uniform – was to experience an unforgettable jolt.

Arriving from junior schools, where brains or sport or hilarity had placed us in predictable scenarios, we found ourselves in a daunting environment where, whatever irrelevancies went on in classrooms, the focus was on becoming a woman – as soon as possible. The jolt was to find that, for girls at Good Hope, there was simply no other criterion of judgement.

'You don't *still* wear a vest,' said Fiona to Flora in a tone of supreme contempt, on the first day, as they changed for gym. Fiona and others looked smugly mature in padded bras hitched to the highest tilt that straps would allow.

Gym was followed by Afrikaans verbs. With the coming to power in 1948 of the National Party, under D F Malan, Afrikaans became more entrenched as the official language, beside English. For Afrikaners, this represented a belated battle of the unforgotten Boer war, and going back further to 1795 (when the English first took over, claiming the Cape as part of a larger naval strategy against Napoleon), a long, bitter struggle of local versus imperial power, of local dialect versus the prestigious international language. I liked the homey humour of the 'kitchen' Afrikaans spoken by coloured servants tossing opinions over our heads as my brother, Pip, and I licked bowls. Their frank criticisms of 'Madam' or 'Master' had a relaxed and fearless sound in the presence of the children. '*O Jere, maar Master is so kwaai as hy gou-gou wil gaan – gits!*' I heard the rapid friction of those soft *g*'s, like low growls, as the sound of indigenous vigour. But when Malan assumed power, Afrikaans became associated with his policies and those of his party.

One of the ways that children of all races expressed their resistance to the regime was to learn as little Afrikaans as teachers would tolerate. This became a serious political stand later, in 1976, during the Soweto Uprising, when black children, fired by Steve Biko's ideology of Black Consciousness ('black consciousness is in essence the realization by the black man of the need to rally together with his brothers around the cause of their subjection'), refused to attend schools that forced on them the hated language of apartheid. The South African Police killed 134 children between 16 June 1976 and February 1977. Many black parents were unable to trace numbers of other children who were detained for indeterminate periods in prison without charge or trial. They pulled their triggers, those blond thick men with their blocked-off eyes, unable to perceive that Afrikanerdom, with its domestic warmth, hospitality, and fresh language of pithy comment, had been perverted by leaders with Nazi histories and by wide-scale brutalization through compulsory army training. As the fantastical programmes of apartheid went into practice from the early '50s to the late '80s, police had to perform bad deeds, called 'keeping order', in black townships like Crossroads near Cape Town. In the '80s, troops were brought in to enforce Pass Laws which gave the army the right to bulldoze the improvised dwellings that had been put together from sheets of tin and sacking. They left children shelterless, with their toothless *tannies* (the prematurely aged aunts, elderly friends, and grannies, who had to care for the household while the mother, often a single parent, worked as a live-in servant in white areas). Did many white mothers consider what was done to the minds of their sons as they performed such lawful deeds against families whose wrong was to have skins of a colour that disqualified them from residence in the purlieus of Cape Town?

Certainly, by the 1980s, women, even some Afrikaner women, were no longer prepared to have sons fight frontier wars to prop up dubious rebel groups against the Marxist governments which took over from the Portuguese in Angola and Mozambique. RENAMO, a rebel group in Mozambique, was notorious for acts of atrocity and indiscriminate massacres of local villagers. It was to this group that the South African army lent support. In 1988 a fashion magazine,

Fair Lady, published a series of articles which questioned the draft, and was taken to court. For these articles touched some nerve in the national readership of women who would usually be reading about *nouvelle cuisine* under the hair-drier and following the colour of nail varnish currently in vogue overseas.

In the '50s it was taboo to mention politics in classrooms. This taboo was part of the unreality of school, and of South Africa at large at the apogee of apartheid: the state understood that it was easier for the populace not to know.

After Afrikaans, came history. Active with ruler and pencil, we underlined in the textbook: it was the familiar story of the heroism of the Voortrekkers of the late 1830s in their search for independence from British colonial rule – smarting, in particular, from the emancipation of slaves under British law. Armed with Bibles (as well as guns), they figured as the Lord's own people, a dream not incompatible with the parched biblical aspect of African horizons. The myth sanctified their advances against the 'Kaffirs', their appropriations of land, their battles. In this they had much in common with American pioneers, except for less success in exterminating indigenous populations. The Khoisan people, it is true, did not survive the Dutch East India Company – with its ruthless greed, its profiteering prostitution, and the smallpox brought by its ships – but the much larger societies of Bantu-speakers, with complex clan structures and durable political systems, proved more resilient.

History skipped lightly from one white event to the next: the text opened with a reference to Da Gama's voyage round the Cape of Good Hope in 1497–8 and then rushed on to the arrival of Van Riebeeck and the first Dutch settlers in 1652. South Africa appeared to be a *tabula rasa* for white invaders. There was no mention of the fact that the Khoisan people had inhabited the area of the Cape Colony for millennia before the Christian era nor was there any note of centuries of black history. In fact, the text suggested that 'migrating' tribes of Bantu-speaking peoples were arriving from the north at roughly the same time that British and colonial forces, moving up from the south, met them at the Fish River in 1811–12. The implication, of course – and this was universally believed by whites, liberals as well as Nationalists – was that blacks had no prior claim to the country. No school book mentioned that blacks settled south of the Limpopo (that is, within the borders of present-day South Africa) from AD 300. Instead, the text made heroes of the Boer guns that had mown down what it called 'hostile' Xhosas in a series of 'Kaffir Wars'. Further, it associated God with the defeat of the warlike Zulus and their wily chief, Dingaan, at the battle of Blood River on 16 December 1838.

Fictions of heroes and conquest – what textbooks called history – were to be learnt as facts for repeated tests. But those stories faded. And then educators said that girls who appeared quick tended, at adolescence, to lose their brains. And, in truth, thinking back, it was not the three thousand Zulu bodies in Blood River that held Flora's attention; it was the humiliation of a vest revealed. For Fiona's withering question carried unmistakable import for the life ahead: would she develop as a normal woman? Or would she swallow the patent fictions of school, and become the model of mental passivity projected by our uniform? The best girls, said Miss Horton, would win badges marked D in gold thread: D for Deportment. Or worst, an alternative not to be contemplated, would she end like our teachers, unfulfilled, unwanted, and compelled to force girls through the routines of Afrikaans verbs, white man's history, and reluctant run-ups to the stuffed horse, a swollen grey-brown beast that stood high backed in the centre of the gym?

The horse was the familiar of the bloated figure of Miss Horton, the gym mistress who stretched to three hundred pounds. She loomed beside the horse, barking commands at those who feared the jump. One by one, she forced us over, her flat, pink face grim and retributive.

'*Some*one has BO,' she announced in shocked and sorrowful tones.

Each girl said to herself, 'It's me.'

So she cowed girls by her power to humiliate in the sphere of the body; the more feminine or timid were her choice victims. Phillippa, moving languidly and speaking in round vowels, took a resigned view: she ran with conspicuous apathy towards the springboard. Myra, who was timid and accustomed to Persian carpets, stumbled blindly across the rough floor with her knees together, to land in a pleading flop, knees still locked, on the top of the creature – while Jocelyn Basson, Fay Thornley and other athletes flung one leg to the side of the bars in the 'wolf' leap or somersaulted over in 'waterfall'.

My diary on Friday 9 September describes a typical confrontation with Miss Horton:

> I am writing this in needlework class.
>
> I am in trouble. My name is up for the 13 and under netball match tomorrow vs. Loreto Convent and there is a practice this afternoon. At the end of the last period, I went to Miss Horton and told her that, as I have a drama rehearsal this afternoon, I won't be able to play.
>
> 'I keep giving you a chance,' said Miss Horton in her hateful voice, 'and every time the same thing happens. If you don't come this afternoon, I wash my hands of you.'
>
> I wouldn't mind if she washed her hands of me if she would only then let me alone. But when she is angry with a girl, she goes out of her way to find fault with everything she does.

Irene Tanchel, who was the baby of the boarding-school (she was sent at eleven from Salisbury, Southern Rhodesia, by her widowed father), recalled a favourite form of punishment: if you displeased Miss Horton, she would find a reason to dismiss you from choir. She used to conduct the choir with buttocks bouncing to the melody:

I love to go a-wan-der-ing a-long the moun-tain track
Val de ree, val de raah . . .

She liked to flick her baton ever so lightly on the refrain, 'Val de
rah ha-ha-ha-ha-ha-ha-ha-haaah.' Girlish sopranos followed in
obedient unison, switching off on the final flick of the baton.
The hearty cheer of the song was a sham – no one wished to
sing – yet dismissal from choir was worse. You left the hall under
a cloud of dislike. 'Do you remember,' said Irene, 'if by chance she
changed her mind, if she said "Next week you can come back to
choir", you felt this flood of grateful relief?' So Miss Horton
played goddess at Good Hope, consigning some to the outer
wilderness, returning others to favour on unfathomable impulse.

With obesity went malevolence as she stalked the school,
haunch by haunch, in her Guide uniform, detecting petty crime:
the disappearance of a purse or the perennial stealing of school
hats. Where Miss Tyfield had a grey dignity as a distant discipli-
narian, Miss Horton conducted a reign of terror. She marched up
and down the school as though on the track of some sinister and
unspeakable misdeed. I see now that she stalked some evil projected from her own inner world of suspicion, but, at thirteen,
simply to see her advance was to feel in the wrong, to pray silently,
'Oh, *please*, let it not be me.' Her bullying denied any possibility
that, in her case, fat was beautiful. My mother remembered her in
the early '30s as a new young teacher, 'such a *lovely* young woman,
rather prettily plump in old fashioned gym bloomers'. For whatever fate had done to bloat loveliness into its present form, Miss
Horton took revenge on girls with unspoiled bodies and their lives
before them. It assuaged some resentment that gnawed at her
spirit, to make girls writhe. But do what she could, she could not
change the prevailing cult of femininity.

To develop as regulation women, only one thing mattered:
physical sophistication. In a dozen ways, from covert to blatant,
Good Hope girls defied the innocence of their uniform: with
padded bras; with tightened belts that emphasized the rounding

curve of young hips; with heels in place of lace-ups; with pony-tails high enough to displace school hats, which perched delicately behind a mound of fringed hair or swooped at a low angle over the eyes. Fiona arrived thirty minutes late for a school-play rehearsal one Saturday morning, 'dressed to a T', as my diary puts it, 'with hat, bag, gloves and high heels'. Make-up, forbidden on school premises, was elsewhere displayed with such lavishness, such Tahiti Pink of outlined lips, such heavy, spot-concealing foundation, that one might have wondered whether the vamp or the schoolgirl was the real disguise.

'There is a craze sweeping through the school of peroxiding one's hair,' I wrote in my diary on Wednesday, 2 November 1955. 'T. T. [Thelma Tyfield] says that it is very vulgar and gave a lecture against it at assembly this morning.' Many were such futile assemblies. To become blonde, if only the limp-white produced by cheap bleach, was the sign of the girl who aspired to become a sex object. To these games of identity there were, though, limits.

Because of the absence until the '60s of a reliable form of contraception, the code of virginity did prevail. Morality backed prudence. Since the '60s, drugs have been the chief fear of educational institutions; before that, the bogey was sex. In the exclusively female society of Good Hope, boys were, in truth, omnipresent – their ghostly moves, tastes, desires trailed in whispers up the stairs and along the lavatory-green corridors. It was their absence, more potent than presence, that haunted the imagination. A boarder was promptly expelled when a boy from SACS [the South African College School] was found in her room. This intrepid boy, dared by his chums, managed to scale the wall of the boarding wing of the school, and a boarder, hanging from her window and hungry for fun, let him in. The escapade was innocent on both sides, arousing nothing more than youthful glee. This the girls recognized, but not Miss Tyfield, who chose to see the invasion, without humour, as a serious threat. The virginity of a boarder, she believed, had been in danger. In actuality, the brief, rather awkward presence of the boy, in the few minutes before his discovery, had been nothing, had Miss Tyfield only known, to her girls' own wilder dreams in the undefiled and uneventful class-rooms of her school. These suppressed passions gave the Seminary the feeling and reputation of a girls' prison. Worse, to the intelli-gent, was the deadliness: we called it, with heavy sarcasm, Good Hope Cemetery.

The rare girl who did fall pregnant became, permanently and without question, an outcast. Such a girl one year did, of a sudden, vanish. Though Janet had been one of the most promis-ing amongst those streamed for university, she never returned to school. When Flora dared to ask Miss Potts where she was, Miss Potts said in a cautious, dead voice: 'Janet is not *well*.' And that was that. There were no further questions and no one spoke of her again. It was as if she had ceased to be, which was the price of losing virginity. Petting, as it was called in magazines from over-seas, was the compensation for virtue.

'I had to gargle for *hours* after the party last Saturday,' Fiona whispered to a grinning Kay Lee as we lined up in pairs after break.

Gargle? Behind them, Flora and I stared. What kind of kisses were these? They did not seem to fit the elaborate seduction in my mother's copy of *Tess of the D'Urbervilles* (which I'd gone over with care, curious at the way Tess slid into a fog and came out pregnant) nor the suspended romances of Tryna du Toit, in which final scenes ended with the thrilling words: '*en hy het haar gesoen . . . innig . . . innig . . .*' (To translate this baldly as 'he kissed her tenderly' can in no degree convey the emotional intimacy of *innig* and the pleasing tension of those dots.) Those slow, hard-won kisses of commitment seemed a world away from the gargling of Fiona, who appeared to have swallowed her boyfriend to the tonsils, only to cleanse his possible contamination with practised efficiency.

The focus on that rigid ethos of femininity had to do, perhaps, with a particular mode of education that was prevalent, and still is, in girls' schools. Femininity was one possible alternative to the stupefaction produced by force-feeding: the glum hours of home-work instead of reading for pleasure, and the reliance on boring textbooks which distorted history and made of geography a welter of mindless fact: our Longmans text on West Africa defined the size of a cocoa plantation by informing young readers that it was the same size as a yam plantation – but of course, no one, includ-ing the teacher, had the faintest notion of the size of a yam plantation nor had we ever seen a yam. And nor did it really seem to matter. Longmans enlightened us further to the fact that the natives who worked the plantations were able to buy the brightly coloured fabrics that those sorts of people liked. The women, said Mr Textbook, cleaned the hut, while children 'played'.

A while ago, I visited, as a short-lived governor, an English girls' school, distinguished for its results – it was dishearteningly like Good Hope. The Sixth Formers, serving tea, managed to convey their irritation with the school's joyless insistence on the kind of hothouse learning that produces the A grade. At the start of each school year, the headmistress would make her 'welcome back to the grind' speech. The effect was fatal to natural interest. One girl, unable to decide on A-level subjects, had sought advice.

'What have you in mind?' asked the Head.

'I'd like to take subjects where there's lots of discussion,' said the girl.

'Oh no, no, there's lots of *hard work* to be done,' reproved the Head. Like Miss Tyfield, she thought not of the girls themselves, but of results. How well university teachers know that product of certain girls' schools: the first-year student, who comes up with her good results, and who proceeds to write down every single thing the tutor says, even jokes; or another kind who remains enervated for months, and who has to be rescued by an agreement never to discuss certain books, like the novels of E M Forster, which were taught at school with grinding thoroughness.

English lessons with Miss Tyfield were a redeeming aspect of Good Hope. She published poems in local magazines, and her book on the uses of English, *The Living Tradition*, was widely used in the schools of the Cape. When we muttered over school, my mother and her Old-Girl friends said: 'There's Miss Tyfield to come – she's worth it all.'

To look up at her, at assembly, from the rows of the smaller girls as she stood erect on the stage, an awesome figure in a black academic gown, to hear the fine flow of words which spelt out discrimination in taste and morality, was to recognize – even the stupid felt it – distinction. She taught only the A stream, those going on to university, in their last two years. So we awaited Miss Tyfield through the lower years of the school. Nor were we disappointed when that day came in Standard Nine for her to sweep into the classroom, fling open the windows, and dispel the inertia of the textbooks with the impact of Shakespeare. For she was alive to literature and we sat up to her judgements. But they were *her* judgements. Though it was part of her lessons to pause for a question about, say, the character of Hotspur versus that of Prince Hal, she was curt with any idea that did not emanate from herself.

Once, she asked a question whose answer did reach her. It was not, in fact, a literary question:

'Hands up', said she, 'those of you who would like to marry Heathcliff.'

All of us put up our hands.

In an odd backturned way she chortled to herself, and dropped the subject. When I related this at home, my mother let slip the secret of her story.

'Long ago, she married a demon of a man,' said my mother, 'and divorced overnight. She happens to know Heathcliff from experience.' Neither Miss Tyfield with her personal experience, nor my mother as moralist, would concede the exhilarating as opposed to anarchic aspect of Heathcliff's ambiguous energies.

It was Miss Tyfield's custom to dictate notes designed as fodder for matriculation examiners. Needless to say, these notes ignored class discussion; they aimed at compromise between her own acuteness and the plodding detail, the laborious learnt quotations, of a system which rewards feats of memory. She did not trust us to read on our own. Every word of every text had to be read aloud in class, which meant that the pace of a play was lost as it spread over months. Naturally, Miss Tyfield took every part. She would hand out roles – but, sooner or later, was compelled to scoop them back. How could a schoolgirl fathom Lady Macbeth saying 'unsex me here'? How could anyone but Miss Tyfield herself convey the twinkling nuances of Falstaff on honour as he dodged the battle? And she did it well, as her thin, hawk-like figure leant back from a round, indulged belly, and the stern lines of her face became creases of jollity.

At the same time, she was teaching our future role of obedient passivity – that we had nothing to offer, and had best attend to the judgers and doers. So we learnt to defer to opinion, and most of us remained silent for years to come. That, of course, was not peculiar to a provincial girls' school. The same deferential silence prevailed in New York as late as the mid-'60s, in classes at Columbia, because it was patent that some teachers, at least, had no wish to hear women's voices. Strange to discover, two decades later, that accomplished speakers like Sandra Gilbert or Elaine Showalter sat silent, as they say they did, in American graduate classes of the '60s. Twenty years ago, at a seminar on the fourth floor of Hamilton Hall, I forgot myself when Professor Ahab stated the truism that Henry James could not treat erotic tension.

'But what about that scene in the carriage in *The Golden Bowl* when Maggie must resist the solicitation of her adulterous husband?' I thought James had shown with great sympathy a woman's struggle not to lose her integrity in oblivious surrender.

Astonished by this interruption, Professor Ahab stopped short and gazed balefully into the distance.

'I'm getting a pain in my balls,' was his eventual response. That shut you up. No woman of my generation failed to leave that department unscarred by abjection. It was the legacy of men of famed intelligence, like the critic Lionel Trilling, who spoke, like Jehovah, through a cloud of smoke as he puffed his cigarette at the ceiling of Philosophy Hall. After some weeks, he asked why the class had frozen. No answer. But I have to own the origin of silence in the authoritarian classroom of a woman teacher. It became recognized, in the '70s, that career-women, like Miss Tyfield, were not wholly unlike elder women in certain primitive societies who identified with the dominant order in its suppressions. For it was she who first forbade us to take risks. She replaced the quirky with the standard word. I lurked nervously in the corners of my correct essays, lacking the panache of Rosie whose marks were decidedly higher.

Once, Flora dared to pour out her feelings in a rush of an essay written after a class in which Miss Tyfield's insights had tantalized hopes of 'empathy'.

'Stand up,' said Miss Tyfield to Flora, next day, as she swept into the classroom, her gown curving back off her shoulders, and the pile of essays stacked neatly against her blouse.

'Yes, Miss Tyfield?' Flora glowed with the release of confession. She was one of those 'enviable mortals', described by Anthony Storr, who 'seem able, from their earliest years, to express whatever they are feeling in the presence of comparative strangers without fear of being rebuffed, disapproved of, contradicted, or made to seem foolish'. Now, now, what lay at the core of Flora's self, what she had managed to express, would make her known to this admired teacher.

'Will you please inform me what is the meaning of this – this – *rubbish*?' Miss Tyfield demanded in her iciest tone, holding up a page of Flora's writing scarred with red slashes.

Flora was crushed. She acknowledged at once that it *was* rubbish, and promised never, never (she spoke with passion) to do it again. Nor, from that day on, did anyone else make the same mistake. Flora, we realized, had written with wild indiscipline and reckless speed, but certainly she would have laid out that vital core of honesty that had made her the acknowledged leader of our year. Horribly incorrect though her grammar may have been, and entirely without what the school called 'deportment', she was so alert and eager as she stood for her teacher's response that one didn't need a Master of Education degree to realize that here was material for constructive attention. But Miss Tyfield, we knew now, had closed off – not to literature, but to pupils. She had her insights, and her idea of education was to pass them on from year to year, and girl to girl, irrespective of difference.

So, at Good Hope, the days crept at their petty pace, underscored by the cooing of the doves from the pines along the lower slopes of Table Mountain. Their coo brings back the very note of mental monotony in the natural paradise of the Cape. I took refuge in my diary, written during the most barren classes, Scripture, Maths, and Needlework. Dug up after decades of shunting between the US and England, the diary of these schooldays is not only banal and, in places, embarrassingly silly, but contains rather less on Flora and classes than I had hoped. It is really more the product of solitude that was one alternative to miseducation on one hand and the cult of femininity on the other.

Since I am writing mainly about friends, I shall not dwell on solitude except in so far as it bears on the context of their lives – their too short lives, that drove too keenly to a self-definition that, to the end, would elude us all. If Flora's end was to become a *Parisienne*, Ellie a therapist, and Rosie a Woman of Today, these labels tell too little. What they leave out, as scientists do in their linear stories of driving discovery, are those experiments that have come to appear irrelevant, and – less distinct – unnoted observations, and – fainter yet – observations not made at all. For Flora, Ellie, and Rosie, were there pauses, like my diary? Or did they feel more insistently than most, a pressure to be mature, to be loved, to be women?

As they fulfilled the obligation to go to parties, they put on a mask of glamour that made them unreachable. I knew them on weekdays; then, on Saturday morning, they were transformed. Each had a standing appointment with Mr Hugo or other hairdressers with artistic, European-sounding names, and to these men who devised their images, they were placatingly close – an intimacy quite different from outspokenness between women. In their helmets of lacquer, bouffant creations balanced on long, poised necks, their focus was men. If they spoke to women, it was glazed, preoccupied utterance with eyes elsewhere. The generation of the '50s was the last to define itself, in this way, solely by the response it evoked in the male.

I soon discovered the boredom and torture of the teenage party for one not destined to be a social success. The first I attended, at thirteen, began with boys choosing partners from names in a hat. To my dismay, I saw the weediest advancing towards me. His name was Michael. He said in a whining baby-voice: 'Are you Lyn Dell? Can you bop, Lyn Dell?' I had been practising all afternoon in anticipation of this moment, but our struggles together were such that I could only welcome the end to that dance.

Worse parties followed, and I saw no reason to endure them further. Flora and Rosie looked upon this decision as a damaging withdrawal – for it put you beyond the pale – and they showed a grit I lacked in their pursuit of what we called 'social life'. Flora at that time was still plump, and her shiny green dresses (green for red hair) were bedecked with bows and frills. Rosie, in the latest shade of shocking-pink, also tried hard, receiving the thrust of chaff with the giggles of a decorative nitwit. Occasionally, one or other tried to lure me back into the realistic struggle of social existence:

> Wednesday, 23 Nov. 1955.
> Rosie Singer invited me to her brother's bop club but I don't think that I shall go. I will no doubt feel out of it. Linn was also invited. I have become very friendly with Rosie.
>   Tomorrow night is the [ballet] rehearsal. I am so happy . . .

Though ballet was my first love, the discipline of the barre had long revealed that I was not built for it. But I still loved centre-work: the slow unfolding movements to music, the controlled abandon of leaps and turns. That month, for my fourteenth birthday, 'Granny gave me two pairs of the latest pyjamas and a L.P. record of "Giselle". Mommy and Daddy gave me the complete "La Traviata". When I listen to it, I can forget even the [end of year] exams, beginning on Monday. The divine music lifts my soul to heaven. While it plays, I imagine it is I who am the tragic Violetta. Auntie Berjulie sent me some jeans.'

Our divergence in that fourteenth year foretold our futures. For Flora and Rosie to stick out the ghastly parties until they conquered that world – Flora as a seductive beauty whom every man wished to marry; Rosie, chosen by *Fair Lady* as 'Today's Woman' – this was a formative ordeal. And formative for me, too, though more indulgent, was the idle reading that may have been the origin of my improbable route to Oxford – improbable, given the fact that, of all the group, I was the least brainy.

Society or academe – our different ways had the fascination of what's difficult. In July 1973, at the Bread Loaf summer school in Vermont, a group of students and teachers discussed the consequences of this curious fascination. We all owned to be following the course least natural, creating what Yeats called 'the anti-self'. A specialist in Puritan New England said that he would have flourished in high finance. My husband, a scientist, thought he had talent for military strategy – 'if only', he added wistfully, 'there were room for cowards in armies'. Though I had just then completed graduate studies in English, I had to admit my impatience with almost all literary critics: the pointless intellectual gymnastics of such as Frank Kermode, the laboured pretensions of such as Harold Bloom, reduced me to groans of boredom.

'So what are you really?' asked the Puritan specialist.

'Oh . . .,' I cast about, 'a suffragiste on a platform.' In 1973 it was a possible note to sound with wary superiors; it dared them to think that women, in their – yes, hurtful – phrase, were becoming 'aggressive', and hopefully, at the same time, in some corner of their minds, to acknowledge the injustice of that automatic rebuff. It also measured my distance from the destinations of Rosie and Flora who, at that moment, near the end of youth, were still alive.

Though our lives did divide from parties on, and though afterwards first Rosie, then Flora, came to look on me with some irritation, we were bonded, all the same, by a crime at school that reverberated both in public and in private for a long time and in all sorts of ways.

The crime was cheating. And it was not one incident but a way of life, and not for one or two alone but drawing in quite quickly a whole class, 10A, at the top of the school. To give the whole truth of the matter may seem like a Hermanesque attempt to explain – to present as plausible what should be regarded as absolute wrong. Yet to understand how a whole class of twenty-five quite decent girls could have conspired to do this thing, and the strength of consequent bonds, it is necessary to see it in the peculiar context of Good Hope. In what I am going to write, there will be no element of retrospective fabrication: at the time of cheating, and at the time of its exposure, we all knew, and spelt out to one another, why it was happening.

The obverse of the glazed exchanges of girls at parties was the quick-fire bluntness of girls at school. From Standard Eight, halfway up the school, this talk hardened as rebellion. We were not without a cause: it was a rebellion against deadness, a sense of imprisonment in a meaningless routine that seemed to exist for its own sake. The confrontation inherent in the cheating episode had behind it a confrontation, two years earlier, in which Phillippa, acting alone, had defied Miss Kenny.

Of all lessons, Scripture was the deadliest. Bovine Miss Kenny, who taught the D stream domestic science, should not have been assigned this subject. She was a slow-moving epitome of a mindless form of schooling, but she got on well enough with household efficiency and balanced meals. The soul, however, was not an idea that sprang to mind when Miss Kenny plodded to the teachers' platform. It may have been Miss Tyfield's indifference to Scripture, as a non-exam subject, that led to that hopeless marriage of the wrong teacher with the wrong class. Miss Kenny coped with faith by leaving us to our own devices.

Officially, her plan was to have a series of girls read aloud to the class while she got on with marking. My diary's first mention of this class reads:

> Thursday, 18 August 1955.
> I am writing this in scripture class. Phillippa is reading to us and I am to read after her. I don't believe that there is a girl who had not got her science book on her desk as, within an hour, we are having a test. Miss Kenny's lessons are a bore! I consider them free periods.

As the months passed and boredom grew, contempt for Miss Kenny became more open. She might have won acceptance had she got to know her pupils. But she seemed almost oblivious to a class as an occasion for contact. This we underrated: we did not realize that it was a mask for incompetence. She simply seemed too thick to react. One day, this misapprehension erupted in an unprecedented clash:

> Thursday, 14 June 1956.
> There was an uproar in our class on Tuesday. Phillippa cheeked Miss Kenny and for once she blew up. It all began when Miss K. clopped into 8A and Phillippa deliberately turned her back and spoke to the girl behind her, with her hands on her hips. Miss K., infuriated, gave her 50 lines. Then all was quiet till the middle of the period, when Phillippa turned to Miss K., and pulled a face (a horrible one) at her. Miss K. jumped up and shrieked:
> 'Get out! I'm taking you to Miss Tyfield!'
> Phillippa, calm at the centre of the storm, replied smoothly: 'You can't control me, that's why you send me to Miss Tyfield.'
> Miss K. went purple. It looked ludicrous with her carroty hair.
> 'You are the worst girl I have ever met,' she bellowed,

while Phillippa sauntered across the room and paused at the door.

Miss K. marched her downstairs to the office. I was called to the office too, and so was Flora, and we were told to behave ourselves in future.

Phillippa paid for that blaze of defiance. Miss Tyfield declared her a banned person: no one was to speak to her for the rest of the day, and she was excluded from the school play and any other form of activity in which the school was represented. She had to stand on the stage for the rest of the day, with her back to the hall, as various classes filed in and out for gym. Miss Horton, busily presiding, was in her element, directing attention to the outcast, warning girls against contact in solemn tones, and barely containing her triumph that, at last, Miss Tyfield was lending her status to Miss Horton's modes of retribution.

When our period for gym arrived, our hearts went out to that lone figure on the stage. It seemed more terrible that the face was turned to the wall. All that was visible was her slim back and the fawn-coloured tail of her hair. As we leapt over the horse in dread silence, Miss Tyfield crossed the hall to fetch the outcast to join her parents, who had been summoned to the school.

As she passed, pale, her hand touched Ellie's for comfort.

'Miss Tyfield,' called Miss Horton importantly, 'that girl was trying to communicate.' It was as though she had uncovered a clue to that lurking but nameless plot that she continued to pursue. Two years later, her suspicions were vindicated when cheating came to light.

The cheating was planned and shameless because we had lost faith in teachers, in schooling itself. Cheating was a gesture against a stultifying regimen of internal tests which were designed to bring the school the credit of good results in the forthcoming matriculation exams. We saw the bombardment of tests as an artificial incentive to learning, a substitute for the spontaneous interest that lessons had failed to promote.

Was this the sophistry of idle girls? I have no doubt that we preferred the beach to the nearish prospect of an external examination that would determine entry to the university. And, yes, the disaffection was too sweeping, like the flourish of 'pointless', not to be somewhat disingenuous. We valued – perhaps not enough – the content of Miss Tyfield's lessons, but were daunted by her manner, unaware that her severity did have its eloquence and that, in the course of a rebuke, the sound of a driving and well-composed sentence had fallen upon our ears.

There was also Miss Hulston. It was not fashionable to like Latin, and we yawned our way through Caesar's *Gallic Wars*, Book VII. The very name, Vercingetorix, can bring back, at this moment, the mortuary atmosphere that his presence diffused in the classroom. Caesar's repetitive stories of *veni, vidi, vici*, and his monotonous detail of war-machinery and fortifications, left girls slumped over their desks with vacant faces. And yet, Miss Hulston's translations did reflect an economy of statement that was new to me and, in fact, more gripping than Miss Tyfield's correctness. I used to read them aloud behind the closed door of my room, and they became a model for what attracts me still in classic arts: a passionate decorum, the intersection of feeling and strict form. In secret, I proclaimed the moment when the gods call Aeneas, urging a further voyage, and promising him *imperium* without end. In secret, I spoke the Sibyl's words of warning, before the visit of Aeneas to the Underworld, holding back, yet releasing a resonance of dire suggestion: '*sed revocare gradum superasque evadere ad auras / hoc opus, hic labor est.*' If I did not forget those words, it was because I never set out to learn them. I paced them and mouthed them with the thrill of saying something which I did not fully understand yet knew to be profoundly true:

Trojan son of Anchises, offspring of the stock of gods, easy is the descent to Avernus. Night and day the door to Death's dark kingdom lies open. But to recall the step and pass out to the upper air – this is the undertaking, this the task.

Yet, at best, we could but regurgitate an elegant translation or the insights of Miss Tyfield. Nothing had come from ourselves. Looking ahead to the end of schooling, we felt the unstocked emptiness of our minds. We faced the future with no idea how to work but to copy. And so, defiantly, we copied – each other's work. The whole class agreed to co-operate in a free sharing of information. Tests were too frequent to be events, and there was little or no surveillance.

It was not sly, not like normal cheating. Graciously, those adept at Latin would display a grammar exercise to one aisle or the other. Those adept at algebra would return the help on another occasion. There was no counting of favours. The mood was generous, as class bonds grew closer.

Then there was some slip which I cannot remember, and the scheme was exposed. It caused a sensation. A special assembly was called in which Miss Tyfield denounced our class publicly as a disgrace to the school. Phil's old punishments now applied to all. We were, as a group, banned: the rest of the school was to shun us as contaminators of conscience. Those who were prefects had their badges of office removed, and new prefects were appointed from the B, C, and D streams. There was much surprise amongst the staff that our class captain, Marjorie, had participated, but it went without saying that the Dux that would have been hers would now go elsewhere. Marjorie, whom the girls had elected unanimously every year, was quietly mature, an unselfseeking and trusted leader. She certainly had the moral courage to resist cheating had she seen fit, but she accepted our argument.

As we saw it, we had replaced a competitive system with one of co-operation. In fact, co-operation is the basis of the way I now teach in a women's college. I encourage women to become working partners, to pool expertise in different areas, and to work out of shared interest instead of hugging to themselves their private achievements. I pass ideas freely from one tutorial to another, assuming women's agreement to a system of reciprocity. So, I am prepared to defend the spirit of cheating as it existed at Good

Hope in 1958. No group could have had more rapport because we gave up any competitive interest in class positions. Results, we had come to see, distorted learning as well as friendship.

At Good Hope we did our learning in the playground, and what we learnt was that all that mattered was the bond of friendship. For this reason the bonds of that time have remained, despite the deadly boredom, despite the cult of femininity, and divergent lives. Our cheating made us a community of women bound by vital feelings of reciprocity.

4

Pasts

When Flora's family moved to Sea Point, she took me up in her irresistible way. This interest had less to do with me than my family. Me, she rather pitied for my looks – as one who lacked the gumption to try harder – but she fell in love with my family. In the '60s, when Flora moved to Johannesburg, she closed with Berjulie as prime guide to a society in which Flora was to shine, but initially, before she left the 'gruesome' stage, she was drawn to my mother who, in those years, was an invalid and always at home.

My mother was at her most riveting at that stage of her life, as she underwent what I have thought of as conversion – though it was a discovery, not change, of religion. While she lay, not too well, on the divan, ideas poured from her that seemed more daring, more spiritual, than anything we had heard. She told us to discard the world with total conviction.

'Listen to this,' she said, opening her favourite poet, Emily Brontë. 'These were the last lines that she wrote:

No coward soul is mine
No trembler in the world's storm-troubled sphere
I see Heaven's glories shine,
And Faith shines equal arming me from Fear . . .

Though Earth and moon were gone
And suns and universes ceased to be
And thou wert left alone
Every Existence would exist in thee.'

It was heady, and a world away from school, from the toiling of Flora's parents, and from what my mother assured us were the barren facts of science and the distorted facts of newspapers. So she filled out the flourish of 'pointless' with the truths of poetry, the sublimities of faith. Flora was avid, thirsty, like a young bud that had been trying to open in the dry bed of formal schooling. Often, now, she accompanied me home while her mother was still at the shop.

'Is she awake?' I would ask Lenie, the cook, rather anxiously, as we tiptoed through the front door, for my mother's fragile wellness depended on sleep after lunch.

'*Ja*, she's waiting. I've taken in the tea.'

'Oh, Lenie,' Flora interposed eagerly, 'is that your lovely, *lovely* home-made cake?'

'Jus' baked. *Gaan, gaan.* Go,' said Lenie, opening the door to the sunroom.

There she would be in her quilted gown, the thick white curtains pulled back to let in the gold light of the afternoon, tea laid out on a cloth beside her, with nothing at all to do but form our souls.

Gripped by her gaze (the more intent for her confinement) and the shaped thoughts that slid down the rays of sun, we were drawn to discussion as she paid us the compliment of assuming that we were equal to insights that seemed to be framed for us alone.

'The Bible', she said, 'is not one book. It is a whole library of books. The story of Abraham is the first great biography, and he lived not only in relation to himself and others, but had a *third* relationship with the Lord, which has been largely lost in the twentieth century. And the Bible has short stories like the books of Ruth and Esther, and there are legends, and history, and the burning words of the Prophets.'

'But it isn't true, is it?' said Flora, who excelled at maths.

'To read the Bible is not *factual* study,' said my mother, dismissing all science with a wave of the hand, because (to her sorrow) illness had prevented her higher education, 'the Bible is *life*-study. In Hebrew the first five books are called the *Torah*, which means Teaching.'

My mother's existence, in her mid-thirties, was about to change with improved medication, and she was soon to go out on her self-conceived mission as a teacher of the Bible. She practised on Flora, as Flora turned to her in open-beaked hunger for anything – knowledge, ideas, though not love, since that Flora had amply in her own home.

My mother's approach to the Bible was essentially biographic, and each story – of Abraham, Jacob, or Joseph – had the same pattern: the journey through various ordeals towards grace. And resonating well below the surface was the parallel, the autobiographic story of my mother's own 'way' to salvation. The implication of a present-day parallel authenticated those far-off tales of desert wanderers of the Middle East, those men with multiple wives and iron wills, committed to serve the new idea of the one and only God. What my mother implied, no less than Emily Brontë, was the startling fact that the central experience, the mystical encounter, could be happening in the present, in some unheard-of provincial place and, what was more, to a woman of no public importance.

What gave my mother her undoubted charisma was an elevation of mind combined with flair for narrative. As Flora munched 'Lenie-cake', she waited to hear what came next: Jacob's wrestle with the angel in his dream on the way to find his bride; the romantic tension of his willingness to work for seven years for Rachel; the trick of his master in passing off the unwanted daughter, Leah; and then Jacob's further seven years of labour for Rachel. Nor did my mother forget the untold lives of women – the longing of weak-eyed Leah for the love that her husband gave to her prettier but less fertile sister. She filled in what the Patriarchs left out: women's faces that reflected our own, at the very time when the war-machinery, the projectiles, ramparts, and fortifications of Caesar and Vercingetorix were consuming many school hours with resentful boredom.

Flora's intense receptivity was always at the ready, for there was no experience too remote for her to touch, taste, encompass. Mysticism she took in with the same enthusiasm as she had for humorous stories.

'Was Good Hope the same when you were there?' she asked.

'Girls are always the same,' said my mother, 'though fashions change. When Auntie Isabel went to Good Hope, a generation before mine, she also read stories under the desk. Different stories, of course: her favourites were *The Bridge of Kisses* and *The Way of a Man with a Maid*.' Auntie Isabel, my grandmother's sister-in-law, still breathed the heavy aroma of romantic emotion. At family gatherings, she was much in demand for nostalgic songs which she sang in a tiny voice but with great verve and jingling of bracelets as she played the piano. Not beautiful, but exquisitely presentable, she dressed her corseted figure in dainty muslins and pressed you to her perfumed bosom. 'Lovey . . .', she would say, with a yearning break in her voice. Years later, when I got engaged, she gave me some very unromantic advice. Drawing Lovey into a corner, she pleaded in her usual breathy way: 'Don't ever refuse your husband.' She nodded, wisely. 'That's all.'

My mother opened her album to photographs of her teachers as Flora leaned over her shoulder.

'Didn't you feel it was *pointless*?' asked Flora. 'That they could never, never *understand*?'

'We had teachers who *gave* of themselves,' said my mother, seizing the invitation to expand on her life before illness had claimed it. 'Here is Miss Krige, who taught English and awakened my love of poetry. She was related to the Afrikaans poet Uys Krige, and also to Ouma Smuts. She was young, you can see, with a sweet smile and curly dark hair – we worshipped her and made up a story about her: that she was in love with a married man whose wife was in an asylum. I was a duffer at maths, but Miss Voss, here, did her best.' She pointed to a clump of girls of the '20s in navy tunics, whispering together in the familiar school grounds, as they were hustled along by a majestic older woman. The caption read: 'What's all this Voss about?' Another photograph showed my mother in shoulder-length ringlets, with two friends, Ray and Doris. The three, with arms entwined about the waist, were styled 'Do, Ray, Me'.

'What the school gave me, above all,' said my mother, 'was life-long friends. When I arrived at Good Hope as a *gawie* [bumpkin] from Klawer, Monica, who was outstanding at everything, and dear Lilianne made me welcome, and have been my friends from that day forward. Lilianne was a thin, nervous little thing, and one day,' my mother's voice took on its narrative note, and we curled up, 'Lilianne got a *third* Order Mark. An Order Mark was for a fault, and if you got three you had to report to Miss Voss. Trembling, for she was still a junior, Lilianne crept into the classroom where the teacher sat on the dais, marking some maths.

'"Miss Voss . . .", began Lilianne in a small voice, but Miss Voss took no notice. "Miss Voss," she said again, a fraction louder, "I've come to report my Order Marks." Then she stood with her head down, awaiting punishment, not knowing what it would be. For a while Miss Voss went on marking. Lilianne waited. Suddenly, Miss Voss rose, and marched to the door. Meekly, Lilianne followed. Miss Voss marched on down a corridor, turned into a room, and shut the door in Lilianne's face. Lilianne went on waiting. Then, to her astonishment, she heard a chain pulled and the flush of water. As Miss Voss emerged, majestic as ever, she said "What*ever* are you doing here?" Unable to explain, Lilianne fled.'

'That's our Good Hope, all right,' said Flora, with her hiccuping laugh: 'yuk, yuk, yuk' is how she set it down in the notes that she spread round the classroom.

'Did you go to parties?' Flora turned to the standard issue of the '50s.

'We had dances, proper dances, not your rowdy parties which no one enjoys. In the '30s, each girl was given a pink card with a tasselled pencil. Partners would then come forward and write their names against the numbered dances. It would have been bad manners to dance with the same person more than twice. I was once invited to a ball at the University of Cape Town – my partner was the head of the Students' Union and there was a pause as he led me across the hall to be introduced to the Vice-Chancellor, Sir Carruthers Beattie. I was wearing a gold lamé frock with a train attached at the waist. At the very moment that he led me forward, this train fell off and had to remain, in a small pool, in the middle of the floor.'

These were oral stories that lived in the moments of telling, dependent on voice and pause. Men have had their own stories, the after-dinner story, the pub story, the barrack-room story, ribald or heroic as the case may be, but my mother's were women's stories of minor disaster, with soft, self-mocking humour.

Flora told stories in the same mode, drawing often on my grandmother for material, dwelling on the difference of Granny's worldliness from the unworldly daughter with whom she lived. Granny and my father, both extroverts, liked to 'step out' together, while my mother lay thankfully on the sofa reading poetry or the newest South African writers: Nadine Gordimer's first collection, *The Soft Voice of the Serpent*, or a story by Dan Jacobson, which she particularly liked, 'The Zulu and the Zeide'. Before my mother emerged from illness and adopted the Jewish community, there was hardly an occasion that held for her any comparable interest. Politically, she stood to the left with Alan Paton's Liberal Party, which proposed universal suffrage, and so belonged to a minute minority in the '50s which accepted the prospect of black majority rule. In 1958, Gerald Gordon, a friend of my mother's, stood for the Liberal Party in Sea Point but was heavily defeated by Jack Basson of the tepid United Party, which opposed apartheid but still upheld white supremacy. The Liberals did not survive for long in a South Africa under Verwoerd and his successor, John Vorster. When, in 1968, multi-racial parties were about to be declared illegal, the Liberals were forced to disband rather than comply.

Though my mother lived in more than modest comfort, she spurned the 'idle rich' of her own milieu, who were then building ever larger and more opulent houses on the slopes of Lion's Head. My grandmother, in contrast, had the ingrained and outspoken prejudice of an earlier generation. She assumed all servants were 'unreliable', and probable thieves, and some of Flora's stories derived from her accusing descent on the kitchen whenever she mislaid her diamond brooch. To Flora's quick eye, Granny revealed prejudice in its most absurd forms. For the dénouement of these dramas of loss was invariably the comic recovery: with expressions of amazement, Granny would 'find' the brooch which, some time before, she herself had hidden in the roll of a corset – to outwit the servants – and then forgotten until the brooch was required for the next 'big occasion'.

No mother could have had a more alien child than Annie Press in her daughter, Rhoda, and no mother could have been more blithely oblivious of this fact. Annie, having no imagination whatever, could not conceive what life was like for those who had it – and my mother lived, like the Brontës, largely in dreams. What made Annie amusing to Flora and me, two generations on, was exactly what made her impossible to her daughter. She had no idea what others thought and felt, and this made her a very happy person, the centre of her world. During the second world war, after she had marched with the WAAFs down Adderley Street, she said proudly: 'I was the *only* one in step.'

My father, Harry, was at the periphery of this women's world. My mother used to order strong, red Lifebuoy soap, which sat on the edge of the bath. 'Don't touch it,' my mother warned. 'The men use it on themselves.'

Harry was the antithesis of my mother in every way. Where she was pure and disturbingly frail, so that we tiptoed about her, he was restless with vigour and easy-going. There were times when I liked to 'step out' with him, to leave that house of nameless suffering, and sit beside him at matches, in the press box, as he did his 'running commentary' for the SABC. I liked to look up at his keen, sunburnt face above the microphone as he related his racing story that rushed faster and faster towards the climax of the goal. 'And it's a GOAL': his stories ended on that thrilled, conclusive note. Those eventful matches called out my father's verbal momentum and he was in his element when he broadcast: relaxed, without nerves. Every Saturday night he would switch on 'Sports Roundup'. There would be the familiar galloping tune, then 'over to Harry at Hartleyvale', and then my father's voice on the air. At seven o'clock we would be at table, with my mother so wearied by this interruption, that soon, grumbling, but never really cast down, my father would switch the radio off. He was touched by the report of my mother's friend Monica, that her retarded son, Michael, was a listener. Michael's flat, fair face would brighten with recognition at the sound of my father's voice.

Neither at table nor in bed was my mother to be disturbed. Only if she were awake was it permitted to say goodbye before leaving for school. On those occasions, she would lie back on the pillows as she tied beautiful bows on my skimpy plaits. Her duties as housewife were limited, as those of all white women, to decorative touches. She arranged bowls of fruit and flowers after the servants had cleaned the rooms. She never cooked, and rejoiced in Lenie who 'had such a light touch with pastry'.

Lenie was there when I was born and still there when, as a

grown woman, I left South Africa: she was part of our family –
there was nothing she did not know – and the calm bustle of her
kitchen provided one alternative to the worry and elevation of my
mother's room. She admired Lenie, not only her cooking, but her
'serenity' which my mother associated with her single state. Once,
when Lenie was ill, my mother took her to Somerset Hospital (for
coloureds). There, it was made known that Lenie, then in her
fifties, was a virgin. My mother proclaimed her pride in this virginity all over Cape Town. Like all white 'madams', my mother in
some sense possessed Lenie, and she partook in her purity through
her feeling for Lenie as an extension of herself.

'Lenie is a saint,' my mother used to tell Flora and me, after
Lenie had led us to the sunroom, and quietly shut the door. She
was a devout Christian with an unforced humility – it was not
servile – and a quietness that was soothing because she was content. Her happiness, like my mother's, lay in conversation. As my
mother, in the sunroom, received Monica with cries of pleasure,
so Lenie, in the scoured kitchen, made tea for her single friend,
Lizzie, when both had finished with evening tasks. Unwilling to
go to bed, I rested against the rhythmic click of their Afrikaans,
not taking in what they said, because what was said was not
important so much as the act of exchange, like two steady
knitting-needles.

My mother's best times were with friends whom she was con-
verting to a deeper and more knowledgeable faith. These formed
the nucleus of a group my father called 'the Heavenly Bodies'.
Admission to the 'Friends' Group', as the women called it, was
much sought after by members of my mother's two public groups,
but almost impossible, for the former was based on old friendship
rather than degree of interest in the Bible. Gwen was one of very
few in the Friends' Group who had not been at Good Hope, and
she differed from the others in her theatricality. She was a dancer,
the only one with a career.

She was tall, with a dramatic presence as of one who wears
robes, not clothes. She came in a cloak and weird hat, which no

lesser figure could have dared to wear and which on Gwen looked spectacular. She specialized in a form of dance called Natural Movement that derived from Isadora Duncan. Gwen's every gesture, even bending down to hand a cup of tea, was an act of deliberate grace that seemed a physical counterpart of spiritual grace. Her flowing walk, rapid or emphatically slow, was not unlike the varying pace of my mother's talk. And though Gwen's theatre milieu was quite foreign to the solitude of my mother's room, they had formed, on meeting in their twenties, an instantaneous friendship based on mutual recognition of their affinity.

In the mid-'40s, ten years before the era of Heavenly Bodies, a street photographer snapped them striding arm-in-arm in rhythmic harmony: Gwen in a flat straw hat, tilted over one eye, with fresh daisies round the brim; my mother in a plain felt hat, with a dented crown in the mannish style worn towards the end of the war, stepping out for once, free and laughing, stepping out as only Gwen could make her, from the enclosure of the invalid and the constraints of marriage. Gwen's husband, an older man, had rescued her from the struggles of her early career. He was the stocky impresario who lured Markova and Ray and other celebrities from overseas. Beaming, Gwen's husband used to kiss all women and girls with gusto; otherwise he had a thick cigar planted between his lips. I disliked those smacking kisses, and can remember my discomfort, at the age of three, when Gwen's husband made me strip to my vest and panties for artistic photographs in their garden. My brown hair was pinned up on either side of my face, and I had to lie on my front, with pointed toes crossed in the air at the back and hands folded under my chin. The idea was to look like a miniature Tiller Girl, but I felt silly, and lay there wishing I could put on my frock again.

In contrast with the welcome of Heavenly Bodies, my father's sporting circle was beneath notice: featureless men with stop-watches, jabbering over the 'times' of swimmers at the latest gala. My mother received them politely, but it was not that best kind of politeness that facilitates social intercourse. She was plainly performing her duty. Occasionally, she made a reluctant appearance at a swimming gala when she did my father the favour of presenting the cups. (My father's own many cups from the Intervarsities of the late '20s were at the bottom of a particularly unimportant cupboard in the nursery, together with his albums. His photographs showed rows of unknown, poker-faced swimmers, their bulging arms folded across the chest, just below the Western Province badge on one-piece racing costumes. In front of their hairy, neatly crossed shins was a large trophy. The captions, unlike the playful ones in my mother's album, were records of serious triumphs: 'Winners of the 1928 Currie Cup'.)

Sometimes, my mother returned from a gala flushed with a triumph of her own: some extraordinary meeting with a reader of poetry or, it might be, an Afrikaner from her remote rural childhood to whom she could talk about the past, with her elevating intensity, without once having to look at the pool where, between races, bathing beauties floated in a formation of opening petals. Her triumph was to overcome her fate as sportsman's wife. She used to sit on my bed in a glow that only the veld could evoke.

'You'll never guess who was there,' she began, 'Judge Van Wyk of Van Rhynsdorp. A Namaqualander. He remembered my father, and the three farms of the Nieuwout brothers in the kloof behind Klawer.' And so she would glide into stories of her corner of the veld bounded by places with funny names: Paddagat [Frog Hole], Pofadder [Puff-adder], Tietiesbaai [Tieties' Bay], Okiep, Nababeep – all these to the north, towards what is now the Namibian border – and to the east near Calvinia, the Roep-My-Nie-Berge, the Call-Me-Not Mountains. I never tired of the strange characters who inhabited this unknown world, complete in itself in so far as it was of the past and cut off from civilization. The stories – devoid of the political issues that have become obligatory in African literature – showed Afrikaners in their pristine state. 'Pristine' was my mother's word for the treeless stretches of rock and veld which bred in them, as in her, a distinctive solitary strength and, often, a religious nature. It became clear that my mother's conversion had been predetermined by that landscape: the miles of stunted 'milk' bush, the stretching horizons, and dominant, overarching breadth of cloudless sky.

Once, she confided her dream to go back to the veld, to Klawer. It would be unchanged, and people would remember her father who grew oranges and lucerne along the narrow fertile edge of the Olifants River – named for the herds of elephant bathing and drinking in the river at the time when the Dutch governor, Simon van der Stel, made the first expedition, in 1685, to investigate the 'copper mountains' of the north-west. There, with the night sounds of the barking gecko and the whistle of the hiekiehee (a transparent grasshopper), my mother would live alone – none of us was included in her dream – and she would wear a 'uniform' (she disliked the bother of shopping for clothes), and she would be a poet.

On her bedside table lay Katherine Mansfield's letters and journal. As an invalid who 'scribbled', she identified with Katherine Mansfield, and read aloud to her children the New Zealand stories about the Burnell family, so obviously like our own. Mrs Burnell was not, in her most secret heart, a mother. She wanted most of all to be alone, or travelling away from her humdrum domestic captivity, away with her memories of her father. Athletic Mr Burnell, leaping into the sea, was unaware and exuberant, like my own vigorous father.

In the first decade of the century, my grandfather had acquired land that, according to his daughter, used to be like the setting of *The Story of an African Farm*. I would reread the magical opening paragraph, trying to imagine that dreamlike past in which my mother still lived: the full moon on the wide, lonely plain, with its utter solitude that breeds in some a mindless animal nature, and in others a godly innocence. My grandfather, coming from Lithuania, was not of it as my mother, who was born to this landscape: it shaped a religious imagination of the purest sort, like that of Emily Brontë on the Yorkshire moors. An Afrikaans novel by Anna M Louw, who was from the Calvinia of my mother's time, conveys perfectly that sense that came to me, through my mother, of the pressure of the unknown, of unanswerable questions, and the strenuous ordeals of the soul on this earth – this bare, exposed veld that brought you close to the testing landscapes of the Bible:

Op pad huis toe het die jong dominee besluit dat kindsheid soos die mense gesê het, 'n aanneemlike uitleg was. Sestien jaar later, daardie Saterdagnag ná die herbegrafnis moes hy twyfel. Was Koos Nek een van dié wat op water leer loop het? Een van dié wat leer balanseer het op die meslem waar God die siel ontmoet wat deur die smeltkroes gegaan het? Was Koos Nek een van daardie soort akrobate? [On the way home the young minister had decided that childlike simplicity was, as people had said, an appealing alternative. Sixteen years later, that Saturday night after the reburial he had his doubts. Was Koos Nek one of those who had learnt to walk on water? One of those who learnt to balance on the knife-edge where God meets the soul that has gone through the crucible? Was Koos Nek an acrobat of that kind?]*

That my mother could eventually align herself, as she chose to do, with the worldly of Sea Point – shopping in flimsy beachwear while servants cleaned the clutter – was an act of imagination: her ideals were stronger than reality, and acquired a firm basis as she adopted a more orthodox form of Judaism. For it was not in her nature to accept anything less than a strict theology. Yet, at origin, her faith came from Klawer, from the unworldliness of that place at the end of the railway before it was even a dorp.

Of course she never returned. All she managed was one school holiday.

---

*From *Kroniek van Perdepoort* (Cape Town: Tafelberg, 1975), p.7.

'The cutting. There's the cutting!' she cried in July 1948, at 5.30 in the morning, just before the night train from Cape Town crossed the railway bridge over the river into Klawer.

'Where?'

'Can't see it.'

Pip and I peered from the sleeper in the dim light. The train was slicing through a dip in the ground, insignificant amidst miles of bush. But to my mother this was home.

Aged four and six, we spent the days collecting coloured stones, while my mother sat on a rock on the edge of the earth, taking in the space and silence. The sharp air bit our throats. In the distance the horizon stood waiting.

Then an old coloured man, with a peppering of grey hair, hobbled up to my mother. '*Is die nie . . . Mnr Press se dogter nie?*' he asked.

'Rolf – can it be *Rolf* – who worked in the bar?'

'*Ja, ja*, Miss Rhoda.'

With her usual intentness, she questioned him closely about the conditions of his life. I couldn't follow his torrent of Afrikaans, emphasized by spread elbows, as he pointed back to the growing town and slapped his chest with the flat of his hand. 'We', he said to my mother, 'are of the past' – of the lard-candle people, is how he put it to her: '*Ons is van die vetkersmense.*'

My mother reminded Rolf that there had been only my grand-father's small hotel, the bar and the shop attached, his farm on the river, the railway station, the station-master, and a few gangers' cottages along the line. As his children grew older, my grandfather helped to build a one-room school, but there had been no church. Christmas was celebrated with *liedjies* [folk-songs] on the stoep of the hotel.

'Is there a church now?' my mother asked Rolf.

'*Ja*, Miss Rhoda, *daar's drie, nou* [three, now].'

The next Sunday my mother attended all three, the main Dutch Reformed Church, the Seventh Day Adventists, and the *Doppers* (who were Baptists of sorts). She had only to stand,

hesitating with her children in the door, for a member of the con-
gregation to ask her in, using the polite form of the Afrikaans
pronoun. '*Here* [Lord],' they were calling, with renewed intensity,
'*O Here, U Genade ontvang ons almal hier in Jesus naam . . . Amen . . .*
Halleluja.'

Flora gained entreé to this past as her questions brought it out.
My mother's feebleness seemed gone.

'How did your father get on with Afrikaners?' Flora asked.
'Was he a stranger, an intruder?'

'Oh, they welcomed strangers. They gave him shelter. Once,
when the river flooded, his cart was carried away. The farmers
pulled out his mules and helped to save some of his goods. In
those lonely places, people looked after one another. Another
trouble befell him. He was going up the mountain, through Grey's
Pass, between Moorreesburg and Citrusdal, when he got typhoid
fever. For one or two days he lay under his cart, unable to move.
Then a coloured boy spotted him, and went to call a woman. She
pulled my father onto the cart, and drove it to her farm. There,
she nursed him, a stranger, for three weeks. He owed his recovery
to this good woman.'

She went on to tell us what she called an Othello story about
her father's visits to a particular farm in the north-western Cape
where there lived a young girl with long, straight fair hair, as
straight as '*n perd se stert* – a horse's tail, the girl said. She was fascinated by the curly black hair of the stranger, who offered her
father interpretations of the Scriptures that he had brought from
his earlier life as a student in the religious academy, the *Yeshiva*.

'Standing behind her father, she listened to him as Desdemona
listened to Othello, the stranger whose exotic experience lay far
beyond her ken,' said my mother, no doubt embellishing the story
in her own fashion. 'So she was drawn to him, and ventured to ask
for a lock of his hair. He had dark blue eyes with his black hair,
but he wasn't handsome. Maybe she fell in love with his mind and
character, for when he came back, on another visit, he found the
lock of his hair in the family Bible.'

'What made him change from wandering across the country to a settled life in Klawer?' asked Flora.

'That wasn't for many years. When the Boer war broke out, he had to lie low. He was not yet a citizen of the Cape Colony, and could have been interned by the British. After the war he opened a shop in Doornrivier [Thorn River], a very lonely place – too lonely to prosper. Once, a group of Africans came into the shop to buy *twak* [tobacco] or *stroop* [syrup]. A man, brushing against the counter, found that it moved; then another moved it a bit more; then, suddenly the whole group caught the idea, and began edging the counter towards my father, inch by inch, to pin him against the wall. Reaching under the counter, he pulled out a gun and fired it above their heads. With cries and waving hands, the crowd fled.

'Then he heard that the railway would be extended to Klawer, on the border of Namaqualand, and he realized that travellers would need a place to stay. So he bought land near the station, and farming land across the river. He built the hotel in about 1910 – about twelve rooms with lavatories and showers in outhouses at the back – and when the farmers said that Jews could not work with their hands, he began growing lucerne (Klawer means clover or lucerne) and oranges which he sold to the South African Railways. Farmers from miles around Klawer would bring their carts on train days, three times a week, and barter their wool, lucerne, and skins for coffee, *versterk-druppels* [strengthening medicine], sugar, flour, *velskoene* [skin shoes], farm implements, saddles and harnesses. Philip himself was a good horseman; he called his horse 'Apple' because he loved that fruit. He was also a juggler and he could do an African war-dance with *kieries* [sticks].

'After his marriage, part of the hotel was for the family, and my mother had a private kitchen with bags of cream-cheese hanging from the ceiling. She socialized the place with balloon dances on Saturday nights. A balloon was tied to each woman's heels and the winner of the weekly prize was the one whose balloon hadn't burst by the end of the dance.'

Klawer had a compelling otherness for girls growing up in the English atmosphere of Cape Town, with its élite of colonials whose consciously refined accents and distancing manners intimidated all other groups: Afrikaners, Jews, coloureds, Malays, blacks, Indians, Portuguese, and the arriving Italians who were opening coffee-bars called Venezia and Harlequin. In 1954 when Anna Louw's daughter, Elizabeth, went to Rustenburg, one of the most English of Cape Town schools, she found the girls singing 'God Save the Queen' at assembly.

After they finished, the Head singled out the new Afrikaner girl, and ordered her onto the platform. 'Why aren't you singing?' she demanded.

'I don't know the words,' said Lizzie truthfully. The girls tittered.

The Head gave Lizzie an incredulous look. 'You will learn them then,' she said sternly.

It was not until I read *A Passage to India* that it became clear how insistent that Englishness had been. In the meantime, Klawer broke through colonial imitations with an authentic Africa of which we knew nothing.

'What do you remember best?' asked Flora, pressing my mother. 'People? Could you follow their Afrikaans?'

'People, yes, so isolated – they became idiosyncratic,' she mused, 'but more than people, a place – uninhabited, pristine. It brought one close to the Creation – "In the beginning God created the heaven and the earth" – and so it brought you close to your Maker. It was a shepherd's world, with flocks of bushes, sky-circled. Only the herb-scented bush, and turban-piled rocks, and wild flowers: silken Namaqualand daisies that would carpet the veld after the spring rains, *katsterte* [cats'-tails], *vygies, pypies, gousblomme,* chincherinchees and the delicately fragrant afrikander. Temperatures went so high in summer – over 40° – that plants, forced to be dormant, spent the summer underground. Then, in August, at the end of the winter, the sudden, extraordinary transformation. The short blaze. The orange Namaqualand daisies covered every inch of the veld. No other desert has anything like it. There was a yellow-green bush and when you wet its hard knobs, it was soapy. At school, on sewing days, we used to wash our hands in "the furrow" (there were no taps) with these little yellow knobs for soap.'

'What games did you play?' Flora wanted to know. 'Did you have toys?'

'Toys? We had our imaginations! We made caves from the smooth oval stones. On my way to school I used to find stones that were striped like chic Parisian fashions, or moon-coloured, or apricot; possibly semi-precious stones: jasper, agate, opal, and rose-quartz. Sometimes, my brothers and I joined empty sardine tins to form toy trains which we pulled along in the saffron-coloured sand under the pepper trees next to the station. My father warned us of quicksand when we went to paddle in the river, and once my brother, Louis, did sink to his knees but was pulled out by our nurse.'

'You remember such detail,' Flora said enviously. 'I remember so little . . . mostly my *emotions*: when I was nine, I got it into my head that my father was having an affair with his bookkeeper in his furniture shop. I fumed over this until one night my suspicions overwhelmed me. My parents were visiting their neighbours. On an impulse, I *tore* out of the front door and *burst* into the neighbours' lounge where a lot of people were sitting around comfortably.

'"You've betrayed her, my mother," I screeched at my father. "How could you . . ." I broke into loud sobs.

'"What are you talking about?" said my father in a voice of weary exasperation – the whole family was fed up with my scenes and with the terrible fights between me and my brother, Reggie.

'"Tell me what's going on with Mrs Breede," I shrieked.

'"Nothing at all. Go home," said my father, curtly. I could hear from the quietness of his tone that I'd gone too far, and he was really, really furious.

'And then, suddenly, as suddenly as I'd got the suspicion, it vanished. Gone. I knew, with absolute conviction, that it *had* been nothing, and then, I felt this tremendous *shame*, and I wanted to say, to pour out to my father how sorry I was to have shamed him by his daughter's *terrible* behaviour in front of his friends. I *empathized* with him, my darling, my struggling father, so tired after his work. But then I couldn't say a *word* – he looked so sternly sorrowful. I just backed out of the room, knowing I could *never* make it up to him, crept back home, and cried myself to sleep. That's what I remember best: my fury with my own, uncontrollable feelings.'

We all laughed: Flora ruefully; my mother touched by Flora's candour and passion for her father; and I entertained by the urgency of feelings that led Flora into repeated scrapes.

'Sounds . . . touch . . . smell above all, the sour-sweet smell of the veld bushes at dawn, the sharp drone of the *kriekies* [crickets] piercing the vastness of the night,' said my mother, returning quickly to her own past. 'The senses remember best, and bring back that detail. Sounds, now: I remember the sound of hoofs, my father off to the farm as I opened my eyes in the morning; the farmers arriving on train days, which were great social occasions. They outspanned at the hotel and drank their coffee out of saucers – sroop, sroop. They sat on the stoep, looking out to the long, low hill across the river, as they slurped through their beards. After the war, the first world war, Italian engineers came to build an irrigation scheme. Water, which had been dammed higher up the Olifants River, at Bulshoek, flowed through the furrow all the way to the Atlantic Ocean, with sluice gates along its course for leading water to the farms. A large group of Africans came to dig the furrow. On the beat of their chant, their picks cut through the earth in unison. The Italians, who stayed with us, brought opera on gramophone records. It was still that old His Master's Voice gramophone with the horn. Lying by candlelight in my bedroom, one night I heard Galli-Curci's voice, fountaining up to the stars over that lonely veld.'

She paused to relive this awakening, but Flora's thoughts had taken a more practical turn.

'How did you manage, there, without the necessities – a bank or a post office?'

'We made visits to the nearest town, Van Rhynsdorp, a difficult journey in my father's Model-T Ford. The road (so called) passed through the Atties River, which ran between thorn bush, so that the car either had a puncture or got stuck in soft sand. Once, when the river bed was dry, our driver, Koos Nieuwout, brought the car to a sudden halt and we watched a huge puffadder slowly slither across the path about five metres ahead. When my father eventually made it to Van Rhynsdorp to take his driving test, Mayor Van Wyk said shrewdly, "I don't suppose that you've learnt to reverse yet."

'Philip shook his head.

'"No matter," said the Mayor, and granted the licence. There were almost no cars, anyway.

'There was a family called Roos, whose grandmother had been a Dutch Jewess who had married an Afrikaner. Theo van Wyk, a son of the mayor and now Judge-President of the Cape, was her grandchild. There was a brother who became an anti-Semite. Along the river at Vredendal, he held a meeting of the Grey Shirts when Hitler came to power. (In the '30s, and even during the war, many Afrikaners were Nazi supporters, in their case out of bitter hostility to Britain that was a legacy of the Boer war – you remember, that when the Boers refused to accept their defeat, Kitchener destroyed tens of thousands of farmsteads and removed women and children to camps where most of them died of dysentery and other diseases.) Well, this Roos grandchild delivered a speech, and afterwards he called to the audience and said, "Tell me" (I'll speak Afrikaans and then translate): *"Sê vir my, as julle een goeie Jood ken.* Tell me if you know one good Jew."

'So someone put up a hand at the back of the meeting, and the speaker said, *"Ja?"*

'And the man answered, *"Jou Ouma!* Your Granny!"'

'So there *was* prejudice – against Jews as well as blacks,' Flora noted.

'Oh yes, as everywhere else in the world at that time, except that here it carried on.'

'Why?'

'Well, for one thing, the size of the black majority, seventy-five per cent of the population, a problem here as nowhere else. After three hundred years the Afrikaners no longer saw themselves as colonials – for them there was no other home. Not like the British in India who could return to the mother country. And then, of course, there is the effect of the Dutch Reformed Church which set up different churches for the different races – and above all the effect of the *Taal*. The descendants of the settlers from Holland who came in the seventeenth century eventually spoke a dialect that cut them off from Europe, six thousand miles away. The *Taal* cut them off from ideas of liberty, equality, and fraternity; they missed out on the eighteenth century, and remained locked in their language, closed off, as they still are, to the rest of the world. Yes, to go back to Klawer, there were cruelties, not only racial cruelties, but those of mental narrowness, backwardness. I remember, as a small child, watching through the nursery window, the transport drivers whipping their long teams of donkeys unmercifully. And once I saw a railway ganger chasing his small son round and round his house with a whip. I saw the child's desperate cropped head and the twin-bones straining at the back of his neck as he fled. Some months later, the boy died and we, in our one-roomed school, made the wreath for his grave. And then there was black-browed, blue-spectacled Mr Boeke. He had a kindly, bird-like wife with a pince-nez whom he called "Girlie". They used to visit us at Klawer in a tiny trap. Later, overhearing the gossip at my mother's teas, I was shocked to hear that Mr Boeke beat his wife.'

'And she *stayed* with him?' Flora was outraged.

'Of course,' said my mother, calmly. 'Women do: they feel attached and forgive the man who is sorry afterwards.'

'But how can they feel attached to a brute?' asked Flora disbelievingly.

'Oh yes, they *can*. I've known many a woman in the grip of a rotter, fascinated, you know.'

'It sounds exciting,' laughed Flora, thinking my mother too pure.

She wasn't amused. 'You are quite, *quite* wrong,' she fixed Flora with her most serious look. 'I must warn you, because you are like my daughter, that your virginity is an all-important protection. You see,' she went on earnestly, 'what happens to most women is that they become emotionally bound to the man to whom they give their virginity. They can't help it, no matter how bad he is. It's different for most men, who are by nature promiscuous. A woman's feelings are roused by the sex act; for a man, when it's done, it's over.'

Flora and I glanced at each other uneasily. Though we invited the gory details from Granny in her matter-of-fact voice, we did not care for these ominous details of adult trauma. I saw that Flora suspected my mother of exaggeration, and that she was uncomfortable. To hear this warning was to feel ashamed of our susceptibility: the helpless crushes, the recklessness of emotions that, at fifteen, remained within the virtuous margin of dream only because they were secret, improbable, and unrequited.

'The woman who is abused, like Mevrou Boeke, doesn't she fear her husband, even if she gets in his grip?' Flora pursued the matter, rather anxiously.

'The woman's fear is more that violence may be in some way her fault – that's the victim mentality. Then, too, she is adapted to authority. I knew one woman who had her house built in the shape of a Cross, and she was a most good-hearted person. But her husband, the *Dominee* [minister], could have been in Dickens. He was a replica of the hypocritical Reverend Chadband in *Bleak House*. He was solemn and portentous. Later, he became a Nationalist MP.'

'Tell us more. About nice people, and tell us more about the funny ones, about the ones you said got eccentric.'

Now my mother was in her stride, I could tell from the

warmed-up tone of her voice. As her stories got longer, she no
longer needed the prompting. 'There were three brothers,
Nieuwout their name was, and they had three farms. They were
in a kloof in the Matsie Kamma Mountain, with waterfalls
descending, three miles to the back of Klawer. Their furniture was
of stinkwood, and in the *voorkamer* there was a long table, so polished that it reflected the three bowls of violets in its black surface.
And there were *karosses* [skins] on the floor. The floors were of
mis: dried dung.'

'Didn't it smell?' interrupted Flora.

'No. It was diluted, and pressed down. It had a lovely sheen
after brushing. And I remember going there to visit Mevrou
Nieuwout, who was a monolithic woman – I called her "the
Giantess". She adopted a small black girl whom she dressed in
crisp white. I don't remember much about the second farm, but
the third, which was tucked right into the kloof, had old orange
trees casting a glooming light there, and you went across a stream
into this grove. I remember, as a child, going into the orchard;
there was this glooming light and the oranges shining; and then I
heard a weird cackling voice, like "Kaatjie Kekkelbek" [a folk-
character]. There was a *dakhuisie* [tiny attic] in this third
farmhouse, and the cackle came from that window, which I could
just glimpse, high up, through the trees. It was like the story of
David Copperfield when he comes to his aunt, Miss Betsy
Trotwood, you remember: the attic window opens and out pops
Mr Dick. Well, this was Miss Mimosa. She popped out of the
dakhuisie window and her voice could be heard for a mile around
as she gave orders in this peacock voice.'

'Please, *please* write it down', pleaded Flora, 'or it will be lost.'

'Oh, it's nothing,' muttered Rhoda. 'One can't take it seriously, these memories.'

'No, you must,' said Flora, in her direct way that all my family
found refreshing. She was unaware of the customary barriers of
age and deference. She said exactly what she thought. She urged
her elders to fulfil their secret wish, and she was nonchalant,

almost outrageous in asking just the questions that led her, by the shortest route, to divination. The shyer the wish, the more special seemed that bond with Flora who drew it out and made it seem reasonable, natural, even wonderful. 'It is wonderful. You *must* write,' she urged Rhoda. And this, of course, was exactly what Rhoda wished to do – but rarely did because, as a housewife, she feared her temerity.

The fuel of Flora's response was irresistible. She succeeded where others' urgings (including mine) had failed. Tentatively, Rhoda did 'scribble' what she called her 'Vignettes of Namaqualand: Forty Years Ago'. She never tried to publish them – that would have seemed to her presumptuous – but, years later, I found them in a drawer, dated 1957. What had been an assortment of oral histories was here fused in a narrative of one Christmas Day at Klawer in the early 1920s. It was signed with the writer's maiden name, Rhoda Stella Press:

I remember light filtering through a seam in the nursery shutter and, silhouetted as a shape, a cock's crow ebbing across the veld, drawing me out of bed, through the muffled sitting-room onto the back stoep. There is a broom in my hands and I am wrinkling away the sand, like a silky brown skin which the veld wind had whirled there. The giant gum tree which wrestled all night with the wind was now still. Leaning on my broom, I look out like a shepherd over the flocks of patient bushes stretched to the verge of vision.

Round the woodpile and under the pepper trees pace the few who cannot go home for Christmas or who have no home. Then the Giantess arrives, bringing my mother *konfyt* [jam] and oval tomatoes. With her is Lice (short for Liza), the tiny black girl she has adopted, in her white starched dress like a fly dipped in cream. The Giantess has a deep voice and matching strong thoughts about something called the 'school board'. But her sister-in-law, Tant Sannie, has the power of kindness. I have heard my father call her a saint.

For me she is her farmhouse in the kloof, with its black stinkwood furniture laced with oxhide strips, the bowls of violets mirrored in the black table, and *karosses* on the floor.

But why is my mother making staring eyes at me? Tant Sannie nods and blinks to reassure me as I am hustled to the door and hidden in the nursery to be washed and brushed.

Now there is the thud of horses' hooves along the road; then voices, and the sound of a fiddle. Soon there pulses from those leaping rhythms the memory of *trek-laagers*, of homestead weddings, or veld-divided lovers, enlarging my small frame with such inflated emotions that I can hardly wait until the last curl releases me like a spring from the hands of our coloured maid.

There on the front stoep, Lice is leaning against the green trellis, rubbing one fly-like leg against another. Wonderstruck, she gazes at the gathering of homeless men, with no church for miles around, singing their *liedjies*. At the core of the singing is Hennie, the blind man, with his fiddle. With his sunken lids, he seems to be dreaming, but his fingers are awake. The blue globes of his eyes turn inwards. My father tells me that Hennie rides alone about the countryside on horseback, finding his way by the sound of the wind in the telegraph wires. There is Oom Albertus with his long beard, slurping coffee from a saucer; Sakkie, the barman, and lurking in the background his coloured helper, Rolf; and Mr Nelson with his sea-blue eyes and panama hat who boasts, when drunk, that he is descended from the English admiral. He has brought his son, Charlie, who has the whipped look of the fearful and is, I know, a thief. And singing with them is the visiting Italian engineer, Salo, whose clever plans bulge in knots on his bumpy, bald head. Often, in my candle-lit bedroom, I have heard his records: the voice of Caruso or Galli-Curci fountaining over the dark veld.

But my mother is making eyes again, through the window, and drumming on the pane with her fingers. She is preparing a huge Christmas dinner for the men on the stoep. She points me away from the singing into the car with our driver, Koos.

I don't recall on what errand we were sent, nor where, because Gert, my father's clerk who was also in the car, began talking about Christmas. He said, 'Jews – they are at the bottom of all the *nekery* [underhandedness] in this world.' Gert's bullet head which had been as homey as our dining-room table, jutted suddenly cruel; and with his changed look, the kindliness of the Giantess and Oom Albertus and even Tant Sannie was changed too. For the first time I was separated from them and from the veld, and I saw the spaces over which the sun walked serenely that Christmas morning, as mere sand and bush.

Between the bushes swung the 'Dancing Doll', the dressmaker, her hips wading in her many petticoats; her tall, gangling son plodding behind, his clothes patched with bits and pieces of his mother's trade. What she had done, I did not know, but it was something disgraceful that made people signal with their eyes. Towards her hut in the mountains they walked in a path worn only by their own feet – separate too.

When I went back to the one-room school after the Christmas holidays, the Brewer children were there. They were dark; but in those days that was not the chief reason that they were slighted. The scandalous fact that stoked the gossip of my mother's tea-parties was that Mrs Brewer 'painted her face'.

'Is it true that your Ma paints her cheeks?' we asked the children.

The two older girls had the impassive fat-Indian look of their father, but the youngest, who was spry and freckled like a plover's egg, explained eagerly: 'Yes, but she powders it over again.'

When Gert's little daughter asked me if I 'was a Jew', I answered quickly, without thinking: 'no, we're English people . . .'

So memory has telescoped events and rolled them down the years.

Flora and Rosie came to marvel at the local phenomenon of a poetic mother. She did not seem like anyone they knew. Her spirituality seemed different from the placid, traditional religion practised in Sea Point in the 1950s. Despite the emotive style of the ancient liturgy and the keening of traditional chants, I was convinced that the men who swayed below us with the most energetic agitations of prayer, were only aping the old forms. Socially, their concern was to air the small vanities of business.

Rhoda's faith, in contrast – a contrast she would deplore – was strenuous. She had the old moral sense to an acute and uncomfortable degree: a sense of life as a series of tests. She had a capacity for suffering and a horror of impurity. And she emphasized an inner life validated by mystical experience. She intimated that, though solitary, she was never alone.

So the rigours and imaginative reaches of this conversion in the latter years of the '50s provided Flora and me with our alternative education. The private 'way' exemplified a long-term alternative to the compulsions of public identity.

5

Experiments

'One's own personality is only a ridiculous and aimless masquerade of something hopelessly unknown,' wrote Joseph Conrad in a letter of 1896. It was back at school, through revolt, cheating, and the bond of outcasts, that we glimpsed a secret sharer, some other and perhaps authentic self who lurked half-defiant, half-craven, beneath the approved identity of Bardot or socialite, as the case might be. It was at school, in our last year, 1958, that we refused to play the game, ten years and more before defiance became, in turn, a social ritual: the automatic drama of the age. Back in 1958, we swerved in the privacy of friendship, groping for something – not knowing what it was – that found rudimentary expression in certain unrecorded gestures: in notes passed between girls behind the lifted lids of their desks; in low talks at the bottom of the school grounds; and not least in communal cheating. 'Rosie', I wrote early in 1958, 'is my exact opposite – a socialite, self-confident, dress-conscious – but we are both very interested in English and, somehow, though we have little else in common, we have discussions on anything under the sun: art, drama, Communism.'

These talks had to co-exist with a 'gruesome' exterior. Gruesome, as conceived by Flora, was not wholly pejorative: though in one sense it ridiculed the girl who went in for khaki trousers and ideology, in another sense it also implied some intransigence that was invited to indulge itself in the protective environment of a girls' school. It must be owned that Phillippa, inscribing 'ROBERT' on her ruler, had no part in the gruesome, but Flora matched it with her own, antithetical adjective, 'foluptuous'. 'Foluptuous Flora' she signed the notes passed behind desk-lids while Caesar marched through Gaul, or while Miss Johns, who was too clever for school maths, foamed at the blackboard. These notes, on torn bits of scribbler, mocked the polar identities we assumed:

> Wednesday, last period: Latin

Dear Flora,
    My name is Gruesome. My measurements are 40–40–40 and I'm a social misfit.

Dear Gruesome,
    I honestly did not think that I'd grow to like you as I do now. Remember when we used to talk about combining our interests although you belonged to the Movement & I liked social life? I didn't think anything would come of it! But it's worked. I really enjoy being with you. Let's go steady (yuk, yuk, yuk).
        Your ever-loving fan,
            Foluptuous

In the '50s 'social life' meant, specifically, to be a party girl who went to Town every Saturday morning to shop for elasticized belts, hooped petticoats, and mascara. Flora was allowed unlimited licence with her mother's account at Stuttaford's. For Mrs Gevint, nothing was too much for her children, though she dressed plainly and rarely bought for herself. Not to go to parties was to be a 'social misfit'. At one end of the social scale, a girl was 'sophisti-cated'; at the other end she was 'immature'.

'No one' meant no boy of interest, as in 'There was no one at the party on Saturday night'. Approved boys were 'smooth'; but those whose smoothness became insinuating were 'slimy'. 'Pointless' was no more than a light flourish: the nihilism of Sartre or Camus was unknown to us; and French culture more remote than can be imagined in Europe or America. French was offered at school only as an alternative to Latin; and where Latin was part of the curriculum, French was an extra. Parents had to pay, and most, including mine, thought it unnecessary. By the time that French culture reached the bottom of Africa, nothing was left but the open-mouthed pouting of Bardot and, since the seasons diverged, last year's fashion.

The wide belts of the '50s showed off the 'vital statistics', and I won praise from my aunts when I cut my hair. A new cut was a sign of sophistication in the new version of Cinderella: in this story – a film called *Sabrina* or *My Fair Lady* – a simple, fringe-member of society put on the clothing of sophistication which transformed her very nature. Once shy, she was now ambitious – ambitious, that is, to get her man. When she made her dramatic entrance at the ball, she ignored all women, as she greeted the man of her dreams who, in the '50s version, was emotionally thick. This prince, translated into a Wall Street tycoon or reserved Englishman, had to be coaxed – by way of an extravaganza of fem-inine wiles – into some dim awareness of love. The subtler message of the age was to accept the limitations of men locked into a self-made fortress, from which they shot dull commands at secretaries who, as working women, had to be dowdy and even more boring to offset the brightly entertaining babble of Audrey Hepburn.

The socialist youth movement called Habonim offered an escape from 'social life'. Its appeal for me was not its affiliation with Israel's ruling Mapai party, but its commitment to reshape the conditions of social existence. Members of the Movement believed in the dignity of labour, communal living (as practised by the kibbutz in its original form), the sharing of property on an equal basis, simplicity and *chavershaft* (comradeship). Most compelling was the heat of discussion: the leaders spoke with an uncompromising honesty which broke through the drone of men, the gush of women, the banter of flirts, and the lies of crooners. I was drawn by its socialist idealism but, truth be told, went also to court the suppressed pain of a succession of crushes. I was dazzled by talkers like Cory Anstey, the expounders of demanding ideals, or the softer-spoken intellectuals, like the law student Edgar Carlin, with his dark-faced warnings of South Africa's path to destruction. At meetings I offered the most earnest echoes: 'It must be obvious, then, that the kibbutz movement offers the best alternative to the decadence of this country.' That was how we spoke. Once you learnt the argument, it was simple.

To be a serious person in this milieu meant to accept the obligation to devise a future that would take you out of racist society. 'Ideals', in the context of the Treason Trial of the late '50s and increased majorities for the Nationalists in the election of 1958, meant some form of action beyond rhetoric and the excitements of ideological allegiance: a radical action that would effectively change one's life – either to do battle against the regime or to clear out in the certainty that to live as a white in South Africa was to be tainted by privilege, no matter how fervent the criticism. My diary favoured the latter choice: it took the line that there would be no solution to racism in South Africa. This was, naturally, the line pressed by the Movement, which urged us to go 'on *Aliyah*' [to emigrate; literally, to go up to Israel]. At the time when the hardliner, Verwoerd, came to power, with a two-thirds majority in an all-white parliament, my diary notes, on 18 April, 'the sadistic fanaticism creeping over the country' and the growing 'madness of power' amongst Nationalists who 'suppress the vast majority of the population'. But though I was against white power, I had no confidence that black power, whenever it came, would be less terrible. The history of tribal warfare was no less barbaric than the history of colonialism. In any case, whites would be irrelevant, I believed, to black struggle. Robert Sobukwe, a forceful orator, was then emerging as an alternative to Chief Luthuli and Nelson Mandela, who continued to work for reconciliation of the races. Sobukwe was saying that since whites benefited from the existing social order, they could not identify with the African cause.

The diary comments were fairly typical of the alarm that came to liberal whites in isolated political moments, from which they sank back into customary oblivion. Anti-apartheid rhetoric was so habitual as to be part of that oblivion, and the Group Areas Act kept the immediate impact of racist legislation conveniently out of sight. One Movement leader, Siamon Gordon, used to go each week, with other medical students, to work in a clinic in Windermere on the fringes of Cape Town. He spoke once of the horror of *seeing* in the Conradian sense.

'At Clinic last night,' he told us, 'I have never felt so helpless, powerless, and ineffectual. How the hell can a handful of ignorant medical students tackle a problem that society refuses to face up to squarely? I'm telling you, we are wasting our time – wonder-drugs and all. What are we curing them for? Can a person cure starvation with an injection? Can you give people hope in pill form? Does education come in readily dispensable doses? The task is so great that it is almost inevitable that one accepts failure at the outset.'

For most of us this was invisible, so we often said the approved liberal things without feeling them. The effect of the Act was to turn each group upon itself, cut off from other groups, each locked in its own narrow cares.

This was a state of mind that was peculiarly warping for white women, who were left with nothing at all to do but lie in the sun, arrange flowers, and offer each other dainty gifts at morning parties. These small rituals – which defined womanhood in those days – assumed an inordinate importance in the triviality of work-less days. The doves cooing through the pines and the foghorn blaring on winter nights spoke of protracted vacancy. When, as a child, I woke to these sounds, I used to think: nothing will happen; nothing will change. As one day of natural perfection fol-lowed another, they seemed to mark unending stagnation.

As a girl, I never conceived of work in the sense of a profession. Emigration was to be the great adventure, not economic, mental, or political struggle. Though emigration was expected of all Movement members, Siamon was the one leader to challenge the vagueness of this future as it would affect women. I was surprised by his notion that I should plan a career.

'Why don't you write?' he suggested as we sat around after a meeting. 'You should try biography. It would combine your inter-ests in literature and history. You should think more seriously of what you could do.'

'No,' I said, 'no, impossible.' I thought of my mother who wrote poems, but kept them, like Emily Dickinson, tied up in a drawer. If she were diffident, I who was not poetic should be all the more so.

'I wouldn't want to live with an idle woman,' he said. 'I grew up in Darling, in the country, where women worked hard. My mother made her own soap, wine, and candles – there was no electricity.'

'Home-made . . .,' I murmured. 'Much nicer.'

'You've got it wrong. It wasn't nice at all. The soap smelt foul while it boiled. My brother and I used to tread the grapes with bare feet. And for my mother, it was a grind. There was no run-ning water: we children had a bath once a week in a tub in the kitchen.'

'Only one a week?'

'What would you do if you had to make the soap yourself and boil the water on a coal stove? It was an effort. I used to like to make suds, and one bathtime made more and more, the tub was full of shining bubbles, but when I heard my mother's footsteps coming down the passage towards the kitchen, I saw that I'd used up all the soap. She was angry: she beat me.'

'Awful.' I was horrified.

'Not at all.' His English was idiomatic, but he spaced his words with the strong consonants and accented opening syllables of country people whose first language is Afrikaans. 'I didn't mind – she was right. A beating is quick; the issue is over. Much better than all that unnecessary talk and festering resentment that goes on in polite homes.'

'Beating, all physical punishment, is cruel.'

'It's less cruel in the long run than psychological punishment. That is what's awful. Up-country, where people worked hard, there wasn't time for fingering the finer feelings. And no one was a lady – ladies are useless.'

I listened uneasily, looking down at his brown slippers – it was whispered in the Movement that he was too poor to afford shoes. I had never before met a white who was as poor as blacks. His father had been a country Reverend, lower than a rabbi, more of a functionary who had served the religious needs of scattered villages from Darling to Saldanha Bay. Each week his father would make his circuit, slaughtering animals in the ritual way for *kashrut*, and training rural boys of twelve to read the *Haftorah* [portion of the Prophets] for their bar mitzvahs.

The Afrikaans school at Darling came to an end after ten years and a local benefactor had sent Siamon to boarding-school, the South African College School in Cape Town. He had read English books, he said, but never spoken the language, and made a fool of himself on the first day by his mispronunciation of 'auto*mo*bile'. At the age of fifteen, while he was away at school, his father died suddenly of a heart attack. His mother then moved to a small flat above some shops, where she took in boarders. He spoke with concern of her hard life. His poverty, his sense of life as a challenge, his scorn of emotional indulgence, and above all those slippers, so careless of appearance, gave him a moral advantage.

And though I was certain that there could be no approach to his idea for my future, I was struck by the boldness of that disinterested thought. Even in the Movement, the ideal for women was to go on kibbutz where their assigned tasks would be, as elsewhere, domestic: the children's house, the store-room, ironing, and cooking. The men, for the most part, worked in the fields. This was not an issue in our discussions; the current debates were over children. Girls questioned the custom of a children's house separated from parents. The *shaliach* [a missionary from the kibbutz movement] would always retort that, on kibbutz, women spent more numerical hours with children because, after work, they had no further cares.

Should I go to Israel straight from school? Was I suited to kibbutz? In the final year at school we were given a vocational guidance test, and I contrived to tick, at every opportunity, the desire to grow things, to tend chickens, and to dig the soil, in order to ensure that the result would prove my natural aptitude for agricultural labour. In truth, I was afraid of bulls, had seen them only from the National Road, and had never planted anything – the black gardener did it all. The *shaliach* urged us in unanswerably idealistic terms to put the needs of the country before the selfish wish to study further, indeed to 'burn our bridges' by not allowing ourselves the alternatives that higher education would offer. Should I go to the Hebrew University? Could I bear to leave friends and family? And what about love? The talkers who sanctioned my echoes showed no interest in me as a girl. The Movement's emphasis on communal living meant that the leaders abjured (for the time being) the kind of private tie that might undermine the group. We had 'functions', not dates. But quite often, a couple did form in the interstices, as it were, of communal purpose.

These issues crept about as I inspected my spots in the mirror. 'Carbuncle' was Flora's word for the blemish that loomed large in the path to sophistication. Tactful silence was not her style.

'You've got a carbuncle,' she scribbled one day with sisterly

directness. 'Oh, it's so juicy, it gives me the Sex Urge.' With rude-
ness went consolation. 'Come to Gevints Fashions,' she invited,
'pick out some dresses.' So she tempted me to transformation.

A week before, I had hiked along Table Mountain, with the
older élite of the Movement, to whose group, called the *Chug*, a
fellow member called Jasmine and I aspired. Jasmine, enviably,
had at that time a boyfriend in the *Chug*, Ralph, who was, as my
diary puts it, 'the link between all the sects and cliques. I like and
admire him tremendously,' I wrote. As we climbed up the rocky
path, early in the morning before the sun got hot, he had turned
to face me.

'Look,' he said with the concerned directness that was the
Movement style, 'you're a mess.'

He stopped in the path, a stocky figure in the blue Movement
shirt with the blue beret on his head, and gazed at me appraisingly
but not unkindly. His brown eyes reflected my baggy trousers, the
khaki shirt that hung over too-big hips, the heavy, rolled-up
sleeves, my untrimmed hair, and hot red face. Yes, I was a mess
and, almost perversely, practised a studied indifference to my
appearance because I thought myself more than plain. In contrast
with other girls, I was irredeemable. I stamped up the mountain in
thick boots, pushing my unwashed hair out of my eyes. Under my
palm, I felt the familiar film of acne. Those days, I could hardly
bear to look in the mirror long enough to tie my hair back, as
required by Miss Tyfield, on school days. On Saturday nights my
friends went on dates; I counted myself fortunate that, at functions, we danced mainly in a circle – since I did love to dance.
Siamon sometimes asked me for the fast and furious Krakowiak
which was danced in competition, to see which pair could hold
out longest. He liked to win, and I knew that he picked me for
stamina, the controlled placing of energy learnt from ballet. I
wrote in my diary that 'Siamon Gordon dances with more zest
than grace'.

At Gevints Fashions, Flora's mother had put aside three frocks
in crisp cotton. one was white with thin green stripes. It buttoned

on the shoulder and had white ricrac around the neck and the armholes. 'See how nice you can look,' said Mrs Gevint, turning me round. 'There you are.' Undeniably, I did look better in a frock.

'Why, you've got green eyes,' Flora said, looking closer at the mirror. 'You should make something of them.' A few days later, I wrote: 'Flora came for dinner. We made up our eyes for fun, and Flora did my hair in a new way which we both thought very chic, but my mother said I looked like Mark Antony gone wrong.'

That spring, when the need to be normal came to have precedence over ideals, I drew closer to Flora and away from the Movement. Our differences dissolved in anticipation of the untested possibilities of existence. Flora looked on existence not as a purposeful coming into being through ideology, but as a heady, immediate moment of experience. From September to November, as we prepared for our matric exams, we shared a life of no event, unless it could be called an event to leave our books for the sand at Rocklands, to let the sun sear our minds away, and to hear the irregular pulse of the breakers coming at us with a burst of spray. The noon sun warmed our bodies so completely that the rays seemed to radiate from beneath the skin to meet the reach of that cooling spray.

Flora was a giver of confidence. Her blunt darts – 'you have a carbuncle' – were honest and humorous, not hurtful. What Flora and Rosie called (proudly) 'maniacal laughter' or (approvingly) 'hysteria' accompanied their bursts of candour that induced moments of the strongest rapport.

Rosie, who was reticent, said: 'She rushes in where angels fear to tread, but you don't resent it, you even welcome it, despite yourself, because she's so rashly impulsive, so impatient, so curious. With heels pounding, she tears into your house, almost bursting the lock.'

The advancing leaps of 'empathy' that almost knocked one over, like Tigger's unruly bounce, had their goal: to induce others to be what they were made to be. She had no rules; she simply lent herself to undefined need, called it into existence, watered it with eager concern, and nurtured it into action. In this way she exploded provincial stagnation: to know her was to realize that possibilities lay all about us, in the provinces of South Africa, in the dullest of schools. Formal learning was but veneer. When, later, I learnt Conrad's corollary to his perception that character remains hopelessly unknown – 'There remains nothing but surrender to one's impulses, the fidelity to passing emotions which is perhaps a nearer approach to truth than any other philosophy of life' – I recognized this fidelity as one that Flora practised long ago, without a philosophy, with only an intuitive grasp of how to be.

In the '60s, Flora became a teacher, but teaching was not her vocation. She formed people, not ideas. She was memorable not in the usual sense of fame – she left no achievement behind her, only her imprint on those who remain. Phillippa, I, and three quite different men whom she loved, would have to acknowledge her continuing presence in whatever we are. Our pasts are laden with collaboration, the unrecorded action of shared lives.

As I withdrew from the Movement, four of its older members, Herman, Edgar, a scientist called Ivor, and Siamon, who was in his third year of the six-year medical course, decided that I had been so unpromising in womanly terms that ten shillings would be offered to whomever became the first to induce me to kiss. Knowing nothing of this bet, I was surprised by various attentions: Herman offered me lifts in his car; funny, white-haired Ivor, a devotee of science fiction, bought tickets for *Coppélia*; swarthy Edgar, whose manner was rather dangerously sleepy, exerted himself to do a few slow twosteps at the law ball; and last of all Siamon took me to a serious French film, followed by a very long discussion during which he asked in his most concerned and helpful voice, 'What is your attitude to sex?', and I answered coolly (on the basis of Granny's gory details), 'Perfectly normal, thanks.'

I kissed none of them, but in the course of the last outing, which took place at the end of 1958, Siamon struck me as distinctly promising. To him I confided the unmentionable: my conjectures about the unnamed illness in our home. And as I uttered the taboo word, epilepsy, it was fearful no longer in the comforting light of his clinical knowledge. Over the next month, we began to go out; after a few years, we married. He never collected the ten shillings; in fact, it might be said that the consequences of that idle bet, and his rather tardy bid to win when others had failed, cost him his future.

One of the main events in this period of the bet was the school dance. The exacting norms of sophistication ensured that we asked partners on the basis of presentability. Flora asked Bernard, a seasoned lover-boy with melting but slightly bulging brown eyes; and since I lacked the pluck to ask, Flora secured for me the obliging Reggie. Confidently, Fiona invited my popular, smiling cousin Leonard – he who used to read 'Dames are my trouble . . .'. But Phillippa upstaged even the sophisticates when she announced in tones of mature *ennui* that Robert, her boyfriend in his final year of medicine, was 'really too old for school dances'. He consented to look in on the private party that Fiona was giving after the dance. 'Fiona's party had a theme of underwater,' I recorded in September. 'The walls were decorated with fishing-nets, mermaids, and octopus. Flora and Bernard drifted cheek-to-cheek, as though they were lost in a dream, but the next moment she tugged me into a corner. "Just look at Phil's *technique*," she whispered. Through the underwater darkness, we watched Phillippa stroking the back of Robert's neck with the tips of her fingers as they danced.' She seemed to us enviably accomplished.

As our final year at Good Hope drew to a close, we began to stay away. Lessons, we argued, were useless. We needed peace to prepare for the coming exams. One day, at noon, I was lying in bed, quite healthy, and revising history, when the phone rang.

'Yes, Miss Tyfield,' I heard my mother say, as I tiptoed nearer, 'there's nothing the matter with her . . . yes, I'll send her to school at once' And she put down the phone.

'How *could* you?' I gasped.

'I won't lie,' said my mother firmly. 'You're to go to school and report to Miss Tyfield's office.'

I phoned Flora and Rosie to prepare their excuses. On the bus, everyone stared at my uniform. Who went to school at 12.30?

I approached Miss Tyfield's office with heart beating. But all she said was 'Go to your classroom'.

Later, I heard that thirteen out of twenty-five girls had absented themselves and that twelve mothers had claimed their daughters were ill. All twelve succeeded in persuading their doctors to provide the medical certificates that Miss Tyfield demanded. Nothing more was said, except for Rosie. Of all of us, Miss Tyfield respected Rosie with her gift for English. Time and again, she called Rosie to her desk, and asked her to confess to truancy. Time and again, Rosie denied it. Miss Tyfield's answer was to deny her the English prize. Any other punishment would not have touched her, but this struck at the one thing that really mattered, that wish to write that was screened, almost sealed, by the careless, airy manner of a flibbertigibbet.

The last scene of school took place each year on what was known as Mad Friday. For one day, school-leavers were permitted to 'go wild' in the presence of the staff – a last fling before the burdens of womanhood. We called it 'My Fair Diary' as we sang songs based on *My Fair Lady*, the musical hit of the year. But our fair lady, the writer of the diary, was not to be rescued for society; she was going in the reverse direction, from bad to worse. A social outcast to begin with, she became increasingly irretrievable as a year at Good Hope wound by, an unrepentant comment on our own descent into cheating and truancy. Rosie played the outcast in the first half of the year, during which Miss Horton was ever on her trail, but never could lay hands on the crib that led to unprecedented success in the midyear examinations. The truth of the matter we confided to the diary, to the tune of 'Folks Like Us' from *Annie Get Your Gun*:

Folks are dumb where we come from
We ain't had any learnin'.
Still that's how we'll always be
At the Good Hope Sem'nary.

Oh, you don't have to know how to read or write
When you sit next to someone who is nice and bright.
You just have to look in her book and find
What the right answer is, or what's on teacher's mind –
At the Sem'nary,
At the Sem'nary.

Miss Horton, a musician,
Has never had a lesson,
Still we learnt to sing off-key,
At the Good Hope Sem'nary.

I played the outcast in the second half. Beginning my entry in
the diary with 'To-morrow and to-morrow and to-morrow', I saw
Miss Tyfield's frozen expression relax momentarily into a flicker of
hope, but it was soon apparent that time creeping at its petty pace
referred to the deathly tedium of her school.

In the scene of the September school dance, which had been a
strictly proper affair – we had been warned in advance that no girl
in a low-cut dress or heavy lipstick would be admitted – we fanta-
sized complete disruption. Flora made a hit as a female Elvis Presley,
who ousted a sedate band to sing 'Schoolhouse Rock' with a madly
rocking pelvis beneath a leather jacket and tumbled, jerking red
hair. Leaping into the centre of the action, as she struck the first
chord on her guitar, she grabbed an imaginary microphone and
hung on to it at an arm's length as she pivoted the hips that horrified the teachers and had the younger girls howling with delight:

The Head threw a party in the Good Hope school,
The school band was there but it began too cool.

The band began a-jumping and the joint began to swing,
You should have heard those knocked-out schoolgirls sing:
'Let's rock, every-ba-a-ady let's rock . . .'

The words were not important, only that intoxicating rhythm that drew the audience – even teachers – into Flora's theatre of excess.

The next day, on the sands at Rocklands, Flora offered God a bargain.

'If exams turn out well,' she vowed, 'I'll go out with Herman.' It was to be an act of charity to a misfit.

And so it happened that a group of us celebrated the end of exams with dancing at the El Morocco: Flora giving thanks to God through attentions to the unsuspecting and jubilant Herman; Ben Samuel, in a jagged beard, with blonde Maria Carnaby, of whom we were in some awe as the intellectual winner of the year above us at Good Hope; and I and Siamon who, at that point, unknown to me, had taken up the bet.

'When I came from up-country,' he told us, 'I felt ashamed of my *brei* [a regional Afrikaans accent with a harsh *r* rolled at the back of the throat], and I couldn't dance. I had speech lessons, and took up ballroom. For essential practice, I used to slip out of boarding-school on Sunday nights, and gatecrash weddings at the hall next door. In my room, I could hear the band strike up. I'd ask each partner, "Are you related to the bride or to the groom?" Then, you understand, I'd belong to the other side . . .'

'I remember you,' Flora interrupted. 'My parents took me to dozens of weddings.' She laughed in her hiccuping way. 'You seemed so at home, sweeping around the floor, sporting your bow-tie, flashing your smiles, always with the best dancers.'

'I used to have a good look, first, to see who'd suit my practice. Then, when the band packed up, I had to dodge back to the hostel. My room-mate, Jonty, from the Free State, used to cover for me. He'd make sure the window was open.'

When we circled the floor, he held me close as he demonstrated the latest manoeuvres.

'One of the things I learnt was that you dance better if you hold the girl *very* tight. The teacher put a record between you and your partner, and if you let it slip and break, you had to pay for the record.'

'You don't have to explain,' I said shortly, susceptible as usual to a lot of talk, especially in this melting darkness. Ben, in contrast, always quiet, became silent, almost withdrawn. Now and then, he leapt, tall and awkward, to his feet, and yanked Flora onto the floor, hardly waiting for her consent. On the floor, he flung her about in a kind of mockery of rock 'n' roll. Either he could not dance at all or it was some weird private joke. The dance over, he lapsed, again, into moody abstraction. Talking it over afterwards, we agreed that his behaviour had been strange, and not very considerate of Maria. We thought him an incomprehensible but not uninteresting creature. He was in the Movement but had become, as we used to say, 'disillusioned' after a year in Israel. To be 'disillusioned' was a rare disgrace. Ben was tight-lipped as he went about his Movement duties – leading younger groups. He never explained his mental withdrawal.

It was part of Movement education to spend a post-matric year in Israel, a lot of it on kibbutz, reading Karl Marx, A D Gordon, Berl Katznelson, and other theorists of labour and communal living. Settlement on kibbutz was regarded as the Movement's highest challenge, as the Movement magazine, *Aleh*, put it in 1959, but short of that, 'It aims to produce *a type of person* who will be in a position to understand, intellectually and emotionally, that *Aliyah* is a challenge facing him personally . . . and be able to cope with this challenge.' Aware that a certain number of Movement recruits returned to South Africa disaffected in some way that they did not explain – for to explain would have been to acknowledge their failure to cope with the 'challenge' – Jasmine and I decided that the problem lay with the ideological programme and not with Israel itself. In October we took a decision to emigrate directly, to be independent of the Movement and go, instead, to the Hebrew University in Jerusalem. The Movement asked its members to 'crystallize' their aims, and bring them to 'realization'; we were convinced that, at one stroke, at the age of seventeen, we would fulfil the 'challenge' of *Aliyah* and 'realize' ourselves as that desirable *'type of person'* who would put ideals before the selfishness of 'bourgeois' lives.

On arrival in Israel, I was taken aback by the gap between theory and actuality – the actuality, at any rate, of the Israel to which immigrants had access. We were ever in search of 'real Israelis' as we passed the 'slimy' loungers in the fly-filled cafés of Natanya, where we spent the initial months at Ulpan Akiva, an intensive Hebrew course. When we hitched a lift to Haifa, a horde of soldiers forced us out of the way, piling into the truck, and shutting the doors against two ousted girls still approaching with their bags.

It did not take long to understand Ben's disillusion, and that of others like him. I loathed the boorishness of Israeli men, and their style of discourse that seemed to exist for the purpose of scoring points. I preferred the company of my mother's elderly friend, Miss Hirshberg, a refugee from Germany, who spoke with quiet civility. From those calms of sense, I would return to the choppy ulpan, with its displaced people, whose boisterous directress, Shulamit Katznelson, gave rousing lectures on the virtues of Israel above all other nations. Her manner was rough and distant: in theory we were valuable additions to the State; in practice we were fodder in her famed enterprise in integration.

'I'm just bursting to tell you this,' Flora wrote in April 1959. She had been to see *The Parisienne* and, according to her date, looked 'just like' Brigitte Bardot.

'Well?' she demanded. 'Oh, don't snigger, you're making me miserable.'

Preoccupied with my inability to adjust to Israel, I did not reply to Flora's question. I thought her as silly as she feared, unaware that I, too, had tried to fit a predetermined image: a pioneer in a new country. Our images were of opposite kinds but within their respective contexts Bardot and Pioneer were, at the time, approved. I thought Bardot a cheap model; yet mine was equally contrived. I was the brainwashed product of the Movement.

While I had squeezed into khaki trousers, refused make-up on principle, and found a superior satisfaction in my lack of allure, Flora had straightened her hair, pouted, dieted, and put her body through an array of tortures: the boned Merry Widow that pushed up her breasts to swell above the deep square of the Bardot neck-line; the various nipping waisties; and the constricting step-in that certainly flattened the stomach but also rode up the bulge of each healthy buttock, cutting merciless lines into the flesh. Such was Flora's impatience to be slim ahead of the diet, that she often wore all three instruments at once.

Last Sunday I went for a drive with Cowboy [she wrote in the April letter]. Have you ever been right to the end of Hout Bay, to the harbour with the little boats flapping in the breeze? It would have been a pleasant afternoon but for the fact that my step-in pantie was so tight that I writhed up and down the seat in mortal agony.

Cowboy must have mistaken the suffering in my eyes for transfixed interest because he kept on paying me profuse compliments and saying that he had never met such a good listener. The fact is that I didn't hear one word that he said. I was too busy trying to slip my hand up my dress so that he wouldn't notice. This kept me occupied for the whole after-noon.

Her focus of attention was her bid for stardom – stardom, that is, in the circumscribed milieu of Jewish Cape Town. Emerging from a girls' school into the mixed arena of 'varsity' (as university was called), she discovered the limits of her group. All too soon, she knew 'everyone'. There was 'no one to meet', by which she meant that interesting Christians were strictly beyond the pale.

She wrote at the start of the 1959 academic year: 'To-day was Freshers Day. But, my God, I've never been so disillusioned. I don't know what on earth's the matter with me. What did I expect that I feel so empty and lost? Something essential was lacking which I haven't been able to discover yet.' She explored the matter more closely in the next letter, writing just as she spoke, with emotional abandon:

237 High Level Road,
Sea Point,
Cape.
5 March 1959

My dearest Gruesome,

I didn't think that it could possibly happen to me – that there are 2 people in the world who can boast a friendship equal to ours. I have a friend who understands all my moods . . . If the various emotions I experienced during the day could be tabulated, the line would jump up and down like a game of snakes and ladders: one minute blackest despair, the next minute unbelievable happiness. I don't know what's the matter with me. I was happy during the holidays, oozing self-confidence; but now, just like that, I'm losing faith in myself.

I trust you so implicitly & I love you so very much that I feel that I can tell you the root of my trouble. The fact is I'm not going out as often as before. I get asked out by Christian boys but not by many Jewish boys at varsity. I try, honestly I try to laugh it off, to say that it's not important but Lyndall it is, very important, & you know especially to me.

It's incredible: here I am confiding something that I would not even admit to myself before.

At varsity there are absolutely no eligible Jewish boys to meet. The Christian boys are terrific but I can't go out with them.

I don't know why I'm writing all this drivel. I hope you
won't think me a silly baby when you've got such
important things on your mind & I hope you won't lose
respect for me. I wish I had kept my big mouth clamped
shut & not worried you with trivial matters. Your letters
mean everything to me.

    Love,
      Flora

She was unprepared for the complications of the promise that
her image aroused. Appearances to the contrary, Flora was to
remain for years to come quite as virginal as others of her set. The
long April letter contains a rueful account of uncertainties,
mishaps, and pounces – from the absurd to the dangerous – at
Herman's party:

Can it be only a few short weeks ago that I went to
Herman's 21st birthday party? He rented the [dance]
studio of Bateman and Berks, and on the walls he pasted
enormous cardboard strips representing his initials. Dear,
dear Herman.

    Before we went in, Rosie and I stood at the bottom of
the stairs in a maniacal fit of hysteria. We were unable to
decide whether to go in or drift down to the docks. [The
latter idea would have come from Rosie: it was then the
vogue for the arty set to go slumming amongst the sailors
and prostitutes of the Cape Town docks. My mother was
quick to recognize the moment the docks exchanged low-
life rawness for the picturesque when she met her most
respectable nephew foxtrotting his cheery way at the
Navigator's Den.] Rosie spent most of the evening with
Reggie, while I drifted from one boy to another. I have
never danced with such a poor dancer as Ben Samuel. He
is a disgrace to the male sex. By the way, he has shaved off
that moth-eaten barbed wire that he had the nerve to refer

to as a beard. I danced with various other so-called
members of the human race.

Linn was having such a miserable time that she phoned
her parents to come and fetch her. When I went to collect
my jacket in an adjacent room, I found Herman and a girl
I'd not seen before in one helluva embrace. How he
reached her mouth with that beak in the way I can't think.
I murmured my apologies and dashed out of the room
before you could say 'Herman's Nose', but before he
would allow me to leave the party, he insisted that I kiss
him. If that wasn't enough to put me off boys for the rest
of my life, Ben dashed up smacking his lips. Just then, a
good-looking boy called Malcolm Finn offered me a lift
and, grabbing him, I escaped.

Now, listen to the sequel to this story. We now come to
the juicy part. As Reggie had the key to our house, I had
to wait with Malcolm until he arrived. I could see lust
written all over his face, so tried to get out of the car.
Then this brute informs me that my door was locked &
that I could only get out on his side. He started to kiss me
passionately. I kept shrieking 'I really must go in now . . . I
really, *really* must go in . . .'. He didn't let me out until
Reggie came.

Flora preferred the safer exercise of stardom: to have a crowd of
cynics in first year physics howling and whistling as she waltzed
into a lecture. She wore wide tight belts, flounced skirts over ruf-
fles of petticoat, and loose long hair. 'The owner of a coffee bar
stopped Rosie and me as we left,' Flora wrote again in July. 'He
said that he had seen *And God Created Woman*, and that I looked
just like B B.' Backed by daily catcalls from the tiers of maths and
physics, confidence returned. Long earrings completed her image.
Her favourite pair were pagodas, three-tiered, reaching to her
shoulders. What she called 'the pagoda-earring stage' followed the
'gruesome' years of adolescence. The letters of 1959 still call me

'Gruesome', but the tone changed quickly from mild scorn to nostalgia for the uncomplicated bonds of school. A more subdued ruefulness seeped uneasily into letters from Rosie – uneasily, for she was less prominent, less obvious than Flora, with an acute mind that needed slow and patient ripening, so that her emergence – whatever subtle thing she was to be – had yet to be defined. Far away, I retained for both a memory of a secure past as they entered on the social tests (evidently, more trying than the mental demands) of university.

The weaker I turned out to be in my inability to adapt to Israel, the more I clung to the same past. With the speedy collapse of the sturdy pioneer, and the humiliation of finding myself unable to sustain the image, it was consoling to dwell on the past, which remained intact in the stasis of memory. At Ulpan Akiva, I shared a room with two disgruntled immigrants from Romania. Hermina, who was middle-aged, fell upon my suitcase, and clawed through shortie pyjamas, stove-pipe trousers, and cashmere twin-sets with cries of joy. As she held a silk scarf against her chest, her companion, Doulka, tried on a string of pearls. For however pioneering I wished to appear, my mother had sent me away with 'the best'. Their rapture over items of clothing seemed almost frenzied, and certainly not in accordance with the high principles expected of immigrants to a promised land. I had assumed that all immigrants would be imbued with the principles of the Movement: the will to live simply and work hard. Pumped with ideals and equipped with luxuries, I decided that never had I encountered such crude greed.

That first night, I went out with an Iraqi immigrant who had offered to show me the sights when, earlier that day, he had driven a *sherut* [shared taxi] from Tel Aviv to Naťanya. It came as a surprise to find that, to Yacov, I was not recognizably a 'nice girl', but a pick-up. Though at home it was not done to go out with strangers, it did not occur to me that it was naïve to assume that, here in Israel, different rules applied because we were all idealists together. I imagined Israel as the Movement on a national scale. In

Africa, I had heard of a promised land, not of Middle East machismo. My prompt agreement to see the sights appeared to Yacov nothing but a signal of compliance: the price of the evening's entertainment was to be mauled in his taxi, parked suddenly, at a distance from the ulpan, in dark byways with which I was still unfamiliar. With the frantic strength of fear, I pushed his face away and struggled out of his arms, trying to reach the door. Luckily, he soon let me go, shouting abuse in a spew of Hebrew that I did not understand but knew to be vile. Stumbling through the darkness, I somehow made my way back to the Romanian room with its tiled floor and three institutional beds. The next day an English girl, who had been to Roedean School and wore her hair in a tight fair plait, made caustic reference to my taste in taxi-drivers.

Natanya, certainly, did not appear in the rainy start of 1959 to be the land of one's dreams. In the main street, idle men with grease on their hair slouched over coffee-tables or leant in doorways, with roving, shifty eyes. I used to walk in a quiet park which overlooked the sea. There, for the first four months, I looked over the Mediterranean, thinking of Flora, Rosie, and most of all Siamon, and what would have happened if I had not come to Israel.

In my most self-pitying letter to Flora, I wrote of being 'without a friend'. In fact, I was with Jasmine – we had gone to Natanya together – and this was part of the problem, as my diary puts it:

Friday, 27 March 1959

My relationship with Jasmine is superficial although there is no reason for it to be so, except that I sense a withdrawal or self-sufficiency in her. Of course, there is my inferiority which engulfs me in her company. It is not her fault that I burn with resentment that she is so much quicker at learning. It is not only in this matter that I am jealous of her, but in all others. It sometimes seems to me that she demands my

subservience. At the same time, she is unaware of my inces-
sant wish to be alone, my dislike of obligatory expeditions,
and amusement at her attempts to act Israeli.

I was most jealous of Jasmine's effort to take on the challenge of
adaptation while I backed away. As usual, the faults of the accuser
were visited on the accused: it was I, not Jasmine, who was with-
drawing from a venture we should have shared. I was 'looking
forward to a sad love affair' – this was not wholly a joke. In my
view at seventeen, it was romantic to go off and live amongst
aliens and there to be lovelorn and extravagantly homesick. Like
'pointless' of old, homesickness was a luxury in which others
could not indulge, least of all immigrants like Hermina and
Doulka who were refugees from a Communist regime to which
they could never return. My mother thought, disapprovingly, that
I missed the material luxury of corrupted whites. But though I did
feel the impact of material change – especially the ugliness of
institutional rooms – my vice was less remediable because it was an
imaginative refusal. Sensibilities that might have made something
of Israel were blocked at once by a wish to shore up the ramparts
of a private space. That space – the past – I guarded with a determination that no one suspected. In this way adaptation simply
could not happen. I was the opposite of the adventurous traveller:
all hopes fixed on the act of return. This Flora, alone, encouraged:
she was a backer of the emotions, even those our group would
have thought unworthy – for the approved scenario was to
enthuse over Israel. Jasmine, aware of my withdrawal and unable at
that point to enthuse herself, told others at the ulpan that I was
besotted with a boy back home.

'She likes a boy who's *fat*; she writes him dozens of letters,' she
chortled after supper as we mixed Nescafé with sugar to make
foam-topped 'mocha coffee'.

Since Jasmine was the only one in a position to know, my
protest against the alleged fatness seemed to confirm a blind love
for the absurd. In fact, Siamon had a reputation for brains, which

didn't matter to me but was just the thing to appeal to Jasmine, who was brainy herself and who once remarked that she could not accept any man who was not her intellectual superior. 'If I were a Member of Parliament,' is how she put it, 'I could only marry the Prime Minister.'

At the ulpan I appeared her twin and shadow. This was one side of what was, in truth, a dual role, for at night in the room we now shared, she was prone to scenes of distress.

'Why did you write that, about having no friend, in your letter to Flora?' she demanded, one night, as we switched off the light.

It was like the pounce of a beast in the dark. We both breathed into the lengthening silence.

'Do you read my letters?' I tried to speak evenly.

'I *don't* "read your letters", as you so kindly put it. That particular letter happened to be open on the table – my eye merely fell on the last line you had written. And I thought: how *can* she say that, when we've come here together, been together all these months, with everyone thinking we're friends? I've thought of myself as your friend. Why don't you count me one?'

'Please, Jasmine, please don't cry,' I pleaded, for she had started to sob 'Why does no one really like me? Why do things break down – what's wrong with me?'

'Please, Jasmine, believe me, there's nothing wrong. Please understand that it was nothing, no more than a passing mood. I felt homesick, that's all. I can't think what I'd do without you.'

She was unconvinced, of course, and wept pitifully during a storm of confession about her failed relationships. It was impossible not to be sorry. After that, I felt compelled to restore confidence and she to try harder, with the result that we locked ourselves all the tighter. She rarely allowed me to be alone, and the need for privacy became a craving:

Saturday, 23 May 1959

Jasmine is trying hard to be a friend. I am trying to respond. But that jealousy of so many years lingers and will, perhaps, always be a barrier between us. I am guiltily happy that she has gone up to Jerusalem for the weekend, while I stayed here in Natanya. When she is not here, I can read all night as I did for the first time since leaving C[ape] T[own], and am gloriously free. Jasmine made me analyse techniques of showing warmth, and now is trying to put this into practice. I hate techniques; I hate it to come from the brain.

Nevertheless, she could be disarming in her sudden candour about her flaws. I was the more unyielding – 'stiff-necked' – and my denigration of Israel must have made it harder for her to adapt.

'All the American tourist ladies carry copies of *Exodus* under their arms,' I observed on a visit to Tel Aviv, 'and they shed heart-broken tears over every Israeli scene. The hero is a tough-guy who, when he can't get what he wants from a woman, walks out on her in disgust. These tourists get ecstatic every time they see a Jewish beggar – and there are many – grovelling on the pavement of Allenby Street. Visitors to Natanya seek the simple pleasures of the seaside after the strain of dressing for dinner every night at the King David Hotel.' That May, three months after arriving in Israel, I was still tossing off the standard flourishes of my fading role as Pioneer.

To criticize Israel in 1959 was to reflect badly on oneself. Siamon's letters, which I thought stern, pressed me to take a braver attitude: 'Don't look for what Israel could do for you, but what you could do for Israel.' The notion of living for others, in place of selfish individualism, was the essence of the Movement type to which we both aspired. To fail this challenge might be, Siamon warned, 'to lose your self-respect'. For this reason, he advised me not to return within a year.

Somehow I got through that year by fixing all hopes on the life left behind that was kept alive by correspondence. During a spell on Kibbutz Yizre'el, I received a consoling letter from Rosie, in reply to one of mine in which I confessed my plan to return:

Dank God! You're still alive! For a while I thought they'd
mowed you under with the potatoes.

This is probably going to irritate you, & possibly I
should not say this:

You seem to be on the defensive about finding that
Israel perhaps, and kibbutz life certainly, would not be a
fulfilling existence for you. You may even feel that in some
way you have failed your ideals, yourself. This, of course, is
not necessarily true. Ideals are often dreams which can
never possibly come true. We can only work to achieve
them, & when we find that our efforts end in failure or in
a disappointing victory, we accept this finality. The
important thing is that we have tried. Life is not a straight
& endless stairway, the steps of which we tick off as we go
smugly on, but a forest of wandering paths. Each person
has his own path, his own destiny, the happiness–end he
can find only by frequently retracing his steps.

I suppose I wrote the above for myself as well as for you.

Now I've got myself all depressed, so let me tell you
about my holiday [with Linn] in Durban before I get
positively morbid. Never, Never, Never, Never, Never
(this is meiosis, understatement, King Lear & all that) have
I had a more wonderful holiday . . . [With Linn] *there was
no expectation or demand for help*. There were no claims, no
feelings of obligation, & because of this, on my part
anyway, I was more willing to help. On the other hand,
frankly, if Flora had been together with us, there would
have been a dominating demand for 'sticking together' as if
we were two child orphans. I don't know if you have ever
felt this almost overpowering demand practically requiring
that you sink your individuality in hers on penalty of rude
abruptness & sulks for differing with her. Of course, I
exaggerate; Flora is a wonderful friend and person but, to
my mind, having so violent & uncontrolled (NOT
uncontrollable) a nature, her demands upon one's

friendship are sometimes too heavy. In fact, I must admit
that I am at present struggling to detach myself from her
influence, while still retaining her friendship. Please write
& tell me whether you have felt something similar in your
relationship with her . . .

I'm looking forward to seeing you next year.
Love,
Ro*se*.

P.S. Nobody dares call me Ro*sie* anymore, unless they
particularly want a knife in their back.

Rose's need to find an identity beyond Flora's sphere of influence, and some self-protective need for detachment that would be a cocoon for transformations to come, was to alternate over the next few years with her repeated capitulation to Flora's engaging rushes across the threshold of Rose's reserve. As they left school behind, these tensions grew. By the mid-'60s, their friendship would come to an end. In the letters of 1959, Flora, too, warned of changes that I did not wish to hear:

Sea Point.
28 April 1959

My dearest, dearest friend,

You know that our correspondence is something more
than a mere transmitting of words; it's almost a giving of
pieces of our very self to each other. I don't regard you as a
separate individual now but as part of me. You're more
than just a friend, you're . . . It's difficult to explain. We're
above petty jealousies and insincerities, and I know now
that I can accept the fact that our friendship is, as you said,
'enduring, like the rocks beneath'.

I must confess that I did phone up Rosie and read her
bits from your letter. I wanted to gloat. All very childish I
know.

I've just been looking through some photos of 'Mad

Friday' and it has given me an awful twinge. You know, our class isn't as united as we imagined it to be. I can kick myself for being so naïve. We've all drifted apart and the 'old days' seem like ages ago. What I wouldn't give for another hysterical session with you and Rosie outside the lab. with Miss Potts hauling us in by force. Life then seemed so simple.

We've all drifted apart. My best friend instead of being with me is in Israel. I'm getting old (nearly seventeen), and there are so many obstacles in life to overcome.

I do miss you and long for the day when you'll come back to South Africa. In the meantime stay as I remember you.

> Love,
> Flora (what do you think of Florian)

Her sense that a passing phase of life had come to an end was a confirmation of an earlier letter from Rose that virtually said farewell to the past. I read it with incredulity, almost disbelief:

> 'Wembley',
> 32 Upper Orange Street,
> Oranjezicht,
> Cape Town.
> Tues., 24 March 1959.

Dear Lyndall,

I'm glad you wrote to me. About the fact that we lost touch with each other during the holidays, I think it went further back than that. If you'll be quite honest, you'll see that we have from the beginning been mainly school friends, each finding social life with a different group of people. It was mainly in the last year that we were friendly out of school. The type of friendship that existed between us then, found its ideal setting in school life, where it was born & the boundaries of which it did not leave for so long. It was wonderful when the two of us were lying on the grass, facing the school buildings, discussing life, the teachers, the girls, and making cracks about them. We were very honest with each other. There was a warmth between us. But, there was something in our relationship which was too polite, not noticeable or even present in school, but when we met socially outside school life. We have both, I think, a natural reserve about intruding into another person's affairs. This reserve melted in the general warmth of school life, but outside, without the influence of school, set up a barrier of politeness which prevented our friendship from developing to a fuller extent. Someone like Flora does not find this difficulty, I don't think. She crashes down barriers, rushing in where angels fear to tread. This is perhaps a good thing because she seems to get right down to the heart of the matter. In the beginning, one may resent her 'nosiness' & prying into one's private affairs. I know I did. Yet now that she has broken down my defensive & protective barriers & opened up her heart to me, we've become close friends, although we often have little disagreements & arguments. Here is an example of the unnecessary politeness between you & me. We never allowed our anger or irritation to show, & instead became even more polite! I think arguments are necessary in every friendship. They bring people closer together – two people angry with each other are joined together by that very emotion. It breaks down barriers, allows for no reserve in one's heart . . . I know I felt very uneasy with you because I thought you regarded me as immature & a baby. It seemed to me that you felt you had changed because of Siamon, & that I still remained the same. In fact, that you had outgrown me . . .

With regard to varsity, it isn't bad & on some days it is even quite enjoyable. I think the difficulty lies in the inability of many girls to mix the educational and social aspects. I always say to myself, 'Now don't worry about meeting people, don't *strain* – RELAX, be natural and smile.' Only when I don't think of this slogan does it work.

I read this, thinking: no, she can't mean it. I remember fending off the message that friendship was over. I had shared with Rose a sense of a submerged being, like some deep-sea creature swimming and diving beneath the surface. Nothing of this had we put into words, but meeting Rose or Flora beneath the sea, had been for me, and I believed still was for Flora, the truthful moment. What I could not accept, as I read and reread the letter, was that Rose could discard this.

One aspect which I refused to face was the element of competition. I believed in my admiration for Rose, but a greater honesty would have revealed some envy of her flair for English, and some exasperation that Miss Tyfield invariably gave her the higher mark. Reading her letter, I was drawn as ever to the startling note of candour. Where Flora's writing did not do her justice, Rose's writing revealed, more than her talk, the quality of her being; and it was precisely here that I felt the special bond. For I, too, was in my element in the act of writing. What we shared, in particular, was an awareness that, through writing, we could express what could not surface in any other form. What I came to see only later, was the effect of marriage-pressure, particularly in the immigrant milieu. This hit Rose and Flora at an early age. In their homes, weddings were a frequent topic of discussion: 'Natie' or 'Gerda' or 'Mervyn', their parents might say, 'is marrying into such a good family'. It was customary to talk of marrying a family, not a person. Letters from Flora and Rose were full of appalled accounts of various contemporaries, often the plainest girls, who had pulled off the feat of an early engagement. Their terms of expression assumed I would share their shock, as in 'Fanfare: Diane is engaged, to a fellow years older, who has pots of money. All right, get up off the floor, push your eyeballs back into position.' In fact, I dismissed such announcements as over the top.

Only later, was I to learn of the terrifying power of the marriage market, and the coercive role it played in the lives of daughters like Rose and Flora. When Siamon, a son of immigrants, had asked me to go out with him, he felt it necessary to warn me: 'You're not the love of my life.' He said this with honest directness, not wanting to lead me on with hopes of marriage, but at the time – I had only turned seventeen – the matter seemed remote. I could assure him easily that I, too, had no lifelong intentions. No sooner had I relieved this concern than it occurred to him that we should, after all, plan to marry, and whenever he posed the idea, I dodged it in the intensive correspondence of 1959. 'I was touched by your picture of marriage to me,' I wrote in May, 'but can't commit myself because I don't trust my stability yet. Although all the girls from my class worry about marriage, it is not an issue facing us yet – we have another two or three years before we are on the shelf. Don't laugh, it is true, and it's terrible. My contemporaries are already turning 18. I'll turn 18 too in another six months, and I don't want to, because it is then within reason to settle down. I want still to be hysterical as at school and do crazy things. I am determined not to spend my life in the kitchen as many Israeli women seem to do.'

Rose's absurd idea that I now looked down on her derived from the ethos of the marriage market. In her milieu, to 'go steady' with a boy was to slot into a superior status, a rung below the apex of engagement. With relentless tenacity, the public ethos was closing its tentacles around her attentive and delicate mind. There was in Rose a strange conjunction of truth and artifice. She had the mind to see for herself – to detach truth from ideology – but for some reason she did not respect her originality, and even feared it. The stranger she was, the more she willed herself to belong in the world which she saw as a market for images. With the help of wired bras, pencilled lips, and peroxide, she transformed herself as the current object of desire, and to be this she had to cultivate oblivion with a cynicism that was not uncon-nected, I used to think, with the dead eyes of her mercenary father. Her favourite song was 'Diamonds Are a Girl's Best Friend', which she hummed with ironic bravado.

The really disturbing statement in her letter was that whatever we had shared had been different for her – incomplete, unsatisfactory, shadowed by a reserve that had come from me – since she had no such problem with the more ebullient Flora. The thousands of miles of separation, and my tendency to reconstruct the friendship in imaginings that bore too little relation to reality, prevented me from taking in the general warning in Flora's letter, the specific denial from Rose. I continued to cling to the hope that friendship, as we had known it, would somehow be restored. I told myself it was too good to fade. I stuck out that year, in deference to public opinion, for it seemed a waste and worse. My failures, of which failing to pass the Hebrew entrance examination to the university was the least, destroyed what confidence there had been. In January 1960 I returned to South Africa a more subdued character. I returned to find that Flora's warning had been true. The old group had drifted apart; it had been a passing phase of life. The old rapport had faded in the remorseless rush of time, faded before the competition of the marriage market and the demands of awakening passions.

6

Changes

My diary recounts an expectant return to the past, denying against all reason that change had, in the course of time, persisted:

Cape Town.
Sunday, 17 January 1960

After two nights on the train, I got up at 5 a.m. and went along the corridors of the coaches to the shower. It was just dawn and I glimpsed through the windows the undulating valleys and vineyards of the Cape. In Jerusalem I read *Cry, the Beloved Country*, and for the past month have kept certain phrases for this moment: 'wake in the swaying coach to the half-light before dawn. The engine is steaming . . .' and the 'fertile valleys and great mountains of the Cape bound them with a spell'.

As the train rolled slowly into the station, I saw my

mother hurrying towards me – I waved – and then behind her – Siamon with his varsity blazer slung over his shoulder. Then I saw Flora, gorgeous and bursting with excitement and, in the background, Ben, looking rather sheepish. As the train jerked to a stop, I thought: This is not a dream. I kissed my parents and hugged Flora, then turned to look at Siamon. He just stood and looked at me.

After lunch we were left alone and when we walked down the road, he took my hand. To walk through the streets of Sea Point again, to see the familiar places . . . It was as if I had never gone away.

Some of the ingredients of change were already present. There was the unplanned appearance of Ben hanging over a platform bench, his head obscured by the diffident hunch of his shoulders, suggesting the difficulty of utterance in his new attachment to Flora. There was a new attachment of my own, established *in absentia* as the somewhat disembodied figment of my imagination, but who now became, before my winter eyes, a sun-tanned young man with flashing teeth and purposeful, light eyes, a separate person, at once more physical and less intimate than the sharer of letters.

'What do you see are my faults?' I asked, perched on a rock at Seaforth a week later, thinking of the feebleness that had made me give up on Israel – but still hoping for indulgence.

He looked grave. His answer was unexpected.

'You don't use your mind,' he said, looking out to sea. It was only then that I took in the fact that he was an intellectual who would expect me to match certain standards of his own. What these were I did not know, but it was clear that some change was required. Far from maturing during the year away, I had returned, in his eyes, undeveloped. A sense of purpose, he said, should replace the sense of the past, all that mental lingering and super-fluous nostalgia.

Thirty years later, writing the sort of memoir that defies that sense of purpose – the expectations of publishers, the norms of academe, and the advice of a husband who thought Flora a bad influence – thirty years later, I would make a case for the back-stitching of the mind that Flora and I, or Lenie and Lizzie, or my mother and Gwen, used to perform together in some rhythm of renewal, in the dim night kitchen, or under the bent fig tree, or listening to the quiet, deep pulse of Beethoven's late sonata, opus 110, or lying with heads together through long beach days, drenched through with sun, in those years before women got too busy. As time moved us inexorably forward, we looked back, retrieving time, not to establish a formula of the past, but in some more indeterminate and open-ended way of coming into being. For, as women of that generation, what we were to be, we could not know – and in not knowing, were in a way more liberated than our immediate successors who made themselves in the image of men. 'I want all the evil things men want,' said a fellow student at Columbia at a consciousness-raising session in 1969. I drew back. The New York model of success was too warping for emulation. Women had yet to see how the past made the present, how the present rests in untold ways on the subterranean world of the past – an emotional equivalent of gravity, a pull against the linear progress of clock-time.

So much for theory. In practice, there was no escape from the transforming effect of time and place. As I looked back in 1959, in the undergraduate years of the early '60s, in the graduate years of the later '60s, back to moments of friendship, back and back again, in the habitual rhythm of return and remaking, change did at that very time go on in the present: change in the world – the winds of change in Africa; Sharpeville in 1960; and the student uprising at Columbia in 1968 – changing myself no less than others.

The night of my return was a Friday, and my mother extended the ritual of the sabbath by inviting an array of relatives and friends to hear my impressions of Israel. They came to hear the rave about the Promised Land, and when I blurted certain truths – about mil-

itarism and aggressive masculinity – the resistance of my listeners
was so complete that I cried in my room, convinced that I had
confirmed myself, before uncles, aunts, grandmother, and everyone who mattered, including Siamon, to have been unworthy of
a great opportunity.

Flora tried to help. 'Sometimes, you're just bursting to say what
you really think and really feel,' she said in my room. 'I'm always
opening my own big mouth and saying the wrong thing, too.
When my mother talks to her friends, she calls me "my impossible
daughter". She can't understand why I quarrel with Reggie, why
I shout and disrupt the home. Why do I have these uncontrollable
emotions? Why do I give my parents such a hard time – that's
what you're thinking, isn't it?'

But I was thinking: 'It wasn't the whole truth. There could
have been another story . . . if I'd gone to Jerusalem sooner . . .
met Maia sooner . . .' I remembered the August day when Jasmine
and I climbed the Judaean hills towards a city of grey-pink stone
that glowed at sunset, the intelligentsia of the capital, the widening uses of language, the arrival of students – and Maia, who was
unlike anyone I had ever known before, unlike anyone I would
ever know again.

In Jerusalem, I met a different sort of immigrant, the idealistic
élite of the European immigration of 1905. I wrote to Siamon: 'At
the home of Nahum Levine, a friend of my mother's, one meets
the intelligentsia of the 2nd *Aliyah*. You should hear stories of how
they crossed the Caucasian mountains on foot and left Russia
with forged passports; and they used to sit and sing in their tents
when there was no food; and when their parents wrote urging
them to return, they refused. What a generation! But according to
Mr Levine, there is even more for our generation to do.'

Until the age of seventeen, I had not seen great works of art.
One Saturday morning in September,

I hitch-hiked into town and went to the Bezalel [museum].
I saw an exhibition of Norwegian Expressionists. One

painting was merely a horse and a man: the horse, plump, solid, rooted in the land and the man blurred, indescribably apart and unbalanced and ephemeral. But the most wonderful work I saw was a sculpture by Rodin called 'Pain'. It was a woman's head in black stone. The mouth was open, but more than the mouth, the pain was expressed in the drawn-in hollows of the forehead and in the tension of the chin. Last night we went up to Mount Zion and wandered around the Montefiore quarter. It was so near the city yet completely apart – I want to do much more of this wandering around. Socially, it is not at all bad. Jasmine and I have joined an American programme for students on their Junior year abroad. To-night, we were called upon to entertain a group of 55 (mainly non-Jewish) students from Europe for supper and afterwards a dance in our *chadar tarbut* [entertainment hall]. Some said that they were thinking of coming to live here, though one Swede said to me but oh, so politely, 'It is a *little* bit hot.'

As the season turned, I wrote, again, in October:

It is autumn now. Twice during the past week I have travelled down from Jerusalem and could hardly believe it was the same journey as a month ago. Maybe it is because of the change in season, maybe a change in myself, but I found it so beautiful, so infinitely beautiful in its barrenness. Only now am I beginning to love Israel and feel bound up in this country. It is the social aspect that deters me from staying on, the fact that I have no friends amongst the Israelis themselves. I might even consider staying if I saw the possibility of a circle, but I haven't remotely found what I am looking for.

All of us on the American course were awaiting the arrival of local students in October, at the beginning of the university year. They looked older than we had expected, and rather self-contained, with eyes fixed on their lecture-rooms, bent in that one direction, as if to say that life was a tough business and there was no time to waste. I was struck by the numbers of the disabled, physically and mentally, the relics of the Sinai Campaign and the children of Auschwitz. I wrote in October: 'It is hard for students to get into the *shikun* [residence] and I feel guilty for being here. Most of the students have tragic histories. One boy was at Auschwitz and the Germans did experiments on him; another girl always wears long sleeves because her arms were nearly destroyed by a bomb, and there is a plentiful sprinkling of Sinai casualties – limps, crutches, guide-dogs, and hooks instead of hands.'

The Americans decided that one way to break through the local barriers and, at the same time, improve our Hebrew, was to split up at this point and room with the Israelis who now filled the residence. Many of them had actually come from somewhere else, and I found myself sharing a room with a history major who had come, two years before, from Poland. Maia, who had been adopted during the war by a Christian family in Cracow, did not look the least Jewish. She was delicately fair, with long blonde tresses which she tied in a bunch down her back. She had the spontaneous merriment of easy aplomb. I had never met anyone so popular: a succession of visitors knocked at our door until midnight, men and women, who would bounce in with a burst of Polish. I liked the generous tones of the women, some of them orphans, all scarred by war, who looked after one another in a sisterly way. If any of their set had a date, the others would gather to do her hair and proffer advice. Maia had a boyfriend, also Polish, who was a student at the Technion in Haifa. She was eager for his letters, and made dismissive remarks about various locals who persisted with proposals of marriage in the face of repeated refusal.

She gave the impression, at the age of eighteen, of one entirely alone in the world: some agency paid for her lodging and tuition; otherwise she supported herself by working half-days as a telephonist. She would groan when the alarm went off at 6.30 a.m., then toss back the covers with resolution, fling back her hair into a quick tie, and dash off to work. She was very poor – I noticed that she hardly ate anything – yet she scorned the material temptations which suitors laid before her. Every other weekend, her boyfriend, Karl, visited from Haifa. He had studied in the USSR and was fluent in Russian: he and Maia would read Dostoevsky aloud to each other in the original. I remember the passionate sound of that language with its crashing rhythms as I used to lie on my bed in Maia's room, letting it wash over me – washes of feeling, without understanding a word. An old uncle of my father's, an immigrant to South Africa from Russia, had told me that the letters of my family name stood for the Hebrew words, *ger tsadick*, meaning 'good stranger', which, he said, was the phrase for convert. Since Jewish society was so closed that conversions tended to take place only in rare cases of intermarriage, it occurred to me that it was, perhaps, some remote Russian blood, far back, that was responding to this language with an instinctive, almost intimate delight.

Though Maia welcomed me into the room, I did think of it as Maia's room and felt something of an intruder. Soon after the move, I went with the Americans on a journey through the Negev. On our return, Maia said, 'I missed you.' She had prepared a meal. I was pleased, and also relieved. From that time, I was drawn into Maia's set, and we began to entertain together, cooking huge omelettes, which we served with Polish sausage that used to arrive from Maia's adoptive parents. I could not help noticing that she corresponded with them constantly, but it was some time before she told me her strange story.

Her story had been written up in the more garish magazines, and what I had heard from others was the sensational version. She was born, the story went, in the ghetto of Vilnius, during the war. When her family was ordered to a concentration camp, her grandmother managed to escape with the baby. The grandmother, herself in danger, handed the child to the first woman she saw who, in turn, gave the child to a well-off family, who sent her to

the best schools and took her regularly to the opera where she sat
in the family box. She grew up a devout Catholic and, it was said,
an anti-Semite, reflecting the attitudes of her adoptive parents.
When she completed school at the age of sixteen, she began to
study medicine. Then, one day, her adoptive mother told her the
truth. It so shocked her that she ran away and hid in a Jewish
house. When her adoptive mother came, crying, to look for her,
she hid in a cupboard. Eventually, she was sent to an orphanage in
Warsaw and, after three months, the Israeli Consulate sent her to
Israel. In Israel at that time, the favourite drama was the reunion
of families separated by war: it reinforced, of course, the very
raison d'être for Israel as a place for the persecuted to survive and
come together. Maia's true parents were 'discovered' to be living
in Tel Aviv; they 'discovered' Maia (who never knew her real
name but, according to the romance of the papers, there was the
inevitable birthmark). Cameras flashed; a banquet given by the
Jewish Agency publicized the dramatic reunion of 'parents' and
lost child. 'Is there anything more you want?' was the rhetorical
question during the speeches. 'Yes,' said Maia firmly, 'I want to
continue my studies at university, and will need support.' It was
impossible, given that moment of publicity, for the girl to be
refused.

That was a newspaper story – the reductive story with con-
cluding lines. The unrecorded sequel I relayed in a letter to
Siamon:

                                                    3 November.

The tragedy is that she refuses to accept her 'parents' as her
parents, and has told me several times that she has no
parents in Israel. I believe that her 'father' has often come
to visit her here at the shikun, bringing presents, and has
talked to her for hours, without response. I think, although
she ran away from her adoptive parents, she feels most
attuned to them. For instance, she can't help believing in
Jesus and has a sense of guilt that she no longer goes to

confession. She also carries on a lengthy correspondence
with her people in Poland, although she refused their pleas
while they were searching for her and hid all the while she
was in the orphanage.

My next letter took up the story again:

> 12 November.
>
> I am very satisfied with Maia, my room-mate. She is so
> considerate and sensitive, it is all pleasure. She works
> terribly hard and gets up at 6.30 every morning to earn
> her living – every bit of money she spends, she has to earn
> herself. I admire her fortitude very much. She doesn't look
> at all Jewish, you know. She is very blonde, petite, and
> Polish-looking. The other day her 'father' came to visit
> her. He brought her a slab of chocolate and he kissed her,
> but she stood like a stone. He is a shtetl type, much less
> refined than she is, and I can see why she refuses to accept
> him, to recognize the fact that he really is her father. It is a
> shame, because I spoke to him for a while before Maia
> came back from work, and he seems a good person and he
> said that he loves Maia very much. After he had gone, she
> told me it is not true that he is her father.

I always wrote 'parents' in inverted commas as more of the truth
unfolded:

> 23 November.
>
> I can't tell you how happy I am with Maia. She is so much
> part of my life now that I cannot imagine how it was
> without her. The other day, she herself told me the story
> of her life – it was even more tragic coming from her lips.
> You know why she says that she has no parents – because,
> after she lived with them for three months, the 'mother'
> decided that she was not their daughter after all. I think

she was jealous of Maia's beauty. The Jewish Agency has asked Maia to keep quiet since the success of her case has been so widely publicized. According to Maia, her 'parents' are only interested in marrying her off to a rich man. They don't support her whatsoever. She is very unfortunate because I do think that, in spite of everything, they really are her parents.

This was still not the whole truth. Just before I left Israel, Maia told me that one reason for her running away was that her Polish father abused her. Her Israeli 'father', too, had shown signs of attraction that had estranged her 'mother'. So that was why Maia stood like a stone when he kissed her.

At last, I knew why Maia was alone. On my return to Johannesburg, I told her story to Hubert and Berjulie, hoping they would give her the support she needed to complete her degree. They did. In time, they visited and liked her but, naturally, she wanted no further ties of a parental sort. After three more years, when we had both completed our undergraduate courses, I returned to Jerusalem, and there was the same resourceful Maia, more grown-up with her beautiful fair hair cut short, now married to Karl.

Maia had recesses of endurance and determination in which I could participate only tentatively. For the truth of her story, rooted in war, had the elusiveness of the edges of history – far away from the familiar jokes of Rose and Flora. The effects of living with Maia and the seriousness of her story distanced, somewhat, the hectic activities of Flora – or Florian, as she had begun to call herself. I began to question her shifts from boy to boy. Her feelings seemed facile in their instant extravagance. I began to question feelings that could enter into my most private thoughts and then could 'empathize' with some smooth man in a red sports car.

Yet, as she meandered in confusion from one love-fancy to another, she knocked, almost by chance, against some unexpected substance in the form of Ben – the taciturn, uncommunicative

Ben – her opposite in every way. Her numerous fancies had been largely induced by the drama of a social star with all eyes upon her blazing hair, vivid temperament, and ready bursts of laughter. Ben was too withdrawn and rather too fastidious to give her the obvious sort of adulation that she craved in the Pagoda-Earring Stage. Surrounded by a horde of whistling brutes, the engineers who were the staples of the maths and physics lectures of her first year, she had looked on Ben, whose eyes were averted, as a butt of her wit: 'I have never danced with such a poor dancer as Ben Samuel . . . He has shaved off that barbed wire that he had the nerve to refer to as a beard . . .'

In July, Flora was in the grip of a chemist, a Christian, who, she wrote, 'looks like an Adonis in his varsity blazer, and has beautiful manners'. She was encouraged by the envy of other girls, their eyes on her back as Johan steered her across De Waal Drive to vanish into the heart of the rose-garden. And she laughed off the gossip. Then her mother heard. Endlessly indulgent to her children, Mrs Gevint was formidable when it came to Christians. She forbade further contact. When Johan phoned, Flora spoke with her mother at her elbow. She had to decline Johan's invitation to view his father's car – that smart new car that told you more about the nature of Johan than Florian's raptures. More curious was her instant capitulation to her mother – Flora the headstrong? I concluded that, despite the rhetoric of madness and thrills, she had experienced only the melodrama of romance: the hero as public image of desire, propped by the equipment of travel (the car replacing the steed of tradition); the much-spied-upon tryst; the stern denial. As Johan dropped out of sight, Flora tried out a new diet and pulled her wide belt one notch tighter. She read *The Rainbow*. She nibbled an apple, and devoured three more. It was then that Ben crossed the horizon of her consciousness: Ben, with his eyes averted, partly in diffidence, partly in the most fastidious of covert judgements entered the Union where Florian sat, dodging lectures, in the fond circle of her admirers.

The next letter speaks of long talks – oddly comfortable, joking talks as she drew out words Ben never thought to say – and her astonishment at some unlooked-for stir of desire. For despite Johan's performance in the rose-garden, this was the first time she had a sensation of this kind:

I have been going out quite a bit with Ben Samuel. It started quite innocently. I sat in the Union one Monday & Ben, all trembly-lipped, asked if I would not go out with him the following Saturday night. We went for a drive all over the Peninsula and then spoke at my house until the early hours of the morning.

The following Saturday we went to a drive-in. I've never been so relaxed with a boy as we teased each other on our way. I felt we were getting the utmost enjoyment out of our company, and that's how I always want it to be. Ben got quite passionate at the drive-in, but I didn't mind because I felt myself responding too (for the first time – remember how repelled we were by boys), to my great surprise. Don't misunderstand me now, he didn't try anything much at all. On the way back he seemed terribly subdued but at my home I managed to squeeze out of him what was the matter.

He told me that he likes me very much . . . Oh, he expressed it so beautifully. He wanted to know whether I reciprocated but all I could say was: 'I don't know, I don't know.'

Since then, I have gone with him for long drives & the funny thing is that it is true what you said – he does grow on you.

Enough for now. More developments in my next letter.
    With all my love,
      Florian

It had been her plan to join a student group travelling to Durban for the winter vacation, a group which included Ben as well as Rose, Linn, and Herman. But two days before they sailed, *The Story of an African Farm* induced a bout of self-criticism that put an end to her plans:

> Never has a book made such an impression on me . . . Do you remember the heroine? Do you remember when she says that life is pointless without a goal; to live, I mean really *live*, you must have a purpose.
>
> What is my goal and my purpose? I merely exist from day to day, happy one minute, sad the next. My first 6 months at the university have been an absolute waste – I didn't work a scrap so, natch, failed all my exams. Lyndall's words [in the novel] so inspired me that I resolved not to go away and to make passing at the end of the year my goal.
>
> But knowing me as you do, you can imagine how much work I did. Next year, dear girl, you and I will be doing 1st Year side by side.

A silence of four months followed, during which I grew to know Maia. Then this letter arrived, frivolous, yes – the *African Farm* had obviously faded – and yet, she had changed:

> 237 High Level Road,
> Sea Point.
> November approx., 1959
>
> My dearest Gruesome,
>
> I am writing this letter from the premises of the most exclusive junkshop in Salt River, Gevints Fashions, where I am supposed to be working until Christmas. I say 'supposed' because my typical working day consists of arriving at the shop at about 11 o'clock, staying just long enough to pick out 2 new dresses, and then happily scooting off at noon to sunbathe on our ledge.
>
> Your mother invited me for a Friday night as soon as

the exams were over. She has the knack of making even
the most trivial incident seem important & alive. I saw
Siamon there, and met again your Uncle Hubert & his
very attractive wife. I was charging down Avenue
Normandie at approx. 7.05 when I was due there at 7. He
gave me such a sympathetic smile as I nearly took the gate
with me, in an attempt to open it, comb my hair, put on
lipstick, and pull up my petticoats all at once, that I'm
afraid I was lost forever. He makes his presence felt
without shrieking the place down – a sophisticated, poised
& confident gentleman. That night I basked in the
atmosphere of your home. The evening had a strange
effect on me – I felt light and airy, one moment bubbly,
then oddly subdued.

Do you know that an eternity has passed in these 4
months because so many things have happened and so
much has changed.

I have now been going out with no other person but
Ben for about 3 months. I have never felt over anyone the
way I feel about him. Isn't it odd – here I have known him
for such a long time and all of a sudden I am in love.
Love – that's a strong word. Do I know what love really is?

I haven't seen you for nearly a year, we haven't written
for months, and yet I write and tell you these things as
though you were next door. Our relationship has not
altered at all . . .

I am completely mixed up, yet have never been so
happy. Ben says that if he could have seen himself a few
months ago saying such things to a girl, he would have
laughed and thought he was the most sloshy idiot on God's
earth. It is difficult to explain everything on mere paper.
However, you do know me; we have discussed intimately
to the last gory detail the way boys repel us. You know
that I cannot fall for anyone easily – *Ben is great*, he really
is.

Your mother showed me some photographs of you that almost broke my heart because you looked so mature. Please write soon. You mean more to me than you'll ever know.

Love,

Florian

Where the correspondence with Florian kept our past dammed and still, the correspondence with Siamon was like a river, gaining ground, with eddies (my doubts) overrun by his certainty that what had begun between us could not be stopped. The momentum of this development came from his honesty, which compelled me to speak the truth even if it was discreditable. I almost resented the fact that I could present a more agreeable image in letters to Florian because 'she won't question what I say. I always am dissatisfied with what I write to you because I want to impress you and when one writes to impress, one only makes a fool of oneself. I am so afraid that you will begin to see me differently through these awful letters.' I owned to 'fierce rebellion' against the step I had taken; to dislike of Israel as 'no better than South Africa, a brutal and ordinary country'; to laziness, anger, and 'hundreds of defects you don't know about'. The main issue was my failure to adapt:

I understand that you are keen for me to adapt to Israel for both our sakes, but I really am not happy here. You seem to look on this as an adolescent crisis – you attribute my present difficulties to the need to grow up. My mother writes in the same vein. But I am convinced that this dislike of Israel is not something transient. The women here are drudges; they do nothing interesting. I want something more out of life than the kitchen. Is it possible for you to see through my eyes the horror and boredom of such an existence, no matter how much I cared for a husband?

Separated for a year after only a few weeks together, we developed what we called a letter-relationship. None of the vicissitudes of contact, none of that variable play of instinct that fluctuates from moment to moment, interfered with the gradual solidification of letter-characters. Siamon signed his first letter 'Your Rock', and that was what he proved to be. Though sentimental feeling was not part of his definition of love, this rockiness and the bare manner of honesty, intrigued me as a kind of challenge. It compelled daring, a clarity of statement that I had not thought to risk. 'Although we are continuing under such unlikely conditions,' I wrote in May, 'thousands of miles apart, I can put down in writing far more than I should be able to say. I think that you, too, would not speak as freely to me as you write. In spite of distance we are still, I feel, coming to understand each other better.'

At first, Jasmine seemed to depend on letters in much the same way. But after two months, she confessed that her boyfriend's letters were 'empty', lacking in mental stimulation. She was put off by the carelessness of his language and grammar, which might sound an odd sort of reason for falling out of love but it was obvious that, engaging as Nathan had been in person, he could not exist through the written word – which, for some, is not to exist at all.

That year I existed entirely through letters. Israel and its people were simply not real to the same degree. In the face of actual transplantation, I cast my correspondents, Flora, Rose, and Siamon, in the different forms of fixed and perfect empathy: the more separate in distance, the closer we would come through transparencies of writing. In letters, I would live on unchanged as my correspondents could be, in all essentials, unchanged. The letters addressed a biographic idea of essence, using the paraphernalia of time and place – the raw greed of Romanian immigrants, the soldiers shoving us out of their way, the sound of the siren at Kibbutz Yizre'el – as no more than props for primal events of love and friendship. I had failed to change countries, had given up with humiliating speed, but a consolation, sharper and to me more appealing than the common wish to recast the self, was this wish to fix the past. I was teased at the ulpan as the girl who wrote letters in the dining-room, under cover in class, at every stop on a *tiyul*. I hung about the table where the post arrived, became a hoarder of letters, and lived for moments of privacy in order to pore over the blue, close-written pages. During the worst loneliness of the winter of 1959 I would keep letters unread for as long as a day or more, stealing glances through the unsealed sides of the aerogramme. We numbered our letters to preserve the sequence, and a related pleasure was to reread the growing batch as it gained substance. Its very substance induced trust in the written word to contain and renew the past.

Back in Cape Town, Siamon was a member of a pioneer group that was preparing itself to settle on kibbutz, only slightly worried by the preponderance of future doctors and other professionals, who were not exactly training themselves for humdrum agricultural labour. As an active member of the Movement, Siamon said I should blame myself, not Israel, for the failure to adapt. All the same, he collaborated in the letters that created our story, to the extent that when, occasionally, I did lapse from past to present – verbally going forward, as it were, on journeys through the Galilee and Negev – he dismissed these impressions as mere 'travelogue', quick to detect the withdrawals, evasions, escapes from the momentum of a story that moved towards the finale of return.

As Flora had set new standards for friendship at school, crashing down barriers of reticence, so now in her love for Ben, she appeared fearless, committed, and unashamedly public.

After my return, we went, in July 1960, to Montagu to bathe in the hot springs at the base of the mountains. When Ben arrived for the weekend, Flora flung herself on him like a love-starved wildcat, almost choking him as she hung about his neck. He greeted this sensational welcome with an air of restraining patience. Ben came from a civilized home. Mrs Samuel, who attended my mother's Bible class, had gentle good manners. Flora adored her refinement – drawn always to homes different from her own – but the mildness that charmed her in Ben's mother, was more disconcerting in Ben himself.

Ben was a diffident man, whose feelings were strong enough in his own dignified and private way, but it puzzled Flora that he should register so little beyond that mild tolerance under the literal pressure of her own passions. She decided to 'starve him' into expressive response, and at the same time work off excess passion with lessons in Spanish dancing. I offered to join her, and soon we were stamping our heels, strutting, whirling, staring, and clacking castanets over our heads in Mavis Becker's studio. But, alas, to no avail. Ben remained imperturbable, oblivious to deprivation. So Flora returned to choking him, resigned to the violence of her feelings.

Passions were difficult for that last generation of virgins, who were not exactly chaste. Our mothers and grandmothers had a clearer code of conduct. 'You are behaving like an engaged girl,' Granny once reproved me for holding hands in public. My mother's stories extended to a sedate kiss in the garden in the course of a ball: 'Roy Fennells took Monica outdoors and asked her to kiss him, and she said no; then he took me, and I said no; then, finally, he took Lilianne, and she kissed him; she was thrilled, until we told her that she had been his third try' – such were chums' stories of clean fun. In middle age, they spoke of men as rather absurd, pitiful creatures whose more unpredictable moves should be treated, if possible, as a joke. Their strongest feelings were maternal. Monica, who had been Head Girl of old Good Hope, best at hockey, and winner of all the prizes, devoted herself to having children. Normally reticent, in her forties she confided to my mother that a well-spring of bliss had begun to rise in her in the middle of the night.

'When he sleeps', she said rapturously, 'I'm filled with love. When he wakes, I hold him in my arms, looking into his dear eyes.'

My mother, taken aback, thought that Monica had become

uncommonly excited about her rather placid, pipe-smoking husband, Bill.

'Why, Mon,' she said, fingering her pearls uncertainly, and
looking briefly at the ceiling, 'how *very* nice for you.'

There was a brief silence.

'He can't drink enough,' Monica went on, her glow deepening.

'Oh . . . you meant the baby!' cried my mother, suddenly
enlightened. 'You've fallen in love with little Selwyn.' They
chuckled at the absurdity of my mother's mistake.

Lilianne's husband was a little 'difficult', to use their word.
Bertie Henry was a Scottish farmer who grew apples along the
cool top of Piketberg mountain, on the route to Klawer. A thick-
set man, he had a masculine air of wilfulness that Lilianne rather
enjoyed in the way women used to enjoy the challenge of a dominant male while indulging his lesser foibles. When Lilianne joined
this rough creature on the mountain-top, the isolation was at first
a little daunting, and she was fearful of gigantic African insects
which emerged from the thatched roof of their farmhouse. In later
years, when Lilianne came to town, she would relate her story of
the spider and the penis.

In the early days of their marriage it had been Bertie's habit to
strip after work and lie naked on the bed, reading the *Farmers'
Weekly*. One day, to Lilianne's consternation, she saw a spectac-
ularly large and hairy spider descend on its thread from the
thatch until it hung, suspended, just above the equally novel
phenomenon of Bertie's penis. The look on Lilianne's face
changed from consternation to horror as, suddenly, with an
exclamation, Bertie leapt to his feet, gave a howl of pain, and
leapt in agony around the room. Lilianne showed us how quickly
she rushed to the kettle for water, how efficiently she filled a
basin into which she dropped antiseptic, and how assiduously she
chased the still-bounding Bertie, trying in vain to get the basin
lodged firmly under the penis in order to bathe the injured
organ. Bertie, still howling and hopping, seemed to reject these
efforts with furious impatience until, as the pain died down, he

was able to explain that, as he'd leapt from the bed, he had stubbed his toe.

For all this, nothing was said about women's bodies, their own needs: unarticulated, these bodies didn't appear to exist except to nurture the next generation. Flora's awakening desires, her public declarations and wilder demonstrations, seemed excessive, if not outrageous, in the context of the passive female manners of the time. My grandmother warned us not only against the dangers of licence, but of the tactical inadvisability of showing emotions. She was not analytic; she simply passed on the rules of women in what was still a man's world. Initiative of any overt sort was unwomanly, demanding, indecent. Flora defied these messages, not physically so much – since it was still obligatory to be a virgin – and not in any calculating or ideological way, but simply by admitting honestly, in outward gesture and plain words, to an impulse that did not arise solely in answer to male invitation.

'I've got a draft up my shaft,' she announced one day as we sat together, between lectures, overlooking the Cape Flats from the windy steps of Jameson Hall.

So began our secret fashion. Too lazy to wash our panties, we went without, not ever on dates but on varsity days, enjoying the wild rush of the south-easter – a daring fashion, given the strong gusts of the Cape. It was a variation on the more admissible pleasure of swimming naked against the silky buffeting of the great waves, far out to sea, on the grey, blowy days when the beaches were deserted.

Of course this was no real answer to the trials of virginity. The main trial was self-control. The decent male attitude could not be faulted. It was: do whatever you think right. This might go with a certain amount of scoffing at the 'platter' ritual: society's barbaric offer of a woman's virginity as a prize for the best bidder. There was no regard for purity as such; it was tolerated as a state which might be harmful to overthrow.

There was one attraction in virginity, and this was the element of mystery. At that time 'nice' girls had only a dim idea of what a grown man looked like without his clothes. There were paintings and sculptures, of course, but we had an idea that the real thing might differ, though no mention was made of erections when the facts of life were relayed, rather as a joke, from one relatively ignorant girl to another in the school playground. Joking was one way of coping with mysteries that might, we feared, come to unromantic ends, as in *The Bell Jar*, when Esther, model college-girl of the '50s, saw that the genitals of her date, Buddy Willard, looked like turkey-gizzards.

Where Esther sought out the gory details for the grim satisfaction of knowing, we held to our innocence, deploring the passage of time that propelled us towards adulthood. Curiously, anorexia was unknown in our milieu, despite its vogue for diets, and this may have had to do with the fact that, before the permissive society of the '60s, the rules that guarded licence provided some protection from pressure to mature too fast, and from the finality of sexual experience as men have shaped it. Schoolgirl confessions of revulsion held no fear of frigidity; rather relief that complete adult temptation had not yet come one's way. And as passions awakened, they were granted a certain freedom of play by the very rules that forbade their final form.

'We were the last of the great kissers,' recalled Leonora Carey, who met Flora later, in Johannesburg. 'We did it for hours because we could do nothing else.'

Complicating this interplay of passion and restraint was the brevity of the time-limit before marriage pressure came into play. My grandmother said that it was silly for girls of eighteen to get too serious over boyfriends.

'I agree,' I said. 'I won't start thinking of marriage until twenty-three.'

'Now that's going too far,' she said.

She was certain that plain speaking was for a woman's 'own good'. She told her niece, Sarah, who was twenty-eight and unsure of her feeling for a reliable businessman: 'You are not going to get any younger – or prettier. Marry him. Or else leave him and find someone else.' The urgency of the situation was not lost on Sarah, who married the man at once. And there were numerous Sarahs who, not calculating by nature but made so, married in haste for fear of being 'left behind'. Two weeks after my return to Cape Town, Rose brought up this subject:

> Saturday, 30 January 1960
>
> It is taking longer to draw towards Rose than Flora, but the other day we went to bioscope together and at interval, while they collected money for the Coalbrook Mine disaster, Rose (who has just turned 19) started telling me how already she is suffering from marriage pressure. I hate the way Jewish girls are supposed to get married before they are 21 otherwise everyone gets sorry for them. Flora is already feeling sorry for girls one year older than ourselves.

This age coincided with leaving university. That was the customary time to announce an engagement – preferably to a professional man, definitely to a Jew. This left only three years after school to find the right husband. No wonder my schoolfriends cut lectures so as to concentrate on the social chances of the Union.

Where my mother saw life in terms of moral tests (even illness was, to her, a test), and where Flora saw life in terms of social success, Siamon looked forward to mental challenge. In order to remedy the deficiencies of my mind and a feminine lack of purpose, he set me definite and, I thought, impossible goals for 1960.

'Anybody with any intelligence', he said firmly, 'should do well in paltry first-year courses.' So, after the long idleness of Good Hope, and the wasted opportunities of Israel, I settled to work in Jagger Library, ignoring the jeers of old classmates and the tug of the Union, in the attempt to prove that I did have brains after all. It did not take long to discover that, even if lectures were not always good, it was possible, in fact more rewarding, to work on my own. I liked to go to the library on Saturday mornings, when it was almost deserted, to collect facts about Byzantium in a niche smelling of old print and dust, and then emerge from darkness into the brilliant light when the library closed at 12.45, and look across the Cape Flats, across neat, toy-like white suburbs and the unknown clutter of non-white townships, unreal and quivering in the haze of heat, towards the faint purple splodge of the Hottentots Holland mountains to the east. One Saturday, I locked this scene in mind and body, knowing that all must change, was changing already, that this period of study was but a respite, a last linger in a place I perversely loved, before being compelled to leave for good.

During these undergraduate years, the most absorbing course was South African history in the second year, 1961. Dr Davenport's unbiased lectures were a revelation after the doctored version of history taught at school. That year, I dropped child psychology after two months because its formulations, at least as they were taught at UCT, seemed pseudo-scientific. Instead, I took up social anthropology which, like South African history, had the verifiable immediacy of the local scene. As Professor Monica Wilson and a black graduate, Archie Mafeje, explained the intricate network of obligation and sharing in African society – say, the role of 'mother's brother' or the manifold burdens on women – the black majority came into focus.

Through my mother's Klawer stories came the impact of a South Africa of which we knew nothing: the old-fashioned Afrikaners of the *platteland* and their inextricable fusion with the harsh landscape of the interior. This was a land for which they would live and die. But that was only a small part of the picture: of black society – the vast Bantu-speaking chiefdoms of Xhosa, Zulu, Sotho, Tswana, and others, who were lumped together as the marginal 'Natives' – of them we knew even less. Such oblivion was the triumph of apartheid, specifically of the Group Areas Act, which decreed that non-whites 'develop' separately from whites, on the distant peripheries of cities or in small, underdeveloped and often infertile wastes called 'homelands'. It was impossible for the vast majority of the country's population to herd, as the government envisaged, in these small, deteriorating fragments; but outside them, blacks had to carry passes, to be produced on demand. Those without passes were liable to arrest. All whites knew that blacks lived in constant terror of the Pass Laws: of losing their pass through unemployment – this kept them servile – or of being discovered to have no pass at all, which meant deportation to a 'homeland'.

A black woman who had been moved to a 'homeland' said: 'When they came to us, they came with guns and police . . . They did not say anything, they just threw our belongings in the [government's] trucks . . . We did not know, we still do not know this place . . . And when we came here, they dumped our things, just dumped our things so that we are still here. What can we do now, we can do nothing. We can do nothing. What can we do?'

Any knowledge of the twelve million who were out of sight in 'homelands' or in separate townships or underground in the mines or just visible as servants – even minimal awareness on the part of three million white rulers – had to be sought deliberately.

In 1961, Flora, too, moved into the School of African Studies with a switch from physics to Xhosa. These switches reflected increasing awareness of the claims of the black majority following the Sharpeville massacre. On 21 March 1960, large numbers of blacks assembled at the police station at Sharpeville, a township near Johannesburg. They came without passes, inviting arrest in the hope of clogging the machinery of justice. The crowd was ordered to disperse and, as it turned to go, the police opened fire. They killed 69 and wounded 180, most of whom were shot in the back. After that, disturbance spread. In Cape Town, on 30 March, a crowd of between fifteen and thirty thousand blacks marched to the centre of the city, towards Parliament which was in session. The police assured their leader, a twenty-three-year-old university student, called Philip Kgosana, that the Minister of Justice would receive him that evening if he would persuade his people to go home. They did so. That evening, when Kgosana reported, the police arrested him. By that date, a week after Sharpeville, they had made two thousand arrests, beaten hundreds of blacks, and compelled them to return to work. The years of violence had begun: the atrocities of the police, sanctioned by a state of emergency; and the inevitable formation (in 1961) of the military wing of the African National Congress: Umkhonto we Sizwe [Spear of the Nation]. Before Sharpeville, most leaders had been committed to non-violence; now, said Mandela (at his trial in 1964), 'it would be unrealistic and wrong for African leaders to continue preaching non-violence at a time when the government met our peaceful demands with force.' The government attempted to wipe out opposition by an escalating series of drastic measures.

The most infamous of these measures was the 'ninety-day clause' that became law in 1963. It allowed the police to imprison any person for ninety days without trial. Such prisoners had to endure solitary confinement, interrogation, many under tortures that ended, like Biko's, in death – called 'suicide' in many cases, in which prison doctors had been known to sign false death certificates. When Albie Sachs, a student at the University of Cape Town, was released after a second term of detention, his first impulse was to run to the sea and plunge into the cleansing waves.

At some as yet unknown date, high-ranking Afrikaners gave their consent to secret 'hit' squads which would act above the law. They were to murder opponents of the regime. It might be an active Communist like Ruth First; it might be Joan Cranko whose only political acts were to make regular weekly visits for fifteen years to her imprisoned brother-in-law, David Kitson, to complain of prison conditions, and to cook meals for hundreds of detainees. She was found battered to death, her jaw broken.*

By the mid-'60s almost all overt opposition to apartheid had been eliminated. Those who were not detained and tortured felt guilty for having survived. And with increasingly rigid segregation, liberal aims for a mixed society seemed more futile than

---

*Norma Kitson, *Where Sixpence Lives* (London: Hogarth, 1987).

ever. Anthropology promoted this impression, for what it taught me – unintentionally, of course – was the hopelessness of factual knowledge: no one, I thought, but a black could fully understand a black society, and my hefty textbook on the Tswana, for all its plethora of social detail, was extraordinarily dull and empty of human truth. As the actuality of Israel had made me doubtful of Zionist ideology, so now I doubted not only the easy platitudes of white liberalism, but the very nature of political thinking with its reductive categories that left out the vital nuance of individual circumstance. We were irrelevant to a black country, I thought, and must leave. This was a common conclusion, and a constant topic of conversation, though many deferred their leaving until renewed unrest threatened their safety.

In 1960–3, before the university was finally segregated by government edict, it remained the one social institution where the races mixed under a normal circumstance of shared study. But I was rather guiltily conscious of the element of pleasure to be derived from the *frisson* of crossing the unforgettable colour bar that edged student friendships with Yasmien in history and Blossom in English. Yasmien came from a Cape Malay family and her father an imam in District Six before the government destroyed that deeply rooted community. I liked to dine in Yasmien's home, to scoop up the spiced Malay food with soft bread, and share in the warmth of her close-knit family.

In 1961, if anyone had asked Flora why she took up Xhosa, she would not have made a political statement but would have spoken of her 'empathy' for large, black Dr Jordan who was head of the Department of Bantu Languages. It was not that she had no political convictions but, for her, personal relations were the springs of action. It was liking for Dr Jordan as a man and his powers of reciprocity – perhaps his benign smile when she burst into his office, pleading special and instant favours – that would have told her in advance how much she would relish his teaching. In a calm, disarmingly placid manner, Dr Jordan alerted his listeners to the abuses of colonial discourse. He did not attack the phrase 'Kaffir

Wars', he simply ignored it and spoke instead of 'the Wars of Dispossession'. His articles on African literature in *Africa South* placed inverted commas around nineteenth-century expansionist phrases about 'empty spaces' (Xhosa lands depopulated by famine and pestilence), or about 'backward areas' where missionaries and 'loyal Fingoes' would 'set the example to the backward peoples'. Under Dr Jordan, Flora studied tribal legends like 'The King of the Waters' in which a thirsty hunter, Tfulako, sacrifices his lovely sister to the King of the Waters, Nkanyamba, in return for a drink. When Nkanyamba comes to claim his bride, he turns out to be a snake of enormous length and thicker than the thigh of a very big man, who at once coils himself around the girl's body, rests his head on her breasts, and gazes hungrily into her eyes. With the snake still coiled about her, the girl runs desperately over the mountains, wailing with a heavy alliteration which Dr Jordan could not easily translate:

> *Ndingatsi ndihumntfan' abo Tfulako,*
> *Ndingatsi ndihumntfan' abo Tfulako,*
> *Ndilale nesibitwa ngokutsiwa himyoka, nyoka?*

> Can I, a daughter of Tfulako's people,
> Can I, a daughter of Tfulako's people,
> Sleep with that which is called a snake, snake?

The snake retorts with alliterative insistence:

> *Ndingatsi ndimlelelele ndinge, ndinje,*
> *Ndingatsi ndimlelelele ndinge, ndinje,*
> *Ndingalali nesibitwa ngokutsiwa humfati, fati lo?*

> Long and graceful that I am, so graceful,
> Long and graceful that I am, so graceful,
> May I not sleep with that which is called a woman, a mere
>   woman?

Eventually, the girl outwits and destroys the bridegroom with the aid of an uncle and aunt. Then she rests until her shudders have subsided. When she is recovered, she resolves to make the snake's skull a vessel for washing, and with this gift returns to her tribe. Her brother embraces her and asks her forgiveness. 'Forgive you what?' she asks. 'Forgive you for giving me the chance to prove that I am the worthy sister of Tfulako, killer of buffaloes?'*

Although Flora found Xhosa more congenial than physics, she did no more work than before. As examinations approached, she went into crisis. Her home was in uproar. As she lay on her bed, crying and heaving, she would hear her mother's footsteps, toiling faithfully up the stairs. Mrs Gevint was profoundly respectful of study; unfailingly moved by Flora's ordeal. She telephoned for help on the night before the Final. When I arrived, Flora was sitting up in the bath, her red hair piled on her head, which was thrown back, tragic and beautiful, while Mrs Gevint, on her knees beside the bath, her face wrinkled with concern, soaped her child's back. The next day Flora wrote a paper that turned out to be on the top borderline; duly vivaed, she got her First. Her compelling personality bloomed in viva: no one was quicker to take a point or accept correction with more fervour. In the benign sun of Dr Jordan's receptiveness, her understanding of Xhosa culture glowed in all her bright colours of empathy.

I pressed on in more earnest fashion; as Howarth, Professor of English, put it in a reference of 1963: 'At times she can touch first class by the dint of toil and effort. She would make a careful editorial or research assistant.' I bolstered my correct essays with Leavis, Eliot, and other approved critics, and took no risks with lecturers who seemed rather splendidly remote. The most remote was a graduate student, J M Coetzee, whose tutorials on South African literature were graceful monologues, exquisitely worded,

---

* *The Penguin Book of Southern African Stories,* ed. Stephen Gray (London, 1985) pp. 19–28.

but addressed to the wall above our heads. It was his first term of teaching, and the students froze in pity for his shyness – or was it contempt? We were not sure, and a chill silence met his rare questions which, like the monologue, avoided eye-contact and addressed the wall. These tutorials used to peter out half-way through the period. With controlled resignation, Coetzee would lift his books to chest level, and rather suddenly float out of the door.

At this time when my mother's health improved, she resolved to join me for the three-year major in English. She proved a dedicated mature student, with the confidence to think for herself. I learnt more from discussions with her, particularly about moralists and religious writers – Donne, Herbert, Vaughan, Jane Austen, Hopkins, and T S Eliot – than from lectures, which were filled with odd bits and pieces of preliminary 'background', but somehow never quite engaged with texts.

'On Friday I bunked my English tut,' I wrote in September 1960, 'and met Myra, Linn, and Rose in the Union and we talked about Françoise Sagan and Yael Dayan. It was like old times when we used to have camaraderie at school.' There was, for reasons I could not understand, a growing separation:

Monday, 27 February 1961

The new academic year begins a week to-day.

I wish time could stand still. I want to be nineteen always. It still bothers me to have missed out the seventeenth year. The older I get, the more a mistake it seems. It was not only a dead year, but I have never recovered the ground lost with Linn and Rose.

Flora has remained wonderfully steadfast. I value her warmth of heart, her spontaneity, and her assurance, that have upheld me in times of doubt. Her letters sustained me in Israel – their frank friendship – and it is through her that I hope to bridge some of the gap that grew between Rose and me.

The diary defines the friendship with Rose as 'not a bond of affection, more an exchange of ideas, something sparkling'. I could not understand how she could let this go. Another entry reads:

I know how much Rose and I have in common – we are really very much alike – and we used to get on well. It is a pity that, since I returned, we have not had one time alone, nor have we talked except one Saturday morning when we met by accident at the Library. I very much want to be friends with Rose because she is the only one with depth and intellect. She asked me last week to meet her for coffee in town and I began to hope that our friendship would revive. But she phoned to say that, as her driving-lesson in town was cancelled, she 'couldn't come'. I'd been prepared to go into town for no other reason than to see her, but for her it was incidental to other plans.

At the time that Flora became 'Florian', Rosie became 'Rose'. And as she took on the glamorous, made-up face of 'Rose' – she never appeared without her nail-polish, her silver eye-shadow, and pencilled perfection of round lips – she seemed to vanish, that sparkling, hilarious Rosie I had known at school. Even her jokes had a contrived air, as though she were playing to herself, practising for some future which she did not expect us to share.

What I had not understood was the import of that long letter of 1959, when Rose declared that to gain a boyfriend at an early age was the most defining of social triumphs; that such a girl, glorying in her safety, would look down on less-fortunate friends. It had seemed to me that she was projecting a notion of outdated crudity, and I dismissed it as passing nonsense. Such an attitude belonged to Jane Austen's silliest mother, Mrs Bennet, to be rejected by her sensible daughter, Elizabeth, and upheld by the frothy Lydia. *Pride and Prejudice* has been called Jane Austen's 'Jewish novel', in view of Mrs Bennet's unrelenting pressure on her marriageable daughters. Such pressure is deliciously funny, but Mrs Bennet may be rightly concerned with her daughters' fate in a society in which marriage is a woman's only respected career. To intelligent Charlotte Lucas, who is not in her first youth, marriage appears to be 'the pleasantest preservative from want' and for the sake of this preservative, she accepts a fool. Such women are sensitive to family wishes: they prefer not to burden the father or brother who may, it is true, jar them with every movement, but to whom they are bound by inextricable ties. To such bonds and concerns, Rose, at eighteen, had already succumbed, and with all the super-added sensitive anxiety of an intelligence too discriminating for her environment. This fine intelligence was compelled to subscribe to a view of marriage as a market, with men as buyers: the most desirable goods would go first; the least desirable would be left. Thus the care with make-up, the closed-off smiles, and studied jokes. All through those pressured years at varsity, she was saying to herself, 'smile', and alternately, 'Don't *strain* . . . RELAX.'

A London barrister who grew up in Cape Town and took Rose out several times remembered 'waiting for ages while Rose finished her preparations, whatever they may have been; the making of desultory and strained conversation with Mr Singer (with whom I felt no particular union of soul); the eye make-up; the straining sweaters or the less than all-enveloping evening gowns.' This Monroe look went with a comic nitwit role designed to soften up men as an alien species advancing over the horizon of Good Hope girls; yet interestingly, Rose switched roles – without switching costume – when she came upon a literate man who was far from the vulgar commerce of her father. 'The tone of her conversation tended to the literary', the barrister recalled, 'as if English literature was important to her.' This struck him as 'an aspiration of an entirely different personality. I felt that I was witness to a process of dissociation, by which two main personalities, neither of which was comfortable with the other, had come into being, creating a degree of paralysis of response to life. I don't think she ever internalized a satisfactory image of what she wanted to be.'

Those girls who could not announce an engagement at the close of their third year at varsity went to Johannesburg. To 'go to Johannesburg' was a euphemism for hunting a husband – for some a last resort, for others like Rose a hope of more exciting 'talent' than might be found in the well-worn circle at home. Greta, the twenty-nine-year-old daughter of Mrs Gevint's friend Feige, had gone as the last resort, and she returned home in triumph – not unmixed with trepidation.

'Ma,' she said over the phone from Jo'burg, 'he's not handsome.'

'Just bring him home. *I'll* decide who's handsome.'

The whole family, with Mrs Gevint and Flora, waited at the airport. Down the steps came Greta and, behind her, Max, a fat, bald man with a mouth full of enormous teeth. Slowly, Feige eyed the paunch as Max approached. He was, after all, well off, and she could see the anxious crease on Greta's forehead.

'A *scheine*,' she cried, opening her arms to welcome Max, 'a *feine*! [a good-looker, a fine man]'

'A *scheine*!' echoed the whole family in relief. So Greta was settled ever after.

In Johannesburg, Rose met a leading gynaecologist. There she married and lived in a spacious house with a large garden. I visited her in the late '60s, en route to Cape Town from a dark apartment in one of the sleazier uptown streets of New York. It was strange to see Rose in this setting – a composed wife of a successful man, a mother, my Rosie of unconventional judgement at the bottom of the school grounds. This Rose drew me over to the cot and, softly, a hum came from under her breath as she bent over the tiny, sleeping head.

So Rose, as I'd known her, vanished. With the farewell wave of that disturbing letter, she disappeared into her time and place, assuming that I had gone before her – changed, changed utterly by the paired mode of being that women's magazines of the '50s hailed as 'togetherness'. In the mid-to-late '60s, I used to wander along Broadway or Madison Avenue, looking for my generation, which seemed to have vanished, as Rose had vanished, into marriage and motherhood. By 1965 I, too, was a mother, and my family disapproved of continued study. Columbia itself disapproved. When I asked for a loan, Dr Ridgeway, behind the administrator's desk, said brusquely: 'We don't give loans to mothers.' I, too, was vanishing – silent in Trilling's class, intimidated by the forbidding style of his Jehovah pronouncements, in tow as 'wife' and 'mother'.

Flora, turning into 'Romy' in the mid-'60s, retained to an extraordinary degree her intransigent and buoyant self. She revived me from postpartum depression in the winter of '67 when she came to New York. Her stories of teaching maths to the E stream at Greenside High made me laugh again. She got on famously with fourteen-year-old intellectual duds. Though she had no hope for their maths, she found they worked better to the strum of a guitar: a boy played it softly in the corner, while Romy kept watch for the Head. She became a little apprehensive when the Inspector arrived at the school, and turned the pages of the hopeless books.

'Your ticks are too large,' said the Inspector severely, his eyes bent on the Bardot neckline.

Romy said: 'For one moment, I thought he was inspecting my breasts.'

Yet, voluble as she remained, she was loyal to the men she loved, and more discreet than of old about doubts, waverings, and imperilled virginity. She, too, vanished intermittently into two successive ties during the decade that she debated the question of marriage.

7

Partners

A card of 11 January 1962 marks the date of Flora's first departure. 'My dear friends [she wrote], at the moment I'm lounging at Salisbury airport and cannot believe that I have a journey overseas only a few hours away. Please excuse this communal note but I shall write to you individually as soon as I establish roots in Israel. Am missing all of you already. Love, F'lora (with an apostrophe).'

The next few days changed the direction of her life. Arriving at her aunt's home in Tel Aviv, she found herself in a kind of salon that did not exist in South Africa: an intelligentsia with access to the centres of power. The diplomats, the intellectual women, the politicians, were a world away from the spurious sophistication of pagoda-earrings and tight skirts. Nothing in three years at university had so compelled her total attention. Overnight, to judge by her first letter, the vague ferment of 'we want . . . but don't know what we want . . .' erupted as an almost unassuageable hunger for new forms of life.

The most compelling were men who were not beach-boys training to be doctors, lawyers, or engineers – the restricted professions of our milieu. F'lora [she pronounced it 'Felora'] now met the accomplished: thinkers, writers, musicians. She noticed, in particular, her aunt's friend Dov, who wrote a daily column of political analysis for a national paper. 'Does South Africa really exist?' she wrote on 17 January:

> I have been away for years, not a mere week. I want to
> tell you not what I have seen but what I am experiencing.
> Of course I shouldn't think so *intensely* after only one
> week away from home, but what can I do! This letter is
> all the more difficult to write because I have been
> comparing myself with you and wish fervently that you
> had not gone when you were so young but now with *me*
> at the end of our varsity career. On Saturday morning my
> aunt has 'open house' to anyone who wants to come.
> What a conglomeration of ambassadors, editors, female
> architects etc., but all so *modest* & uninhibited. The
> trouble with South Africa is that everyone is always
> showing off to the next person. I don't think that in my
> whole life I have felt so independent and sure of myself as
> I have since I left.

What she meant by 'showing off' was the necessity to be seen with a partner. It was common for even the most popular girls to pretend they were never alone. When Ellie's date fell through on her twenty-first birthday, she could not disappoint her parents. She went out, eyes lined and hair sprayed, in her sleekest outfit. Where she went was next door. She passed this milestone in the obliging company of her neighbour's twelve-year-old son.

Far off, F'lora, distancing further from the partnered state, questioned a society that propelled girls 'blindly' into marriage. This question seemed so dubious – and so disloyal to Ben – that she asked me to '*burn* this letter after you have read it'.

Successive friends were announcing their engagements to the younger professionals of southern Africa. One of the most eligible was an engineer in his mid-thirties, Jacob Danziger, who came from Livingstone to the Cape for annual vacations. He was the youngest brother of one of my aunts. It was Aunt Ruth's worry that Jacob, bridge-building on the backwaters of the Zambezi, would not marry a Jewish woman. Soon after F'lora's departure, she spied Myra sitting with me under the promenade on the cooler edge of the Snake Pit.

'Introduce me to your friend,' she said with her disarming smile, as she placed her dancer's limbs in a pose of reclining grace. Her loveliness in her white bikini left us conscious of deficient shapes.

'So – what will you do now you've got your BA?' The concern of Aunt Ruth accompanied wandering attention as she weighed the attractions of Myra's responsive blue eyes and stable background that showed in the tasteful sun-dress, imported sandals, and pleasant air of undamaged protection.

'The postgraduate education course,' said Myra without much conviction.

'*Perfect* for Jacob,' Aunt Ruth mouthed at me behind Myra's back.

I was sceptical. Men of the world like Jacob, on brief vacations, had little time for timid girls like Myra. Reluctantly, I agreed to arrange a double date. Poor Myra, I thought, during the subsequent dinner at The Little Gryphon: why go through this? Jacob talked easily through the evening: his encounters with crocodiles, his secretary, his Livingstone home. Myra listened. I pitied. Siamon, rather withdrawn when he saw little point to a social occasion, mulled over the curious habits of the macrophage.

Two weeks later, a car flashed past us on the High Level Road. There were calls and waves. Focusing slowly, we saw – could it be – Jacob and Myra? I had never seen Myra so radiant. For, yes, they were engaged. She had been swept off her feet, we agreed. How could they trust their feelings? Somehow, the assurance of Jacob and Myra made us uneasy: we joked about the bouquets of roses that Jacob sent punctually, three times a week, after his return to Northern Rhodesia.

That summer, at the end of the second year at varsity, I stayed with my grandmother in Muizenberg. I used to come back from the beach, the salt stinging my cheeks and my wet hair sending the occasional cool drop down my back, peel off my costume, and roll up in the pink warmth of her eiderdown. As she sorted and re-sorted her valuables, I remembered to tell her: 'F'lora wrote at the end of her first letter: give my love to all your family and *especially* to Granny.'

'What about that boyfriend – what's-his-name – Ben?' she asked, coming straight to the point. 'What does she expect of him – what does she think she's doing?'

'Perhaps she's unsure of her feelings,' I ventured.

'Feelings? Well I never! Kissing in his car for two or three years, she's had enough *feelings*. She has to know her mind.' She locked her jewel-case and cast about for where to hide the key.

I lay back with my eyes closed. The midday sun had fallen across the eiderdown until its deepening warmth stole through my sea-chilled limbs. The new year stretched out invitingly: History III, English III, talks in the sun on Jammie steps or times with Siamon, away from the wards, under the craggiest peak of the Twelve Apostles where they stretched their feet to the sea, the breakers crashing on the rocks, the acrid smell of seaweed, and the brilliance of the Southern Cross as I'd lie back on my arms . . .

'. . . So, what will Siamon do after his housemanship?' Granny's practical voice, switching abruptly from F'lora to me, dispelled the scene.

'He'll go overseas, partly for training, partly because one can't live here.'

'And he's talked over his plans with you?'

'No . . . not yet . . .' The future seemed comfortably distant.

Time enough for decisions, for not bearing to leave this place that I loved. Though I had resolved not to stay with apartheid, the failure of my first attempt to live abroad still rankled, and there was no pressing wish to try again.

'If he hasn't spoken to you, he's going to leave you, and you'll have given him the best years of your life.'

I sat up, furious. 'I don't, *myself*, want to think of marriage. It's far too soon to decide one's whole life. You shouldn't interfere.'

'It's for your own good. You must take care not to be left behind.'

'Left behind . . . left behind . . .', the warning echoed in pursuit as I stamped from the room. Shamelessly, I charged Siamon with Granny's suspicions.

'Don't be pressured by your family,' was all he said. It seemed to confirm a doubt even as I shook it off. 'The best years of your life,' she had said. Were they over? Had girls nothing to offer but their passing youth? I wrote to F'lora who replied at once:

Kaf-Tet November 65
Tel Aviv, Israel.
6 February 1962

My dearest Lyndall,

I read your letter, yesterday, as though it came from another world – but of course that is perfectly true, another world altogether. What do people live like in South Africa? – I seem to have forgotten. How unimportant the marriage problem seems now and how narrow-minded – no not narrow-minded but single-minded – we are. Our minds move in one direction only: that if by 21 one is not married there is something radically wrong. *FORGET* about it completely, Lyndall; don't let yourself be pushed into anything. To think that I was debating whether or not I should go overseas! Oh my Lord! It has been the most exhilarating experience of my rather inexperienced life. You know the high standards we

have set for ourselves where men are concerned: I know
now that if I had gone blindly into marriage I would have
regretted it for the rest of my days. When & if I go back to
South Africa and when & *if* I decide to marry Ben it will
be with the knowledge that I have had experience with
men different from him. At the moment am very
undecided about my feelings.

So many ideas that I had previously have been altered;
so many things that were important seem trivial now. My
aunt can't tolerate the word marriage at my age. She says
that I should not even begin to use the word until I am
about 22. I am going to be sentimental now and call you
my very dear friend: we have led a secluded, sheltered, and
naïve life in our restricted community. My eyes have been
opened also to the more sordid aspect of marriage.

Write soon. I need your letters.

Flora (Frumi, <u>Roumi</u>)

Two months later, another letter warned more urgently:

If you at all get the feeling that you have been missing
something, listen to that voice or you may regret it for the
rest of your life. In Haifa I have met a woman of 28 who
married when she was 21 having only known her husband.
She now has a daughter of 6 and though she loves her
husband very much, she confessed an overpowering sense
that she has missed something – a restless, inexplicable feeling
that you and I and people like us will understand. Her
advice, like that of all women of her age and older, was to
take all the opportunities that come your way while you are
young, live to the full and experience everything to the full.

As spring came, she wrote more of Dov.

When people say how much they would give to have their

youth again, I never realized what they meant until Dov took me to the Galilee. We stayed at Tiberias, ate fish at Ein Gev, visited a little night-club called Minus on Lake Kinneret, and went for a ride in a boat at 3 in the morning. The boat filled with water, we practically drowned and yet all we did was giggle like children. When we made it to the shore, we raided the kitchen of the club. Dov says he is in love with me, and is reluctant to let me leave Israel. For my part, I really don't know – and haven't made any rash statements which will commit me. I have learnt my lesson about using the word love too loosely. *Please don't breathe a word to my mother of what I have told you.* I honestly don't know what I am going to do about Ben. Tell me what your plans are for the future.

My own months of indecision were no more than a gesture in the direction of self-respect. From the moment I stamped out of that room at Muizenberg, marriage became inevitable. It was inevitable that I should blurt out Granny's suspicions to Siamon; inevitable that he would give the issue his calm reflection. When he decided we should certainly marry, his words were drowned by the deafening band at Naaz, a multi-racial club popular with students for its easy mix and Cape Malay food.

'. . . Mutter . . . mumble . . .' I heard as we danced on the tiny, crowded floor. He looked expectant.

'I can't hear a thing,' I shouted above the trumpet.

'I've asked you to marry me,' he shouted back, laughing.

'I'll – think about it.' After all, he had no choice – this scene was not of our making. Nor was it recognizably a proposal, not like the declarations of Jane and Rochester as the great oak split with the lightning that raced through that romantic English sky. Years later, at an Oxford high table, I heard a don relate how her staid husband had once gone down on his knees after a college ball and proposed as dawn broke. She had found the scene funny but convincing. Here, in the dark nowhere of District Six, such forms did not exist. Here, surrounded by flat colonial accents, in the close and noisy Naaz, were words of love implied – or was this the cool, almost jokey decision that it appeared to be?

More compelling than dreams fed by the wedding-bell plots of innumerable novels, and more persuasive than admiration for a person of high purpose, was an idea of my worthlessness that Granny's warning seemed to confirm. Far from taking the random chance of 'life' as the transformed 'Roumi' proposed, I must take the chance of marriage before it passed.

I used to listen to my mother's words of comfort to the gloomy graduates who were unattached. 'One meets a partner when one least expects it,' she would say. I relayed this comfort to Jasmine who, in her third year at the Hebrew University, had not managed to fall in love. In March '62 she replied in her rational way that she had reached that stage of disillusion when, if my mother were right, it was precisely the time for a partner to make his appearance. 'In other words, an almost primitive belief like that becomes so conscious that I am constantly aware of it, and so there is never a time when I am not expectant!'

At that low point Romy (as she now called herself) arrived in Jerusalem. Jasmine wrote: 'Her exuberant personality soon got us going, and we sat up half the night, talking. I forgot time and place as I entered into her atmosphere. Funnily, I felt all along that you were here with us, the bond between us. I really could see traces of you, in Romy.'

She confirmed that Israel had given Romy an opportunity 'to form that sense of judgement which, perhaps, her relationship with Ben, in SA, did not allow her . . . After all, marriage is the greatest decision we have to make in our lives, and the one which is going to undergo the severest trials.' In her more sober terms, she suggested that I might try Israel again, and offered her home and support. Yet she was too rational to promote false hopes.

Not for a moment did I contemplate this course, and in May, Romy did an about-face to lend herself to a position that was antithetical to her own: 'I give you my word of honour that you are missing absolutely nothing. I feel that I have expressed myself in entirely the incorrect manner. Don't ever dream of giving up love for the sake of "experience". I realize that the difference between us is that you have been in love whereas I was not in love with Ben and could not admit this to myself. In your imagination going out with men is different from what it is in reality – and forgive me for being honest, but you don't have the temperament for it. You would only succeed in making yourself miserable.'

The letter ends with a celebration of a woman's feeling for another. 'I believe', she said, 'that 90% of people go through life not knowing that such a relationship between woman and woman can exist. And because I have known this – this almost spiritual intimacy with you, it is difficult for me to do without it. I have known the best there is. If only I could express myself clearly. We have come close to perfection and that occurs only once in a lifetime. I feel love for you . . .'

It was at this point that I let her down. Some questioning and obstructive reserve did not trust her and did not respond. Her rush of words was, I thought, an overflow of feelings generated not by another, not by me, but by her own effervescent and awakened self.

The months passed. There were times when I no longer knew where she was. Her next letter did not arrive until the close of '62. Reproachful but forgiving, she lamented the end of things as my engagement came about, punctually, on my twenty-first birthday:

I still have not quite decided whether to be happy, not only at the news but at my ability at last to communicate with you – or whether to cry a little because I had forgotten for a while how very dear you are to me. Your letter brought back everything.

I remember one day in particular when I was returning from Haifa to my kibbutz. I sat in the bus wrapped in my thoughts and watched the rain beating against the window. Suddenly I had such a feeling for Cape Town and such a

yearning for you that I could positively *smell* it: the feeling
of driving with you in 'Cherry' [a red Morris Minor]; of
Wolfie [Pip's dog]; of university – the atmosphere of exam-
time; of Lenie-cake with your mother in the sunroom. Oh
gosh, I could go on like this forever but, as I write, I can
feel my heart contract a little because we will *never* have
those things again – our youth. Do you remember those
madly philosophical discussions we used to have – how
terribly intellectual we thought we were? If I had to see
you now, would it be the same, as free and natural as
before?

It was strange to meet Myra here, on honeymoon. They
were, of course, good to me but I thought (although I
don't know Jacob at all) that she was simply transferring
her protection from her parents to her husband. At that
time, though, I had just ended my relationship with Dov,
not knowing whether I had done the right thing or not, so
perhaps it was not quite the best period to renew
friendships.

How great my attachment to Dov had been I never
realized until after I finally decided not to see him any
more. I believe (and must emphasize the word *believe*),
though am not sure, that I loved him, but yet know I
could never marry him. That certain *spark* of a 'kindred
spirit' was lacking between us. Of course this he could not
understand. I had spent nearly 24 hours of the day with
him, we were happy . . . and yet I said that I would never
marry him. 99% of the girls we know would have given
much for a chance to go out with him. He is handsome,
charming, successful, and all the most interesting artists,
playwrights and journalists were those I met through him.
But I knew that I *could not*.

I had no one to speak to about this, certainly not my
relatives. To my parents I wrote nothing. So you see that if
ever there was a time when I needed you it was then. I

hinted as much to you in my letter. Perhaps you misconstrued this letter; perhaps you did not understand. I waited and waited, & with that waiting something went a little dead. I knew you were busy at the university, but hoped that you would have spared me a little of your time.

Some months later, after a reply from you would not have had the same value, I received a letter from you hurriedly scribbled off on some beach with not even the remotest mention of my last letter.

After that, I simply could not write. Every time I tried, it was more of a strain, not the usual pleasure. And it hurt.

Please forgive what I have just written, but I seem to be cleansing out my system after such a long time and already feel better for it.

Now I want to talk about you and Siamon. You are so much a part of me . . . How can I explain it to you? Although I want to be honest, I may sound strange . . . I feel I am losing a segment of myself. I am not going to cry how happy etc. I am for you – that I could do for Myra and Linn, but NOT you.

Although the news is something that should have been expected, it had the impact of a minor bombshell. I am happy because you say you are happy but I also feel a twinge of sadness because I know that it marks the end, the absolute end of our girlhood.

I want to close now since I am a little drained.

    Love,
      Romy

The diary, which I had kept since the age of ten, came to an end with my wedding on 7 April 1963. In one sense, the story of growing up had come to the foregone conclusion. In another sense, I was vanishing along with my generation into the rituals of the tribe: the engagement party (everyone who sent good wishes had to be invited), the numerous family visits, the kitchen tea, the seven bridesmaids' dresses, the choir, the walk up the aisle. To become engaged was to enter a way of life in which attention, which had centred on books and friends, was compelled by an unceasing clamour of obligation. The bride appeared to function as the latest focus for tribal affirmation that expressed itself, in part, through ritual displays of power: the bridegroom's family trumped the bride's by presenting a wedding list of double the agreed size; the aunts replayed their friction through urgent pleas to consider white versus green slippers for the bridesmaids (each pointing to the misguided taste of the other); a prospective relation offered herself as Matron-of-Honour. A fashionable cousin booked the latest band, whose saccharine climaxes were repeated with maddening monotony. The caterer, the one and only Krafchik, talked of green balloons that would hang from the ceiling in the shape of grapes. The facials, to improve my appearance on the radiant day, stung the skin and brought out an unprecedented array of spots. These, I was assured, would be suitably masked when a professional came 'to make you up'. I felt a certain kinship for Xhosa boys in the process of *abakhwetha* [initiation] whose clay-white faces peered from the bush on either side of the National Road. Some walked in a line, with blankets on their shoulders, and sticks in their hands. The flat white paint left two black holes from which the eyes of the creature flickered uneasily. Some waved in a show of cheer at the cars that passed. Others turned away to the improvised huts, low on the earth, like shiny cocoons. After three weeks, during which they must fend for themselves and wear nothing but the customary blanket, they rejoined the tribe as full-fledged adults.

'The engagement is the happiest time of a girl's life,' my grandmother liked to say. In fact, plans for the wedding absorbed all emotions. Though I groaned over the length of the guest-list or the cacophonous band, it seemed futile to take on the whole battle. Could a girl risk her future in a fling against codes of lavish hospitality and female compliance that went back to the Hebrew Bible?

My only friend was my husband-to-be. He advised detachment. 'You'll get nowhere,' he said, 'and it's not worth your
concern. The wedding', he repeated slowly, 'is *not important*.'

Those were the magic words. I assumed that we would play the
game, together, of not being there. All the same, I remained
unready. I did want to marry, but not yet and not in this way. One
night, close to the event, I scribbled something of this to Berjulie.
She replied:

> I wanted to write this personal and private note to you
> after your last sentence in your pencil-written, dread-of-
> night note of a week ago. To tell you that there is not one
> happily married girl who did not have the self-same
> thought the last month of her engagement period.
> Somehow in the middle of the night, one sits up, recalls
> even mild arguments that have taken place (as to how
> many each side of the family is asking to the wedding), and
> the odd moments of tension, and one wonders 'am I doing
> the right thing?' The feeling of 'not being ready' is so
> typical. The tragedy of it all is that a bride-to-be is not
> warned of the feeling and takes it so much more seriously
> than it warrants. The responsibilities of the future seem so
> ponderous at this stage. I hope you will get the feeling that
> I am talking from the heart. And can I say that once the
> wedding is over and you are alone and your time belongs
> to you both to share as you wish, you will not have the
> feeling of losing your privacy. As a matter of fact, a far
> bigger feeling of improved status emerges and suddenly
> one feels truly GROWN-UP, a true free individual of the
> world and no longer the child of one's parents. Have I
> expressed myself clearly?
>   XX Berj

Far from that 'true individual' that Berj herself represented, I
was increasingly dependent on a responsible man. As the brides of

'62 and '63 and '64 vanished, on the dot of twenty-one, behind
the wedding veil, to re-emerge as bodies swollen with the next
generation, Romy was travelling over some horizon – tossing
back the occasional letter which suggested her growing confidence in a new life of improvisation.

In August 1963 Romy went to visit Ben, who had settled in
London. Testing the past, or unable to let it go, she landed impulsively, exploding the quietude of Ben's habits. They did not live
together, but did embark on a long tour of the Continent. She
wrote from Venice; they were going on to Rome; but it was clear
that she would leave Ben and return to South Africa.

She returned as 'Romy' after two years abroad, taller, slimmer
than ever in her tawny shifts, with a lock of flaming hair falling
over her eyes. On the two-week voyage to the Cape, she fell in
with a group of Englishmen who were going out to sail. On
arrival, she danced every evening on their yacht in Table Bay. As
far as Mrs Gevint was concerned, Englishmen were out of bounds;
so were the docks with their dark alleys and fishy byways, a haunt
of prostitutes. Though Romy continued to dance with her
bottom out, tossing her mane and pouting her lips, consideration
for her mother compelled her always to sleep at home.

In the course of one party, the yacht got free of its mooring and
drifted towards the heaving sea beyond the harbour. Romy's first
thought was for her mother: the anguish her daughter would
bring upon her – not by drowning, but by spending all night, as
her mother would see it, with a group of drunken sailors. It was
too much to contemplate. As the yacht floated wide of the last
dock, Romy took a desperate leap. She landed, yelping, in the sea,
and there was much ado to haul her out.

We barely met before our paths diverged. In January 1964,
Siamon and I left South Africa and worked for a while in London.
In December I found myself pregnant.

Arriving in New York in April 1965, I was dismayed by the
authoritarianism of American doctors. A consultant at New York

Hospital laid down the rules of childbirth: fathers were not allowed to be present – 'they got in the way'; the woman's hands were tied down, a general anaesthetic administered, and the baby delivered with forceps. I wrote a letter of protest, declining to be his patient.

Another rebellion took place in the course of an afternoon tea given by one Professor Mirsky who had invited Siamon to work at Rockefeller University. On the way to our host's apartment, Siamon explained his claim to fame:

'In the late '20s, Dr Avery, at the Rockefeller Institute, did the experiment which showed that DNA is the carrier of genetic information – which may turn out to be the greatest discovery of the century. Dr Mirsky, who was a rival, argued that it was not DNA but some contaminating protein. He was involved in this bitter polemic throughout the '30s. He could not accept defeat.'

'So we're to meet a man of some arrogance?'

'He did make one of the great mistakes, but that was thirty years ago.'

We entered an apartment house on the Upper East Side and sped up in the elevator. A smallish elderly man opened the door, and greeted us with strong handshakes.

'And I see that you have plans for a baby,' he said, nodding his head in sanction of this biological destiny.

'Actually,' I said, 'I have just applied to Columbia University to do a Masters in American literature.'

The smile left his face. 'You should stay home with your baby – my wife found that she could do anything she wanted, here, at home. Isn't that so?' He turned perfunctorily to his wife, Reba, who gave soft sounds of assent. 'Anyway, the MA is nothing; it's for the second-rate. The first-rate do doctorates. Why don't you just let that go? You don't realize', he added, nodding firmly, grey and sage, 'how much time, and care, and energy a baby will need. And your husband, too, working long days and nights, giving his all as a man of science, will depend on you for *unselfish* support.'

Afterwards, as we crossed the monotonous grid of the uptown

streets, the sheer towers, thrusting for the sky, seemed to embody, in the clearest architectural terms, a celebration of power which asked derisively: can you pit yourself against this?

Natural childbirth, as I tried to practise it from handbooks, turned out a disaster. My mentor had been Aunt Ruth, who had been a patient of a pioneer of natural childbirth, Grantley Dick-Read. Aunt Ruth never mentioned pain, except to say that all through the ages, pain was the result of the wrong approach: fear, not joy. 'Giving birth', she said, 'should be a joyous experience.'

I discussed this with Nancy, a sparky New Yorker in a pre-natal waiting-room. She opened the conversation, she said, because I wore a Marimekko shift, not a pastel maternity smock 'with bunnies on the pocket'. Nancy, who knew everything and made plans to the last detail, said in her scoffing tone: 'I wouldn't count on joy.'

Aunt Ruth toured New York in the eighth month of my pregnancy. I was homesick, and her demonstrative fondness was comforting. We fought our way through the July humidity to the World's Fair on Long Island. As we trudged dutifully past unmemorable exhibits, she gave instruction on how to conduct oneself in the delivery room. 'Say a firm NO to offers of drugs. All you have to do is pant lightly' – she arched her beautiful body and performed a few shallow pants, looking into my eyes and smiling with the simplicity of it – 'as you ride the wave of the contraction'.

Hit with pain that seemed unendurable, I wondered where I had gone wrong. Almost with disbelief, I heard myself scream in the midst of a late contraction, as busy orderlies dumped me, like a sack of potatoes, onto the delivery table. It was then that a partial *placenta praevia* was discovered, so it had to be forceps after all.

I came out of that labour a changed person. Nature, Wordsworth said, was the nurse, the guide, the guardian, but nature, I now knew, was not benign; it was a relentless force for generation that would not stop. 'Wasn't it *awful*,' Nancy confirmed in unusually subdued tones on the phone from New York Hospital. Her truthfulness was a relief. It cut through the radiant myths, cut through the clinking of toasts that echoed down the telephone line to Cape Town. My mother rejoiced to hear of little Anna's charms – her slanted eyes and high, fair forehead – but seemed surprised that I was lonely in New York.

'Geography doesn't matter,' was her reply. It meant that those in touch with their Maker would not be alone.

A failure in soul and courage, and without the will to adjust, I sank into depression. It was at first intermittent. Siamon urged me to go to Columbia. He believed in the stimulus of some pursuit, but I was intimidated by the success ethos of New York. At Columbia I gave papers on Thoreau's essay, 'Civil Disobedience', and on the poetry of Emily Dickinson. Both were driven to speak the truth, in the woman's case truth beyond words – buried in the questioning silence of Dickinson's dash as, with relentless precision, she prised words apart to finish 'knowing – then –':

And I, and Silence, some strange Race
Wrecked, solitary, here –

This echoed through my growing horror. For in the months that followed I was compelled, as in a nightmare, to hear, over and over, that inhuman scream that seemed to break open the façades of social existence.

It was a creature stripped of cant who went back to South Africa for a few weeks at the end of '65. Until then, a delight in the loveliness of Anna had offset the savagery of what I termed 'the truth', but as I got off the plane with this flourishing baby, my family swept her off with reproofs at her wetness and (they claimed) inadequate cover.

'You'll *kill* her – with blankets,' I shouted at their busy backs.

Romy liked to re-enact the scene when my grandmother presided over the ritual of the baby's bath.

'You don't mean to carry her like that, uncovered, down the passage,' she exclaimed, in renewed reproof, as I lifted the child from the water.

'It couldn't be hotter, and she's *fine*, I tell you.'

Granny could not agree. Stretching her arms to bar the bath-room door, in what Romy called 'the crucifixion position', she cried: 'Over my *dead body*.'

After two years abroad, the fuss over minutiae of health and cosseting, and the sycophancy of female cooing, its rhetoric of gratitude, and its assumption that men's lives had an absolute importance, all appeared as oblivious as a white liberalism encased, I stated rudely, 'in furs and diamonds'.

Truth is a savage pursuit; it can devastate all structures on which life seems to stand. My course now lay with my husband's future at Rockefeller University. All exclaimed at his fortune to have entered this temple of science. I knew its distinguished history in the fields of bacterial infection, immunology, and cell biology, and had heard of the great work – Dr Avery's genetics or the dis-covery of Peyton Rous, that infectious agents could be a cause of cancer – but, again, I withheld imagination. All I could actually see were the sterile residence rooms in Sophie Frick Hall (where children were not allowed), the ramrod tulips in rows, the invari-able cheer which seemed strangely mechanical, the crude success-ethic of Dr Mirsky, and the dressy lobster lunches where wives exchanged platitudes about the nobility of science with the donors of New York society in their uniform of green and pink, furs and loafers. Such was the prestige of Rockefeller, in its heyday in the mid-'60s, that to voice doubt would have seemed mad. It was not until the late '60s that I met a co-doubter. A woman with grey hair in a white lab coat shared a table with me in the library at Rockefeller. Mrs Garfield, who had been a silent-movie critic in the '20s, now worked in Dr Dole's methadone programme: she was compiling a library on drug abuse. It happened one day that we looked up simultaneously as the swing doors opened to admit a large group of biochemists.

'Such dead faces,' said Mrs Garfield, suddenly, in low tones. She looked straight at me; our eyes locked. She was seventy, I was twenty-nine, but we saw, like children, that certain emperors of science had no clothes.

In 1965–6 it was still the norm in all societies for a woman to follow her husband and contrive to be content. Lady Medawar, in her biography of the Nobel Prize-winner, Peter Medawar, presents a model of this kind. Though in the '30s she had been a scholar at Somerville in the same biological field, she became a selfless helpmeet, silencing her impulse to speak when her husband indicated activity of mind, rejecting 'I wonder' from her vocabulary since it offended his regard for verifiable fact, and satisfied to have washed 'five miles of nappies' by hand for each of her children. Lady Medawar made a just claim when she said that 'it worked', and it worked because many women of her generation still had an unquestioning capacity to sink their existence in that of their husbands. As late as 1965, to become aware of the persistence of a life of one's own was to be 'spoilt'. This was the judgement of Uncle Louis in his deck-chair at Muizenberg. Uncle Louis said how much I had let myself go. A wife should not lose interest in her appearance.

Understanding, that summer, came from Ellie. We were in Ellie's car, driving at night around the Twelve Apostles towards Hout Bay when I found it possible to speak of what was wrong, absurd, monstrous in women's history and their lives.

'I'm with you,' Ellie said strongly into the darkness.

'She made me feel heroic and not the hopeless person which I know I am,' I told Romy on the return journey through Johannesburg.

'She kept on repeating that the evening she had spent with you had been the saving grace of this "holiday",' Romy wrote to Ellie. 'I cannot possibly, for my own peace of mind, relate the traumas of those two days. She did not want to go back to New York.'

My inability to adjust to New York became increasingly hopeless and propelled me into a depth of depression from which there seemed no return: I lay inert through all the hours and minutes of the day, hardly able to speak.

There were periods in St Luke's Hospital, on 111th and West End Avenue, but they did no good. The patients used to wander up and down a wide, featureless corridor, past the glassed-in cubicle where brightly indifferent nurses chattered over cups of coffee after the morning ritual. This consisted of lining up selected patients, drooping in their dressing-gowns. They would call out the names of the more resistant cases for a brisk jolt of electro-convulsive 'therapy'. (Two years later, when I passed again through the locked door on the eighth floor of Clark building to fetch a fellow student for class – Marty had attempted suicide following the deterioration of her multiple sclerosis – there sat the staff still, behind their partition, with the same bright fixity, the practised indifference to what crept past them, day by day.)

As a second year passed in that lit-up city, I experienced the effect of meaningless time that creeps at its petty pace – once a joke on Mad Friday. In August, Romy wrote to Phillippa, who now lived with Robert and their child in Camps Bay:

> I received a letter from Lyndall about a month ago, a very controlled letter, in which she stated that she would like me to come to the States. It included a poem which she had written while she was in hospital that made my blood curdle.
>
> Phillippa, I gather from Berjulie that there was talk of her going into a Home but that she would have had to sign herself in for a year . . . Both the emotional and intellectual parts of my very being have rejected this as the body rejects something foreign.

The alternative was shock treatment. In September, ten shocks brought no change. Silvano Arieti, in his book-lined consulting-room on the East Side, chatting in his literate way about my mental obstructions to the wonders of New York – its towers, culture, success – ordered five more. There could, I saw, be no end to it, as Hopkins perceived in that most terrifying line in all poetry: 'No worst, there is none.'

But salvation came, and not through praying, nor through

treatments, but through Virgil. One graduate requirement was to
pass a course in Latin. That fall I registered for Virgil, if only as a
gesture towards action. So, in the mornings, I went to Clark 8 for
a dose of electricity, while in the evenings I crawled, line by line,
with the aid of grammar and dictionary, over several books of the
Aeneid. It happened then that certain sombre lines stirred some
dulled response: the resolve of Aeneas, and his plea to comrades,
to press on in the face of hopelessness:

'O you who have still weightier trials borne,
These too the god shall end. You have come near
Mad Scylla and her deep resounding rocks . . .
Call courage back, and banish gloomy fear,
Perchance in time to come you may rejoice
As you remember this. Through varying luck
And many risks to Latium on we press,
Where fates disclose us undisturbed abodes;
There heaven allows Troy's realm to rise again;
Bear up, and keep yourselves for better days.'

I now read Book VI with the advantage of first-hand knowledge of the difficulty of the return from the Underworld, yet the
words, '*hoc opus, hic labor est*' – 'this is the undertaking, this the
task' – offered the resonance of an imagined challenge. During
November and December, each sixty lines of translation for the
following class were the first, hesitating steps of a return to the
living.

Then, late one night at the end of January, Romy came: a saviour in high tan boots, with streaming red hair framed in a white
bonnet, alighting at Kennedy Airport, tired from her flight, but
bent on transformation. She had feared, she said, 'the worst', and
her 'shock at seeing the person I knew' came out in a burst of
tears. So she gave me back that person. She brought letters from
Ellie and Phillippa which addressed that forgotten being; she
praised my 'Brontë look' as she unpacked her present, a short

tawny shift with cutaway shoulders in her own more sophisticated style; and best of all, she challenged the fiction of illness, in words I could not have dared to say. 'Was she really ill?' she wrote to my mother. 'I know that I must believe those who told me that things were bad, but it is inconceivable. We haven't stopped speaking since I came.'

We took off on a journey in a storm, travelling to Buck Hill Falls, Pennsylvania, through silent woods, along dark rivers packed with ice-floes. It was twenty-eight below freezing. The roads, almost impassable, were drifts of snow; the Greyhound driver picked his way from memory. We crept along for many an hour to reach, at length, an inn that *Cue* had called 'spacious' but turned out to be cavernous in its empty seclusion. We were the only guests before the fire.

That night Romy told me about Mark Cass. This was serious, she said. He was older, a senior lecturer in French at the University of the Witwatersrand, wise, sensitive, philosophical – the most humane person she had met. The month before, on vacation in Cape Town, he had read Jewish stories aloud to her – Bernard Malamud, his favourite – leaning against a rock on the deserted Glen Beach, his pale hat shading his eyes. She had watched his lips, edged with deep lines that ran from nose to mouth, as the stories gave shape and humour to that broken past of eastern Europe that lay behind her transplanted parents, behind – herself. Never had she been so moved. Yet there were, she added guardedly, 'problems, doubts, complexities which remain to be resolved'.

When our paths had diverged at the start of '64, Romy had settled in Johannesburg. She had lived at the Jacaranda, in Hillbrow, a residential hotel for single women. As the place for out-of-town women in search of husbands, it did not provide, Hubert thought, 'the right background'. He told Romy to 'bring your dates to Willow Stream'.

To Romy, Willow Stream was heaven: the great willows that

followed the line of the stream, the thick pile of the sloping lawns that were watered in the cool of the day by a myriad spouts, the perfection of Sunday lunches where even the peppermints matched the tablecloth, and the polished guests who included Esmé Berman, the art critic, Chippy the flautist and – it must be said – also her husband, Percy Yutar, the state prosecutor in the Rivonia Trial of 1963–4 when Mandela was condemned to life imprisonment (it was said that only international opinion prevented the death penalty). How much Romy knew of Yutar's activities I have no idea, but she did not leave. She was, said Hubert, 'a little shrewd. She once said to me: "I couldn't do such-and-such because it would have looked too shrewd."'

'Romy lived by an internal rhythm that overrode what you call duty,' I said to Berj, 'and yet you couldn't disapprove of her. Was it the attraction of opposites?'

'I think so,' Berj agreed.

'Was it a mother–daughter relationship?'

'It was a friendship,' said Berj emphatically.

'In one letter,' I recalled, 'she said that you "revitalized" her – not that she needed animating, I'd have thought. But did she need you?' I pressed her, knowing that Berj would have responded to need.

'She had to talk, you see, about virginity – I was older, but not her mother. She could talk about her conflict. There was her duty to her parents – and to herself. She had to look after her interests, not throw herself away.'

'Romy, I'd say, had no difficulty whatever in looking after herself,' said Hubert, amused. 'She was strong, with a temper. She once told me what she did when some chap "started with her" on a landing: she took hold of him and literally threw him down the stairs.'

Romy 'partied' her way through 1964 while, very much in the background, she did teacher-training. She drove a tiny Mini Minor, the back littered with maths books. The course at the Johannesburg College of Education was, she said, 'a joke', but there she met the abandoned Leonora Carey. Together they dated 'the two Jerrys', good-looking, unstable, and fun, who invited the 'girls' to black-tie dinners at their home. Romy and Leonora, aged twenty-two, would arrive in ball-dress. During the Easter vacation, they drove alone to Lourenço Marques where they flirted with naval officers who presented each with a Portuguese doll – their game was to 'spoil the ladies' in hope of favours. Leonora ended up in the cabin of the commanding officer, having (as she put it) 'a hot affair', while Romy got away with a few of her extravagant, pouting kisses. They raced back to Jo'burg with a huge bag of cashew nuts between them on the seat. Then there was a puncture. It was customary to await immediate help from the next car and, sure enough, four men stopped, leapt out with alacrity, and changed the wheel. Romy's role was to hand round the cashew nuts in the manner of a hostess.

Leonora Carey presented a new challenge to experience: a challenge, as Leonora saw it, to sexual maturity. To women of our time and background, women were either virgins, or tarts, or married: Leonora was none of these. When you met her, you did not think – is she pretty? – because you were arrested by her fire and grace. Unloved, as a child, by a cold mother, a photograph shows her twirling her Spanish skirt with a mix of fire and shyness in her eyes. Her rhythm came from within, and she still had it in 1990 after more than twenty years of marriage to a farmer in the remoter reaches of the Free State. We met in the foyer of the glossy Rosebank Hotel in Johannesburg, on 13 January 1990. I knew her at once, as she came towards me, the black-haired Leonora of the '60s – not quite so slim, perhaps, but passionate as ever in voice and gesture. The truth, an intimate and bodily truth, fell easily from her lips.

Leonora, opening the door to maturity, had told Romy that the time had come to use tampons. Romy retired to the bathroom to try them out and, fairly soon, came back wailing, her panties around her ankles, her pelvis thrust forward, holding a tampon in the preparation position. 'I can't find my vagina,' she wailed, laughing at the same time. 'Can you imagine being so helpless?' said Leonora, remembering. 'She didn't know anything about that part of her anatomy.'

In 1965, during Romy's first year of teaching at Greenside High, she took a flat in Tyrwhitt Avenue, Rosebank. It was furnished with Berj's cast-off armchairs (it was the time when Johannesburg took to antiques). Romy shared the flat with a fellow student from UCT who had taught for some years at a night school for blacks in a church near Wits (the University of the Witwatersrand). Careen, the flatmate, then discovered she was pregnant and there was to be a rushed wedding with her mother arriving from Cape Town. It happened in the midst of this crisis that one of Careen's pupils came to their flat. Careen later declared that 'pupils never came to the flat', but it may have happened that one arrived to see her on his own initiative. Romy found herself dismissing a man, with suit and briefcase, who stood at the door having travelled 'from God-knows-where'. There is no way of knowing why Romy thought he had come by appointment, and that she had been left to 'get rid of him'. Someone with the social conscience to teach at night school is unlikely to be a callous person, but Romy assumed so, broke with Careen, and did not answer Careen's invitation to be a bridesmaid.

It was through Careen that Romy met Isabel Summers, big and protective, with a warm manner. She was a fighter for human rights: she had been a social worker in Sophiatown before the state bulldozed it in the '50s, and she was now a fearless lecturer in South African law at the University of the Witwatersrand. Isabel's parties were neither the gourmet dinners of the two Jerrys nor the well-heeled lunches of Willow Stream: they were occasions for political debate, agitated disagreement over the consequences of the distant ideal of one voters' roll: the implications of full suffrage that would switch the South African electorate from three to twelve million. Most of Isabel's circle welcomed 'the inevitable black majority' but feared, at the same time, 'the inevitable blood-bath' that would bring it about – that was realistic thinking in the mid-'60s after Mandela, as leader of the ANC, had called for a 'defensive policy' of armed struggle, a defence (as he put it) against the brutality of apartheid. At these debates of university lecturers and other liberals, white and black, a newly agitated Romy was introduced in November 1965 to the rather jaded Mark Cass, with a cigarette between his lips and dark hair swept back from a quizzical forehead, for he had heard the arguments before.

'His father', Isabel whispered to Romy, 'was a Communist with other intellectuals of the '30s. There was a picture of Stalin over the fireplace, that is, before the war, before one heard.'

'Why does he look so . . . so pained?' Romy whispered back.

'Because he *is* in pain: a month ago his car crashed twenty feet down an incline. He's broken two vertebrae, and done some damage to his spine – the doctors aren't sure. They can't give any prognosis, so it's not only pain but also a certain amount of worry. And there isn't enough money: he's got various dependants'

Soon after, school closed and Romy left for the Cape. To her surprise, Mark was at the airport to see her off. He had taken the trouble to find her flight. On her way to the plane she waved back at that short, rather interesting man who had left his Camus, Hemingway, and Henry Miller for a smile and a word. As she lounged at Clifton in her black bikini, surrounded by muscled males oiling their legs, she thought more than once about Mark, his one hand pressing the small of his back, the keen glance from behind his glasses – as though he looked through her beauty to her soul – when they said goodbye. She wondered whether he would be waiting for her when she returned.

He was. They went to Pinter's play, *The Homecoming*; they read Nadine Gordimer's *The Late Bourgeois World*; eventually, they went away for a weekend. On her return, she told Leonora that she had experienced intense but almost desperate love – desperate, she said, because she had come back a virgin. 'But don't get me wrong,' said Leonora. 'It was, in its unique way, a passionate relationship.' By the end of 1966 they were a couple, and the question of marriage arose.

Mark Cass was, without doubt, the man who was commensu-rate, at last, with Romy's specialness. Like all men, he wished to marry her.

'So why didn't she?' I asked Leonora on that hot summer morning in 1990, as we sat at breakfast, with croissants and orange juice, fourteen years after Romy's death.

'Why did she persist in her virginity?' Leonora countered.

'Because it was our code – we are the creatures of our code.'

'But to continue to be a virgin at twenty-four, twenty-five? To go repeatedly so far, and no further? When she went away with Mark, he wasn't a boy – he was older than the rest. If living was her credo, I return the question: why didn't she?'

'Too complex,' I brooded.

'I'm asking a simple question,' Leonora persisted, 'and I think there's a simple answer. She appeared to have left the *shtetl* behind her, appeared to be impetuous, adventurous, tempestu-ous, yet when it came to sex, she was afraid – scared to lose her control.'

'We stop here.' I was not convinced. 'Stop at this gap – it's what we don't know.'

Leonora refused to leave her idea. 'It wasn't done to hold back in the circle in which she mixed. Losing virginity was part of being an intellectual, being at one with all the literature and pas-sion you were reading about. Mark, remember, was a Francophile. He liked Henry Miller.'

'The code', I explained, 'was a habit. It wasn't genuine moral-ity, but one of those unbreakable habits of provincials whose minds are closed, locked, to alternative possibility. We *were* provincials – Romy's sophistication was her mask. She may have longed to open the closed doors of inhibition – the last portal to experience as she understood the word: experience, that is, on a woman's own terms. And all the time, that other girl would have been there too: the marriageable daughter of her *shtetl* parents, born to offer her precious virginity to the best bidder at the tribal wedding – that "good daughter" who would grant her parents the *nachas* [social credit] she owed them – and who, in the end, she could not bring herself to be.'

'I hated introductions to eligible men,' Leonora said heatedly, 'those lords of creation who might care to confer their favour. I could have laughed in their faces, so full of stupid importance. One day, a neighbour dragged me into her flat to meet this farmer – a boer from the backveld. *Me*, he thought to meet, a person who read literature, who had a vocation – yes, a vocation – for teaching. I was deliberately rude to him; said I had to leave at once to finish some marking at school. As we went down in the lift, he vowed (he told me later): "You bitch, I'm going to bed you even if I have to marry you." He was used to women who were keen to meet him – he was rich, see – but, unconsciously, he was looking for a woman who would be tough enough to stand up to his mother *op die plaas* [on the farm]. Actually, I liked his natural-ness; he would pick up babies or little animals with equal ease. When, *eventually*, I agreed to marry, my mother said: "What have you got to be tense about? From the day you were born I've been planning your wedding." But my father was different – oh, how I miss him. He told me, at sixteen, that virginity meant nothing. "My dearest," he said, "you must never sleep with a man because you feel obliged; you must never violate your feelings; but nature's impulse is there to be enjoyed."'

This extraordinary advice from a father in the late '50s had been the making of Leonora, who lived for passion – not promis-cuity, which is a form of power, but an expression of her own. In this she bypassed contemporaries who experienced passion, if at all, in lending themselves to others' desire. What Romy had known with Ben and Dov was this reflected excitement that asked, only, a tantalizing, partial act of surrender. With Mark it was different: her passion seemed more desperate.

Leonora thought: 'Mark tiptoed emotionally round her, fraught with the same dramatic intensity. She needed a man who would DO it, not debate it so carefully.'

I shook my head, doubtfully. 'You're too certain, Leo. How can one know – and should one know – a matter so intimate?'

'Lawrence argued that we should, that it is in the passional places that the tide of awareness has to flow, cleansing and freshening – *Lady Chatterley's Lover*. But it has to be done with respect, he says, respect for the struggling creatures we are.'

'Leo, when Romy came to New York, in January 1967, she stopped in London. Can you guess? She went again to Ben. I remember her telling me at Buck Hill Falls – with a storm outside – not much, but that it was "important". She went to see Ben when he was about to marry a gentle English girl. She was impetuous, as you know, and she couldn't let a tie go – no more than she could tie herself finally (yes, she feared finality). I got the impression that, just then, it was hard to give up Ben in a final way. I can imagine her dramatic entrance and the way she would have left Ben, who was building the ramparts of safety, exposed to the disturbance of unfinished emotions. Her affairs with men were highly charged; she sustained and recharged them, not wilfully, but because they had become a part of herself which could not be left to die. That older, simpler part of her was still vibrating, perhaps, when she came on to New York and agonized over the complexities of her bond with Mark.'

Here, again, there is a gap. The electricity had, after all, some effect. It left this blank: I cannot recall exactly what Romy told me when we sat before the fire at Buck Hill Falls early in 1967, when she struggled with her virginal demands, her worshipping, unconsummated passion for Mark Cass. All I remember was her scream – over ill-connected lines, a cry that had to carry and reverberate over the nine thousand miles between 114th Street on the Upper West Side and Berea, Johannesburg. The sound had carried through the small apartment, penetrating the bland surface of my treated mind. But why did she scream? What inarticulate need – in that most articulate of women – drove it out?

Mark was shattered as he put down the receiver. So said Peter Keating, his friend and colleague in the Department of French. 'She was too much for him,' Peter said.

This was one of recurrent fights. At the centre of their struggle, in Mark's view, was an issue of allegiance. Mark had obligations: to a widowed sister, ten years older than himself; to her sons as surrogate father; and to his elderly mother with whom he lived. She was a *shtetl* mother, but to Romy less vulnerable than Mrs Gevint: too demanding of her son, too unwilling to let him go.

Leonora put the case in this way: 'If Mark were to leave home, it would have been for marriage. Romy demanded that he leave home anyway, to assert himself and to provide the space in which their future could develop. Mark's mother nursed his back; Romy wished to take over – which was unrealistic, to say the least. Since she couldn't live with him, she would have popped in and out, done something here and there – Mark wouldn't have had the same care. The crux of the matter is that Romy made this demand without committing herself to marriage. Mark had to do this first. To placate her, he did take a small *pied-à-terre* in Berea which he shared with a lunatic artist. It wasn't easy; and it cost too much. This Romy didn't consider: what it meant not to have money.'

The call from New York made another demand: Mark should come at once. He told me later: 'She was devoted to you and said, one day: "She needs me. I'm going." She left the school – fed up, anyway, with teaching.' Similar action was required of Mark. To Romy, it was a call so urgent (for whatever reason) that it had to surmount all other considerations. To Mark, it was caprice: a man could not drop his job, forget his dependants, and rush off across the globe. It was another round in a draining battle; for Romy, it was (I would guess) a test of Mark's willingness to act in response to private need. It was a conflict of obligation versus feeling, and this battle Mark fought also within himself, for he had the sensibility to acknowledge in full the claims of both. For Romy, there was actually no issue: her refusal of non-being (gallant or outrageous as others saw it), her transforming power, infusing others with her appetites, quickening them with her irresistible spirit, she was laying before Mark – her splendid offer. The private moment – exhilaration or empathy or desire – was her *raison d'être*. Her scream registered its denial by the very person for whom she cared more, now, than any other.

This may well be a superstructure. A gap remains around that scream, sealed further by the day-to-day events of Romy's visit, as recorded in letters of the time:

31 January 1967: Romy arrived on Sunday evening. We waited above the luggage hall at Kennedy Airport, scanning the arrivals. When Siamon spotted her, we charged down to the passengers' exit. While others waited obediently behind the barrier, we stormed the door . . . The first morning we went to Rockefeller Plaza and up the RCA building for a view of the city. Romy was so responsive that I took possession of New York in showing it to her. It was beautifully clear but bitterly cold – when Romy took her bonnet off, she nearly lost her ears – and down below the skaters circled in little skirts. At Bloomingdales, she bought a 'kookie' yellow dress in the new Baby Look, demurely frilled but very, *very* short. She said defiantly that 'others wear their hems up to the navel'. Nancy phoned to ask if Romy would like to meet 'a real live American'. It is so good to have Romy here that I can hardly bear to let her sleep: I have to hear about everyone I care for in South Africa. All through the night I devoured Albie Sachs's book [about his imprisonment] which Romy had brought. It was very moving and disturbing. It so often happens that, during trials abroad, one remembers with longing the natural paradise, and closes the mind, to some degree, to the horrors of inhumanity that have made South Africa the unreal dream it is. One forgets more, here, where it seems so far away. Though people know of apartheid, they seem unaware of its finer abuses.

5 February 1967: Poor Romy immediately caught a heavy, chesty cold but has been very game for outings and most enthusiastic about New York. After two days she said she would like to live here.

5 February 1967: [To Phillippa] When Romy described the summer in Cape Town, especially you and Ellie, I longed to have been there with you. Many thanks for the beautiful frock you sent for Anna. Normally, she lives in trousers and the old ladies, on their bench in the middle of Broadway, say 'sweet little fella', so that today when she strutted out in the frock, she caused a sensation.

The other evening, Siamon was stopped by a traffic cop for, he claimed, numerous offences. Romy stepped in with a practised performance. 'Oh Officer,' said she, 'PLEASE don't spoil my first, my very first Saturday night in this city.' The cop burst into welcoming smiles and started saying, 'Well, yeah, public relations . . .'

7 February 1967: At Buck Hill Falls, the sun shone on the flawless snow. We skied for the first time and, as we flew across the vast, untouched expanses, became independent and young – so young that a waiter asked sternly if we were over 21 before showing us the wine list.

13 February 1967: Romy has been coming with me to classes, and delights in the beat types on campus. She met a Ph.D. student at the West End Pub around the corner, and is out with him to-night. The other day, when she asked another student where to change on the subway, he took her all the way and brought her back. Romy looks stunning in a dark green corduroy suit with a little boy's cap. Men can't help looking at her. One doddering professor, in the elevator in Philosophy Hall, said: 'You look like a picture I've seen somewhere before.' I like showing her off to friends, and friends to her. Ted [a college teacher] took us to the East Village where the addicts hang out. He pointed to The Head Shop, which sells not drugs but everything connected with them, e.g. syringes. At the end of last semester, a student came up to him and said: 'You're the swingiest teacher I've had – here's a present.' It was marijuana. While we drank coffee, we saw a gang taking their house-plants for an airing.

19 February 1967: I wish Romy could stay indefinitely. We talk and talk – the time with her seems so precious that I won't let her go to sleep until I've had my say. At about 2 a.m. she starts protesting feebly. Siamon says we could be back at Good Hope, and asks if he has to make an appointment a week in advance to see me. He has a great sense of Responsibility, worries when Romy stays out late, and warns about pick-ups. An academic at the West End asked her out: mindful of Siamon's dire predictions, she told him that she was leaving *immediately* on a tour around the country. The next day she bumped into him on Broadway to her embarrassment, but this time consented to consider his credentials. She warned him, 'I have friends who are seriously concerned about what happens to me.'

20 February 1967: She is a marvellous companion and an easy guest In fact she isn't a guest – she washes up, peels vegetables, shops. Yesterday, when I took Anna to Columbia, Romy stayed behind on the pretext of 'sleeping late', but when I came back, she had cleaned the whole apartment. She is, of course, dieting, and groans that she is 'starving hungry'.

Romy isn't used to putting things out of a child's reach. Anna keeps trotting to me with her glasses and tiny earrings. The other day I spotted Romy's pearls lying at the bottom of the lavatory. After a week's search, we found her address book in the vegetable rack.

Romy will tell you when she gets home the intimate

secrets of the way we live. We try to quarrel quietly in Anna's bathroom, but somehow it reverberates through the apartment!

On Friday we spent the afternoon at the Whitney Museum. There was an exhibition by Andrew Wyeth, who's all the rage now. Many paintings bordered on the sentimental. There was one of flowers on a grave with an equally soppy caption. At the Museum of Primitive Art we saw a New Guinea sculpture of mother and child. I was struck by the face which was the antithesis of a madonna: it was savage, brutish – true enough.

27 February 1967: We watched Ruth First's program on Channel 13: a re-enactment of her 118 days' detention under the 90 days law. It reinforced my feelings after Albie's book: revulsion and shame. It must be difficult to live there now. I am so sad because I love the country so much and wish I could live there in peace.

5 March 1967: We have just returned from a magnificent concert at Philharmonic Hall – Romy and I. After the Haydn symphony, we rushed down the aisle to the stage in order to get a close-up view of Leonard Bernstein. Afterwards we met Nancy and Tim for Viennese coffee on West 72nd, a refugee area where little old men converse in *Mittel*-European accents while munching through thick chocolate layers of Riga pastries. On Saturday night we had some New Yorkers for dinner; then on to see Martha Graham and her company. She is about 70 but still appears on stage with a marvellous Presence. Her first action as Hecuba was simply to walk across the stage – but what a walk: strong, proud, and rhythmic. She used many ballet steps which were 'opened out' into a more sensuous use of the whole body. Afterwards they came back here for coffee and we talked late, mostly about racial issues in SA. The

program on 90-days made an impact here on those who
saw it.

5 March 1967: [Romy to my mother]
My dear Rhoda,

We have just returned from an exhilarating experience
at the Philharmonic. We are lounging around – Lyn in her
turquoise negligee & yours truly in shocking pink. Siamon
is wallowing in his bath and Anna at whom I have just
peeked is rosily asleep. I feel so very much at home & so
deeply entrenched that I shall probably find it difficult to
leave . . . I want to assure you that all is 203% well here.

   All my love,
      Romy

22 March 1967: After the long winter, we have had a few
warmer days and a picnic near the zoo in Central Park. We
turned up our faces to catch shafts of sunlight and new bird
sounds. Anna sang a little spring song as she rolled along in
her stroller. On Romy's last Thursday night, we went to
hear a panel of playwrights from Off-Off Broadway. They
write for cafés in the East Village. One woman who has
written a play on sodomy kept shouting 'achtung!' and
'reactionary!' whenever this work was criticized.

   Please forgive this letter's lateness. The reason is that
Romy left last night, and towards the end I had to draw
out every minute of her company. Neither of us could
believe that she was really going until she had gone. She
fitted so completely into our life, made so many friends,
lived with such intensity and yet so naturally that we went
on as though she would live here always and, now that she
has gone, I feel her absence very much.

Romy's departure marked a new beginning for me: a resolve to
build up the good deliberately, as she did instinctively, and affirm

it with all one's strength. What she suffered – whatever deviant thought or feeling stirred her scream – she kept alive but out of sight as, presumably, generations before her. 'How safe, methinks, and strong behind/These trees have I encamp'd my Mind', wrote Andrew Marvell in about 1650, a revolutionary guarded by the mask of caution. I saw, now, the possibilities of that double existence: to hold firm to truth and, at the same time, to make terms with the world in order to act within it. 'You can't fight the world,' Arieti told me. 'Don't waste your energy,' Siamon advised. Men took for granted the rules of survival. 'No point in going under,' they were telling me. 'Do something; and compromise in order to be effective.' I could not agree in principle but, in practice, there was no doubt, my husband was a model of effectiveness who had managed to adapt to the success-mania of New York without loss of integrity, as he had gone with detached tolerance through what had seemed to me the distorting scenarios of a tribal wedding. His control was never at stake. Was this the power of confidence? Was this maturity? Or was it that all structures, professional or marital, were – whatever their trimmings – designed for male convenience? Gender, degrees, prizes: were these not all fictions of order beneath which lay dreams, cries, whispers, and the elusive moments of existence itself?

And yet – Existence – some way back –
Stopped – struck – my ticking – through –

So wrote Emily Dickinson in her room of her own in Amherst in 1862, holding the 'bomb' in her breast: 'Nay – Hold it – it is calm –'. That was one model. The other would be my husband in his searching aspect: the man who said that to be a scientist was to recognize the vastness of the dark in which we lived, existing on some tenuous outer fringe of knowledge – a far cry from the insistent image-making of Rockefeller's news-sheets about prizes and promotions. But that, Siamon said, is what you ignore. 'You concentrate on work. Do what interests you, and let the world take care of itself – for the time being. In the end you'll do some-thing useful.' I began some research, on the basis of this plan.

In April, I wrote to Linn, whose happiness in her engagement to Morgan, after her divorce, seemed a parallel start:

Since Romy left, I am leading a very quiet life, enjoying a new-found peace in being alone. It is much warmer, and every morning I take Anna to Riverside Park. It is peaceful there out of sight of buildings and traffic, and Anna can roam on the sparse grass and dusty-dead leaves the last of the snow has uncovered. She brings me fistfuls of brown leaves that crumble the moment she grasps them. Lying there in the sun, I read *Four Quartets*. Its truths are so elevated by simplicity of expression that they did not hurt in a sick way. It is only truth unrecognized that hurts in this way – unrec-ognized by oneself or by society.

As I feel myself unfold again, I want to be unchannelled, free to live beyond political and religious differences that have proved the most evil forces in history. Perhaps one day I shall think differently, but at the moment want to identify only with good people and natural beauty – things that belong to the world at large.

Between May and August, I wrote a Master's essay on the development of religious ideas in T S Eliot, with a long chapter on *Four Quartets*. I thought it out during walks on the beach near Sedgefield in the Cape, where we spent some weeks in a bare house above the waves. It was winter and deserted. On the way back to New York, we stayed at Willow Stream where Romy gave a party to introduce her Johannesburg friends: Leonora, the politi-cal Isabel, Peter Keating and his wife, Bonnie, a vivacious interior designer in stylish clothes. Mark did not appear. As the evening drew on, Romy stopped laughing.

The next morning, as I came down the stairs, a strange man waited at the bottom. He was dark, with thoughtful eyes and a kind smile – it was Mark. Romy burst through the front door. She was exuberant. Evidently, they had made up. Mark Cass was everything Romy had led me to expect: gentle, civilized. It was Romy's way to precede introductions with a private build-up that wove the affinities of her network. I had been prepared to like Mark for Romy's sake, but succumbed in my own right. This was the man to marry: I no longer know how far Romy had prepared my mind for this conclusion but, from the first, he had my support. As we strolled in the garden, he spoke about books, in particular a new South African novel, *The Keep*, by Jillian Becker. It was about the artifice of a Johannesburg Jewish family, living in a dream-like, Europeanized superstructure that contrived to ignore the intransigence of Africa. In the copy he brought me, I have underlined the deviance of the indigenous child, Josephine, from family habits of selective oblivion: 'Europe was a tale of war and death, but Africa was pervading certainty, like the sunlight, not particularly to be noticed, but the general condition of being.' Mark had a delicacy of mind that set him apart from randy South Africa or driven New York. He had lived in Paris, and seemed more French, in a literate, analytic way, than anything else.

Impressed with Romy's choice, I disregarded their fights, certain that differences could be resolved. How could they not, when Mark appeared to fit the story that I was inventing? In place of schoolgirl romance, in place of kitchen sink and other destructive forms of domestic drama – the birth of the baby-demon in *Sport of My Mad Mother*; the savage, unspoken tensions of *The Homecoming* – there was to be this story, as yet dim and in the making, but a hopeful story in which adults, including women, would go on learning through a chosen field of work. There was to be life after marriage: a new kind of partnership. I saw in Mark the promise of a man who would encourage a woman to go on to Volume II: some yet-to-be-defined but searching sequel to the stale fictions of Vol. I. If Romy married Mark, she might share in the making of Vol. II: we could devise it together. But this scenario proved another fiction.

From the beginning of 1967, Mark doubted a future with Romy. In Cape Town he met Ellie who was taking a graduate degree in psychology. She had cut her hair short as a boy's; it glistened in the sun like a shining cap. Beneath it, her slanting, light-blue eyes looked out with quickness.

'I might have been happier with Ellie,' Mark remarked to Bonnie, on his return, showing a photograph of Romy and Ellie, who were talking intently in a back room at some party.

'And would he?' I asked Bonnie and Phillippa, many years later, in 1989, as we sat on Phillippa's verandah eating pasta with shredded chicken in a sesame dressing. Phillippa was trying out Easy Entertaining for her next piece as Food Editor of *Cosmopolitan*.

'No – he wouldn't,' said Phillippa decisively.

'Why?' I wondered. 'Ellie was intellectual, more so than Romy.'

'*No*,' said Bonnie and Phillippa together. Bonnie explained: 'She was impossible; drank too much. She used to break up parties – she'd fix on someone with flagrant fury.'

'Did Ellie drink?' I was surprised. 'I never saw it.'

'You came so rarely,' said Phillippa. 'You never saw her crazy states. Mark would have coped even less well than he did with Romy.'

In September 1967, Mark told Romy that he did not wish to see her. For him, the 'spark' had gone. Their love, which they could neither eradicate nor consummate, turned out to have been 'destructive'. For this, Romy blamed herself in a letter of bitter self-criticism, written some eight weeks after they parted:

My darling darling Lyndall – At the very moment after reading your letter all I want to say is that I love you – that I love you dearly. Your letter has eased the tight knot at the pit of my stomach. I write to you regularly: at night when I lie in bed I have conversations with you. I tell you things and I ask you things. I wanted to tell you what has happened, but could not bring myself to write. I wanted you *here*, to talk to me, to react to me. I told you before that I felt selfish over your return to New York, but did not realize how much I was going to miss you because, really, you are part of me . . .

I didn't break off with Mark. Mark decided he didn't want to see me. Not that I blame him. His back wouldn't have broken him as I nearly did.

One evening about 8 weeks ago, Mark & I went out for dinner together – and for the first time I was ready to tell him that I had come to terms with so many things: the situation between us, his back, his family. He used to tell me that I would, & now I did, but by this stage he just didn't feel anything. He decided that there wasn't any point to our seeing each other and that he would make the next move.

I can't go into that ghastly terrible evening but very soon afterwards I slept *for the first time* with a man. It probably was a masochistic act on my part. I had to punish myself in some way & punish myself I did. It was so very painful and I bled a lot & he was so 'gentle' and 'considerate' & of course no communication. The irony of it, Lyndall. I have had 2 deep, emotional relationships with Ben and Mark & not slept with them, & then this. It happened 3 days before I went to Cape Town [for the ten-day school vacation in September]. There, I couldn't act the prima donna because there was no emotion. And I couldn't tell anyone at home. How many girls are there in this world who share my secret, who have had deep relationships & then lose their virginity to the next guy who comes along? But it was a cold, premeditated act on my part & I have no regrets.

Last Monday was Mark's birthday and I phoned to wish him & we went out for dinner again. I did not use this as a reason to possibly see him. He wanted to see me.

It was strange. We decided not to discuss anything intense but were both rather disturbed. We discussed

Philby, Mark's forthcoming lecture in Rhodesia, your
letter to Berjulie, and the fact that you enjoyed *The Keep*,
but nothing personal. He looks so much better, the
separation has done him good. He is still in much pain
which he tries to ignore. We came back to my room
because he couldn't sit for too long & we listened to
Shirley Bassey singing songs like 'And We Were Loves' and
'Too Bad, Too Bad'. But he hasn't phoned since.

I try to occupy myself. I just will not allow myself to
brood.

Reggie had a flower party 2 Saturdays ago which was a
panacea for all ills. All my friends came. The punch was so
potent it nearly blinded us. Leonora commented that you
and Siamon were conspicuous by your absence & that
depressed me.

Leonora has a serious boyfriend who flies into
Johannesburg in his own private plane from his farm in the
Free State. She is very happy and hoping for a diamond so
large and heavy that to wear it would mean the
development of left arm muscles like those of a tennis
player. She sees Mark regularly because they are fond of
each other, and this pleases me.

It was something of a relief to be in Cape Town, short
though it was. I spent a morning with your mother & was
sorry to leave her. Reggie came to fetch me & your
Granny, thinking him a beau, was so eager to meet him –
until she discovered that he was my brother. She quickly
lost interest. It was good to see Ellie & Phillippa again, and
of course you were our main topic of conversation.

Berjulie returned from Lusaka last week & I spent a
marvellous afternoon with her. She always revitalizes me. I
enjoy her so much. Her stories about her family were
hilarious.

The letter ends abruptly, at the bottom of the fourth page, as though it were unfinished, and begins anew a fortnight later:

> *20 November 1967*: *So* much has happened since that
> afternoon when I poured & poured out to you. Please *do
> not* worry about me – the first two pages may give the
> wrong impression. I am not unhappy. This was one reason
> for hesitating: I don't want to upset you, my love, & you
> must not be upset.
>
> Leonora has become *engaged* this weekend. Her fiancé,
> the farmer, says that his older brother was at boarding-
> school with Siamon [the room-mate, Jonty, who covered
> for Siamon when he slipped out to dance]. He is down-to-
> earth & though not as sophisticated as Leonora, he is very
> good for her. They are getting married in February & I am
> to be her maid-of-honour.
>
> I have seen Mark approximately once a week &
> although we are both a bit bruised, we are slowly building
> (or at least I hope this is true) on the ruins of our
> relationship.
>
> At the moment he is in Rhodesia & will probably be
> leaving at the end of November for a research visit to
> France. In the meantime there is contact between us & I
> am satisfied with that . . .
>
> The kids [her pupils] will be writing their exams soon
> & then I shall be going home to Cape Town for four
> weeks. If only you were there to talk to, to be with, to
> laugh with.
>
> Please write soon,
> Romy

What had happened in the space between the two letters was
the supportive presence of a new friend called Winston. As she put
it in a later letter: 'Although there was nothing to the relationship
for quite a while, mainly because I had nothing to offer, it gradually deepened with time.'

Winston had grown up in a rural town, Vryburg, in the northern Cape. He had been a Springbok, and was now climbing the corporate ladder at IBM. Hubert thought he had 'a first-class brain'. Leonora reported that he was a fast driver and hard drinker. He was self-contained in an easy, good-natured way. He might have seemed rather detached, even unemotional, but gradually Romy came to see that he was not a casual partner with whom she might pass a few hours of her longing for Mark, but a man capable of the strongest commitment – the strength of which almost frightened her. For some time she could not tell him of her attachment to Mark, but continued to go out with him through the summer of 1967–8. When the time came for Leonora's wedding, Winston was invited as the escort of Leonora's best friend; while Mark was invited as the great love of Leonora's best friend and a friend of Leonora herself. It was unthinkable that they should come together. Who had the greater claim? Leonora said that, at this point, it was impossible to say. The public aspect to the private dilemma was resolved, temporarily, by a happy chance when Winston's brother decided to marry on the same day.

'. . . I remember everything,' Leonora said proudly after twenty years. She had told Romy's story for five hours, sifting barren facts from the facts that suggest and engender. These she circled with insistent question. Why, she asked, the craving for adulation? Could it be that the frumpish teenager lived on in the svelte Romy of twenty-five; was Romy still Flora, that ill-dressed girl of fifteen, with her spray of unkempt curls, tethered to anxious parents at the weddings of smirking eligibles? Why did she resist marriage with her desperate stubbornness? And why, not marrying, could she not let the man go?

We wandered together, crossing, criss-crossing these gaps, coming to rest in a garden in Rosebank on a Sunday afternoon, heavy with unbreaking thunder, when birds called from falling water. On the table were photographs. It was February 1968: Leonora's wedding. Romy – the Maid-of-Honour – came towards us down the aisle in her long, cutaway, provocative dress of immaculate white, her blazing hair caught back from her pale, set face at this time of loss and longing and virginal destruction, when whatever she was doing had to be done alone. We marked her thinness and self-protective air of slight hauteur. And as we murmured, two women in their late forties with heads bent and lives now receding behind them, Romy herself seemed to breathe upon us, hear our questions, and tell us – as she used to – that she went on impulsively, from moment to moment, unable to say why she acted as she did.

8

Futures: I

In 1968 Romy lived in the aftermath of her loss of virginity, that penance for her failure to commit herself to Mark until it was too late. Some time after, she told Mark – how much, I don't know. Was it a provocation, or a bid for pity, or was it some frenzied assumption of the fate of women who have not loved at the right time, those women who, she thought, must share her 'secret'?

That reckless act failed to free her from the past, from Mark, for in one sense it was the climactic event of a 'destructive' relationship in which they remained locked. They were confounded that emotional affinities – the rare, momentous, irreplaceable – could not be good. They were simply not good for each other. Their mutual dramas, igniting the responsive fuse of similar natures, exploded in confrontations that could not be resolved by union.

Romy's long-term future remained for a while obscure. She

had forced herself through sex with a stranger when, in despair over Mark, she had nothing to give. The effect of defloration was a degree of self-loss, so that the exuberant Flora of our school-days and the experimental Romy of our early twenties became, at times, invisible, replaced by a distraught young woman of twenty-six and twenty-seven and twenty-eight, trying to go forward but unable to move.

Romy's friends found it almost as difficult as she to relinquish the idea of Mark. When we met later, we agreed: in her exhila-rating way Romy had built up an image of love that had stirred us with the same stubborn hope. Only Phillippa remained untouched, absorbed by the death of her mother from leukaemia, followed by her younger sister, Eileen. Phillippa, who did not speak of these deaths, said, 'I missed out on Mark,' and we knew what she meant. She was the one to support Romy's transition to Winston. In this, I gave Romy no support at all and, gradually over the years, a divide crept between us.

Where Romy's future turned on the question of marriage, mine turned on work. In 1967, it was not widely understood that women suffer as men do from confinement and stagnation. When young mothers crawled out of cramped, dark apartments to gather, on better afternoons, at the sand-box at 111th and Riverside Drive, they said to one another: 'I'm climbing the walls.' After their years at Smith, Vassar, or Barnard, they found them-selves locked in the routines of childcare. They did try to interest themselves in books on rearing, but these could not suffice to fill their minds. The round of diapers, feeds, and broken nights, and the ceaseless clamour of little voices, left them too depleted for much reading beyond cook-books and the toddlers' favourite, *Busy-Busy World*. This being New York, the gripe was a rich mode of expression; where the English take comfort in humour, New Yorkers relieve their feelings by uninhibited griping – and yet, it seemed, nothing might be done beyond the odd night course. It was a point of honour that no activity should impinge on husbands and children. So, for a mother to take on full-time course-work in the fall of '67 with a view to graduating in the summer of '68 was, in itself, to swerve from a norm.

To do this was not a proud act. It seemed to my family back in Africa, and to some extent also to me, a precaution against 'illness'. Work seemed a diversion which other and more resourceful women could do without. Even the gripers had the initiative to infuse the domestic sphere with more interest. Leaving Anna at playgroup, I would dash to Columbia and come back to find that other mothers had stayed. As the door swung open, I saw an array of mothers bent over toddlers to hand them the next educational toy when their attention strayed. It seemed as if a great fount of energy in each woman poured through this narrow channel into one precious child, infusing the child with all her life – and, in the process, vacating herself. At the sand-box, the future belonged to husbands and children: the careers husbands were forging, the books they would write, the schools to which toddlers would eventually go: should it be the advanced Bank Street school, or the artistic pretensions of Dalton, or the classic training of the classier girls' schools, Chapin or Brearley? These women looked past their own needs to those of their children. A cynic might call it the selfish gene; I prefer to call it altruism, to see the long training in altruism as the most hopeful of human attributes – not the elevated, unfamiliar 'Love' of *Four Quartets*, but love as familiar, daily practice. So, as I crossed between the stimulus of Columbia at 116th and the sand-box at 111th, I began my existence in-between – rather quiet at the sand-box about this other life that was surging with possibility as Columbia itself advanced towards the uprising of 1968.

'Subversive' was the word in the air, uttered by students with the 'right on' sign: to 'opt for' subversiveness, to engage in 'confrontation' was a form of 'action' against 'the military-industrial complex'. It was not only the war in Vietnam – the safe, push-button bombing of civilian villages; the poisonous napalm gas; the My Lai slaughter after which American soldiers pleaded that they acted 'under orders' – it was not only this debasement of the nation, as students saw it, but a question of the nature of power itself: its cynical economic goals; its fundamental callousness which stems from deadened imagination. Literature, with its commitment to sharing and to the imaginative complexity that defers crude forms of action had, for the young, a political prestige – above all, American literature with its sanction of individual revolt against society. Emerson's offer of an alternative form of power, that of the developing soul, seemed the answer to the dangerous conformity of blunted minds.

'Power . . . resides in the moment of transition from a past to a new state,' Emerson wrote. 'This one fact the world hates, that the soul *becomes*.' I read these words as I lay on the grass under the opening blossoms of a magnolia tree near the library at Barnard in the spring of '68. It was then that I resolved to become a teacher and communicate this form of power. Subversiveness conjoined with scholarship: these would be the means to discover truths which cannot exist, frozen, in ideology or doctrine, only through perpetual search.

During the academic year of 1967–8, I made three new friends. All three were married, but their domestic aspect seemed peripheral as we trailed our fingers in the rather murky water surrounding the right-hand fountain in front of Low, the carpeted administration building where an excess of typists filed red claws, where Dr Ridgeway declared that it was 'not Columbia's policy to give loans to mothers', and where a lot of other busy men had no time for 'dialogue'. They demonstrated the continued presence of the fourteenth-century Man of Law:

Nowher so bisy a man as he ther nas,
And yet he semed bisier than he was.

Faith Williams was writing a dissertation on Emerson, and she looked rather like Emerson in a less craggy version: she had chopped-off fair hair and her face, narrow and rather pale, was mobile in its quick changes from high-mindedness to amusement as she gave out her dicta in a quirky Emersonian voice, accompanied by a hoot of laughter at her own rashness – or absurdity. It was a time when 'wild', both in the usual sense and in the current sense of intellectual and moral daring, was the approved adjective on campus. Faith's simplicity of statement was 'wild' in the second sense. She dared you to think her simple as she tossed off insights born of integrity. She seemed to bear out Emerson's vision of 'the genuine man' – transmuted into woman. She lived simply, wore no make-up, and strode along in trousers with her books in a kitbag over her shoulder. Although the women in her family had long ties with Smith College, she had gone to Radcliffe, and came to Columbia because (like me) she had married a man whose job took him to New York. Stephen Williams was a lawyer who was to become a Federal judge during the Reagan administration. Even then, Faith kept her retorts flowing, while her role as Washington wife she carried off with a wave of the hand, as an act of no particular importance. 'I just have this little silk dress and throw it on when I have to,' is how she described her social obligations – while her real energy went into writing poetry and startling law students at American University with demanding questions on 'Evil, Guilt, and Justice'. That was the title of her course.

'How few women have written about justice! Injustice, but those are such squeaky voices, and such narrow ones,' she wrote to me in September 1989. 'South Africa is a chic topic these days, but I think easy and faraway compared to the real homelessness and sadness in this city. I'm going to make the students take field trips.'

Faith's next letter early in 1990 enlarged on the alternative she offered her students of 'a visit to the penitentiary or a ride-along with the police in night-time DC. For the latter, you go in pairs, for four hours, riding in a squad car. One student had a grumpy, discontented cop who told him he carried a "drop bullet" – a bullet to drop on the floor so that he'd have cause for a search. He said others brought drop drugs in addition, but he drew the line.

I'm trying to get Steve to go too, although I'm sure the middle-aged get no such revelations. It would be sort of like King Lear experiencing the life of the ordinary.'

Faith's letters over twenty years presented a life of many challenges: to keep teaching without tenure; to adopt two daughters (one a Vietnamese orphan) in addition to four boys of her own; to cope with the death at birth of her second-last son, which caused prolonged grief, as did the sudden death of her brother, Steve Morrow, a foreign correspondent in Peru. For all that, no woman of my generation seemed to exist as imaginatively as Faith in what I call 'the between'.

Where Faith was a Quaker, Rachel was Jewish: a type of convert like my mother, a searcher who happened on her inheritance. After college, she had emigrated to Israel where she had married a religious academic. She still had the fervour of the convert and her husband, who took religion for granted, used to grumble good-naturedly at the uncompromising strictness of her observance. One Friday night she would not accept flowers because I had picked them on the sabbath. She explained that the religious life must be grounded on the Law, the painstaking, innumerable laws that govern the minutest acts of daily existence, from the preparation of food to ritual cleansing of the body. Rachel said that devout women go to the *mikve* [public bath] at set times: after menstruation and on Friday, before the sabbath begins at sundown. Through such observance, through given prayers, the spirit can infuse every common and physical act. She spoke modestly, but she was stating the possibility that all of existence might be blessed.

Rachel was a pupil of the Henry James scholar, Dorothea Krook, who was then teaching at the Hebrew University in Jerusalem, but who in the '50s had been a fellow of Newnham College, Cambridge – there she had taught Sylvia Plath to their mutual satisfaction. Before that, she had been, rather improbably, at Good Hope in my mother's time – my mother called her 'Doris', for some reason. Dorothea Krook had sent Rachel to Columbia to continue her work on *The Ambassadors* under Lionel

Trilling, who, it turned out, was always too busy to see her. Rachel was only relieved. She dreaded an interview with a man of such importance.

We met in a seminar on the Novel where we found each other voicing feminist notions – which we continued to discuss after class with the teacher, Carolyn Heilbrun (who was to become more widely known as the detective writer, Amanda Cross). We sometimes lingered for another hour at the top of the stair on the sixth floor of Philosophy Hall.

This encouragement provided a contrast with the repressiveness of Trilling's seminar on Wordsworth, where I met Lynn Freed. As we waited on the first day for Trilling to arrive, a girl rather sportingly dressed in a tie was reading an aerogramme from South Africa. Her navy pinafore stood out from the shaggy, ethnic outfits of other students with their beads, fringes, and Afro'd hair. She looked rather like an Indian with her uniform complexion, high nose, and long black hair, which she tied in a neat tail. It was unusual, then, to meet a South African at Columbia. Though some went to the Business School, that did not count. Like the Law School, it was regarded – in the jargon of the time – as hopelessly 'Establishment', in other words at odds with the anti-war, anti-authoritarian ethos of the rest of the campus.

All through that semester we listened to Trilling in nervous abjection. We slumped on our elbows. No one ever spoke. His lofty manner seemed to preclude the possibility that we could say anything worth hearing by a man of his eminence. We read through *The Prelude* and other poems, line by line. This required of Trilling no preparation and, disappointingly, there were no larger ideas of the kind to be found in his famous essays. What I remember best from that seminar was the confusion of one girl with a drawn face and lank, white locks who ventured one word during the analysis of 'Resolution and Independence'.

'Of whom does the old man crawling across the moor remind you?' Trilling asked languidly, blowing the smoke from his cigarette towards the ceiling

'Lear,' murmured White Locks, involuntarily.

'*King* Lear to *you*,' said Trilling, with the look of a man who expected as much.

If it was meant as a joke, no one laughed. There was a long pause. White Locks, whiter than ever, stared down at the open text as if she would like to sink out of sight. She was a frail, helpless sort, a temptation to bullies. She committed suicide some months later, for reasons unknown.

Trilling saw himself as a gentleman, and was convincing as such to equals like the dons he encountered during his year at Balliol as Eastman Professor. But to behave towards inferiors with conscious arrogance is not, really, a mark of a gentleman (if we take Mr Knightley as model), and it was precisely this manner that Trilling's favourites and imitators disseminated through the Department in the late '60s and early '70s. As Trilling became the eminent elder, his acolytes took over the Department. Where Trilling was a genuine thinker, these men copied what they took to be the manner of thinkers: they became unavailable and lofty. They took unto themselves only those students who, in turn, reflected their image. Students got the message that the way to get on was to hitch their waggons to the self-styled 'star' – 'star' being another word in the air, what teachers aimed to be. Students, then, took shape as groupies. Gila Bercovitch, later editor-in-chief for *The Library of America*, noticed that if women were hired at all, they were the second-rate. The inheritors would not tolerate originality, least of all in women. So, said Gila, 'you got the Good Girls'. Obedient sycophants, they kept to established paradigms to prop the fragile egos of their 'stars'. It was, for some, a fatal course. Their respect for power was overdone; their intellectual trust, a rather pathetic insistence on femininity, based on a tacit agreement not to question or better men.

Professor Groper, who wore embroidered waistcoats and fancy buttons on his fly, warned that my findings in the Eliot papers would, as he growled, 'get ya inna big trouble'. As the personal basis of Eliot's poetry became more obvious, I was swerving from the critical dogma of Eliot's celebrated 'impersonality'. Uneasy, fearful, playing Good Girl, I wasted months trying in vain to tug the dissertation, against the evidence, back to Groper's ways of thought. He declined to attend the eventual defence because, he said, he could not accept the biographical approach that did, in the end, prevail.

The most original of the College teachers was a Modernist called Professor Syracuse, who had his favourites. He backed my work with generosity and, darting from his room on the fourth floor of Hamilton Hall, seized me in rapturous academic embraces. Yet there came a day when he said with slow, almost luxurious sadness: 'Your eyes . . . are . . . *so* rebellious.' His reproach was for certain extravagant words that I had neglected to say. I had failed some test of sycophancy – a test I did not expect of him, but nothing less was acceptable.

It would be inaccurate to say that all Columbia was made up of vain men. One of the exceptions was E Talbot Donaldson who gave urbane, witty lectures on Chaucer. Donaldson, Heilbrun, and other exceptions taught mainly graduates. The Trilling coterie dominated the undergraduate College, which was then exclusively male. These men looked down on the Graduate School as an inferior institution which admitted women – in some way, women were bound up with its supposed inferiority. It was because of this prejudice that Trilling behaved with such condescension during the only graduate course that he gave in the eight years I was there from 1965–73. He was said to behave differently to young men of the College.

It was odd, in retrospect, that Lynn Freed, of all people, should have been part of that seminar, for she had the least abject of natures. Some years later, she wrote an amusing and truthful South African novel, *Home Ground*. Lynn, who came of a theatre family, was naturally at the centre of attention, exuberant like Romy, but more disciplined. Her theatricality was playful, a conscious style learnt from a mother trained at RADA – she was in amused control of her extravagance and never carried away, like Romy, by her dramas. She entered on flirtatious exchanges with construction workers as we crossed Broadway on our way to Columbia. With the face of an Indian goddess, she swung along, lithe, radiating power.

'Say, you're cute!' men called, automatically.

Such inadequate praise drew from Lynn a perfunctory, withering glance. 'I am afraid that I *can't* say the same for *you*,' she would throw off to one side in her mother's RADA voice.

Lynn and I were amongst the few who sat the repeatedly postponed MA examination at the end of May 1968. Apologetically, we squeezed past the barricades in a shaken and disordered university in the aftermath of a student uprising so vociferous that it gained international attention as an indication of the level of protest against the war. There were also, of course, local issues that did not make the headlines but were, to students, amongst the evils perpetrated by the Establishment: for one, the uncaring relation of Columbia to the surrounding black community of Harlem. There was also the 'lack of dialogue' between administrators (who were said to be in cahoots with the 'military–industrial complex') and students, a vast number of whom feared and dodged the draft.

West Point, the military academy up the Hudson, had a special arrangement with the English Department at that fraught time. They were sending select recruits to take courses in American literature. The idea may have been to instil the higher patriotism. Ordinary students, unathletic, unkempt and, truth be told, unwashed in many cases, used to strike a pose of open-mouthed wonder at the sight of two or three West Point men, in their khaki uniform and polished shoes, running abreast, in exact unison, two or three steps at a time, up the six floors of stairs in Philosophy Hall to their next lecture on Whitman or Thoreau.

One of these, Art, got a little too deep into Thoreau for his total comfort. It was noticed that he had begun to walk around a meagre pond at the barracks, reading *Walden* and 'Civil Disobedience'. He was asking, it was noticed, too many questions.

In short, he had begun to think. Without warning, in mid-course, he was shipped off to 'Nam. There was no time to say goodbye. Long after, we used to worry about dear, innocent Art, and wonder what became of him in the 'theatre of war'; then turn to Emerson on 'the integrity of the private mind' or Dickinson shutting the door of her room behind her as she remarked to her niece, 'Here's freedom, Mattie'.

1968 was the year of my long-delayed adaptation to America as I absorbed the moral positions of its greatest minds. Sacvan Bercovitch declared to the American seminar that 'to be an American is to have a vision in your head. There are *two* Americas,' he went on, 'the geographical United States, a place of scramblers as the West opened up, and the America of the dream, Winthrop's dream in 1630 of "a city on a hill" – that's how he saw it in his prophetic sermon on the *Arbella*, the flagship of the Great Migration: a vision of the exemplary society that would become a model to all the nations.'

One did not, then, have to adapt to the success ethic, the gross materialism, and the sordid streets of New York, filled with tramps and addicts who were left to rot amidst heaps of garbage, collected less often where the poor lived all about us on the Upper West Side than on affluent Park Avenue. This was not that real, idealistic America which students were reasserting in a native tradition of revolt. They stood up to police who came to force them to accept the corrupt America of the rising Nixon, the military, and the underhand aspect of Gatsby's glamorous fortune. It was a time to lift a voice against power, and women raised their voices as well. When Kate Millett called the first women's liberation meeting at Columbia, the huge auditorium was so crowded that women seemed to hang from the ceiling. I stood with Rachel on a bench, squeezed against a wall. From the start, I did not hold with the imitative feminism of Millett: her call to answer power with power. I hoped to find a mode of being that would be inimical to force. In 1971 I edited a women's issue of *The Little Magazine*, a poetry journal founded by a group of students at Columbia. The editorial voiced this position: that women still have to move into a future in which they must discover their nature which remains, at present, undefined:

> We looked for a rhetoric different from the strident voice of the women's liberation movement. We looked for phrases and ideas that had moved beyond initial stages of anger and alertness, for something more flexible, more sophisticated, above all more humorous.
>
> Olive Schreiner wrote in a letter of 1909: 'The true freedom of woman is something that cannot be given her, that she has to work out within herself.' Yet we also tried to select writing that was not tediously self-absorbed, merely an extension of the emotional indulgence of the encounter group. The woman of this issue feels her life with both hands, turns it around, but not to scratch its sores, only to see if it is there. She is, in fact, disturbed by her preoccupation with her life because she is not by nature detached or alienated, but deeply responsible.
>
> This batch of writing, taken together, seems to divide spontaneously into two groups. Some pieces are retrospective: they rethink traditional experiences of women in sex, marriage, menstruation, birth, abortion, menopause, and family relationships. The other group is not so easy to place in one phrase, but essentially it is made up of poems which look forward to new possibilities, new moods, visions. What seems to recur most insistently is a waiting mood, not deathly stasis – although there are many images of death – but a defiance of settling. The woman holds her energy intact and survives a rigid and lifeless order.

Amongst the contributors were Joyce Carol Oates, Marge Piercy, Susan Fromberg Schaeffer, Joanna Russ, and Mary Gordon, and there was an interview with Denise Levertov. Elizabeth Bishop criticized the venture in the following letter:

I don't want to scold or preach – but I have never believed
in segregating the sexes in any way, including the arts . . .
It is true that there are very few women poets, painters,
etc., – but I feel that to print them or exhibit them apart
from works by men poets, painters, etc., is just to illustrate
in this century, Dr Johnson's well-known remark – rather
to seem to agree with it.

This defensible position was supported by a reader called
Edward Butscher, who conveyed his opposition with less
restraint:

I see from the latest issue of *The Little Magazine* that you
intend a special issue devoted to female poets. Shame on
you. May your collective penis get stuck in the collective
zipper in the Fifth Avenue Men's Room on Sunday night.
The next thing you know the poet-esses will be
demanding the right to vote and the use of three names in
their pseudo-plumes. My mistress is already restless.

Another criticism came from Marge Piercy together with a poem
entitled 'The Nuisance' which began, 'I am an inconvenient
woman . . .'. She disagreed with the notion that freedom is something you discover within yourself:

But as for it being an inner thing, that's a kind of leisure-
time proposition. No welfare mother will buy that nor will
any woman in New York who's pregnant and hasn't the
bread for an abortion or in a state where it's still illegal.
There's nothing like having the bite come down on you to
make the environment suddenly rather real.

I went one evening to hear Ted Hughes read at the YMHA to an
enormous, adulatory audience. One poem was about a man
forced to carry three women across a turbid river. Each time, the

woman's oppressive weight almost drowns him but, with stoic fortitude, the hero struggles on.

Absorbed in the counter-struggle, groping into a new future, there were times when I forgot South Africa and forgot to linger in the past.

On 20 November 1968, after a year's silence, a letter arrived from Romy, enclosing two aerogrammes written earlier: these letters, in their honesty, plunged me back into her story. She was in the midst of a crisis that required urgent action, but it was in the very nature of this crisis that it could not be resolved. After going out with Winston for a year, it was expected by her parents, by society at large, and by Winston himself, that she would now marry but, though she had grown to care for him, she could not bring herself to do so.

'I cannot move forwards nor backwards,' she had written on 20 September. 'I cannot possibly think ahead at the moment. I live very much in the present,' she repeated exactly two months later on 20 November.

The inconclusiveness of the letters, and their self-laceration – they 'reeked', she said, of 'miseries' – suggest the difficulty of a situation where words failed. This was the last time that she made the effort to explain herself:

>   Killarney,
>   Johannesburg.
>   Friday 20 September
>
> My dearest Lyndall,
>   In a matter of days I have received news of your visit to Cape Town from both your grandmother and Berjulie. Mrs Press senior wished me a Happy New Year and hoped to hear 'good news' from me.
>   Your letter came just before my birthday [in June], and during the dinner I kept drifting back to the previous year. So much was different: Winston instead of Mark, Leonora with a husband – and not my friends, Lyndall & Siamon.

The irony was that although Mark was constantly in my thoughts that evening, he had completely forgotten that it was my birthday when he contacted me a couple of days later.

I met Winston about a month after Mark had told me that he didn't want to see me again, and although there was nothing to the relationship for quite a while, mainly because I had nothing to offer, it gradually deepened with time. I don't know how to describe Winston to you . . . that is why I am going to enclose a letter which he wrote to me in July from Paris. I have no qualms about allowing you to read it because I want to share it with you – but it is for you alone.

I would marry him tomorrow except that after a year Mark is still part of me. I cannot get him out of my system.

Winston was very upset to know that I cared for someone else – he had never anticipated anyone else. Neither had I. I had loved Ben, many years later Mark, and too soon – still wounded – I loved Winston. But I could not conduct two relationships. I wanted my relationship with Winston to take its natural course but it has not ended. I care for him, but I cannot forget Mark. I cannot move forwards nor backwards . . .

Johannesburg.
3 October 1968

My darling Lyndall,

I wrote aerogramme 1 just prior to my departure for Lourenço Marques with Winston, and decided not to post it before I had a chance for another look. You know how emotional I can get. It was so wonderful to get away for 4 days. This country is going from bad to worse – I am unable to stomach what is going on, the distortions, the damn logical illogic. The disgusting thing is that South Africans are apathetic and apolitical and, as in the States

and France, the move is towards conservatism. The
thought of Nixon as President of the USA is too awful . . .

I have re-read Winston's letter and it is so intimate that I
should be having second thoughts about sending it. Yet it
is the loving Winston I know – because his exterior belies
the warmth and feeling underneath. It was the first love-
letter he has written and he was very lonely and it is the
most precious thing I possess. He would never forgive me
if he knew what I was doing but I want dearly to show it
to you & share it with you. I know Siamon wouldn't
approve & understandably so – so please read it alone and
return it to me . . .

Johannesburg.
20 November 1968

My darling Lyndall,

The kids are writing their end-of-year exams, and
although I should be invigilating, I feel the need to write
to you. Impossible to believe that I shall see you within the
next few weeks.

I have resigned from teaching as from the end of this
year. Four years are long enough. I need a break from the
infantile world. I have absolutely no idea of what I am
going to do next year but I cannot possibly think ahead at
this moment. I live very much in the present.

The other day I found these 2 aerogrammes lying in a
drawer. This is so typical. I write sporadically to you, but
hate my letters and don't send them off. The references to
Winston's letter are rather sickening. If I wanted to, I
would probably find another 4 or 5 letters lying around
somewhere, reeking of my indecisions, miseries, and
complaints.

My situation is unaltered . . . I cannot make the move,
take that final step into marriage – because of Mark. He is
still there in my thoughts, in my heart, but I *must*, damn it,

move forward. I cannot go on like this any more, weeks
into months, and months into years, with my life
unresolved. Time is supposed to resolve one's problems
but, damn it, this is a fallacy.

Winston has been wonderful. I don't know how he
stands for my crap but he does — with patience, with
tenderness, and with love. I seem to sail through life
hurting the men who have cared for me — but one never
emerges from a relationship unscathed.

Enough of this. It must be good to have Hubert &
Berjulie in New York. I miss them very much — more so
than I care to admit. They are my anchor and my stability
in Johannesburg. Even during periods of severe emotional
crisis, whenever I went over to Willow Stream, nothing
was as tragic as I had imagined. I can't wait for their return
to South Africa — and yet Berjulie would pooh-pah me if I
ever tried to verbalize this to her. She is more, much more,
than a friend to me . . .

After July, Ellie came to deliver a paper at the
psychological congress in Johannesburg. God, it was
marvellous to have her with me even for only a week. She
told me to do what makes me feel comfortable — in
retrospect sound advice. She is almost at the end of her
thesis and, knowing how important it is to her, I hope it
goes well.

I had lunch with Mark on his birthday at the end of
October. He is now lecturing on Sartre to postgraduates at
Wits. I had not seen him for a long time and, although I
had thought of him so often, it was a shock to see him
again, to be confronted with the reality of Mark — Mark,
that I felt my throat closing up.

Leonora sends her love, and so does Peter, Bonnie, and
Isabel — I still see all Mark's friends.

    Love,
      Romy

Back at the Cape, the Gevints greeted her in a fever of expectation. Marital plans were regarded as the rightful preserve of
community opinion – to be discussed loudly in Stuttafords, on the
beach, at dinner parties. Romy's family, pestered with questions,
could themselves imagine no between-ground of shadows, doubts,
the flux and reflux of impulse, as a couple advanced from going
out to engagement to wedding.

When Romy and Winston did not at once announce this
anticipated engagement, Feige went to see Mrs Gevint. She came
straight to the point.

'Vot's the problem, Clara? Vot's up?'

'I just don't know,' shrugged Mrs Gevint helplessly. 'She laugh –
she say she can't make up her mind. She tell me not to vorry. And
how can I not vorry? A daughter who's twenty-six and a half,
who'll one of these days be thirty, and still can't know her mind . . .'

'She must be told, firm now, Clara: she must get engaged.
After all this time with him! For vot is she waiting? An angel? He's
a big, strong chap, healthy – a Springbok, a *feine*, a *scheine*! Vot
does she want – to be left on the shelf?'

Mrs Gevint, shaking her head, laid out her palms in a gesture of
incomprehension.

'She'll be the death of us. We told her: "Fruma," her father said,
"you'll give me a heart attack."'

Had she been too soft? Feige said she spoilt Fruma. Feige's two
daughters gave their parents the *nachas* of good bridegrooms, good
send-offs – Krafchik weddings – everyone invited. Those were
daughters to have. So what had gone wrong with her Fruma? It
must be her fault. She nodded humbly to Feige, and shook her
head as Romy tore out to the beach when Winston came.

We met at Fourth Beach, Clifton.

'Meet Winston,' Romy said. She watched me.

He was, yes, a Springbok – the muscled, ruddy figure of a
sport. He lounged on two elbows in the familiar South African
posture with a shirt half-buttoned and legs spread in a way that
took up a lot of space.

'Well?' she pounced when the men went off to swim. It was more than a question. 'He's good for me – won't let me fight. If I start, he says, "stop this nonsense", laughing at me. We get on together – that is, after the start. Gruesome, I have to tell you something: what happened at the start.'

It was not like her to hesitate.

'What?'

She sat still, looking out towards the swimmers as they jumped the steep breakers which could fling bodies, hard, on the waiting expanse of sand.

I shook grains of sand from a cheap copy of *Villette*, already coming apart.

She said suddenly: '. . . That stranger I slept with, you know, for the first time. It was Winston.'

I stared.

'He had no idea of the complexity of the situation – no idea how desperate I was to get rid of the virginity that had become a burden. When we met, I behaved like an experienced tart. And I disliked him – he seemed empty, his hockey matches and crude words and Vryburg thoughts, so far from Mark – Mark who didn't want me. I threw myself at Winston like some mad or wounded wildcat. He was taken aback to find he was with a frantic virgin. Then things changed. He showed an understanding that I didn't expect. My coldness dissolved. He's changed me, made me know what it's like to make love fully. But can I marry him?'

'Romy, do you think it possible that a woman can love a man without the entire surrender of what she is – or at least, confining that surrender to one form of action? You're special. You know that. Whatever you do, don't surrender that specialness – don't.

'You don't think I should marry?'

'Not unless you're quite sure. How can anyone know, really know, your relation to Winston – however truly you may try to convey it. You want me to know the loving Winston who could write that letter you never sent – but you couldn't, and rightly so,

share it without a sense of betrayal. It is sealed for the two concerned if it is to last.'

'Oh, you! You think it out too much. I need help. Simple:
help. I was depending on you to help me, to make up my mind.
Go on,' she coaxed, 'just say what you think of him.'

'I don't know him yet, of course, but from what you've told
me, he's strong, determined. That sort of virility has its undeniable
attractions — it says to you, "don't think you'll get away" and,
before you know it, you've succumbed. As females, we're conditioned for this to happen. All I can say is: don't let it blind you. In
May, just before my exam, I came across a poem by Emily
Dickinson in which she speaks as one who's done better than
marry: "Betrothed — without the swoon/God sends us
Women —". She pities others "Born — Bridalled — Shrouded —/In
a Day —". She sees the exact price: the obliteration of women who
give all of themselves to a conventional marriage. Through the
ages, marriage has been held up as the reward for the highest
virtue and courage. Emily Dickinson questioned this at a time
when there seemed little else for women to do. She ends the
poem:

> My Husband — women say
> Stroking the Melody —
> Is this — the way?'

I have wondered, in after years, at my complicity during that
obsessive summer when we huddled over this question until we
shredded further the conventional marriage to the negation to
which it pointed. Winston thought Romy sole author of her
dilemmas. He waved away the confession that I put down here:
our lives shaped together. What I said on Fourth Beach did play a
part, a not altogether innocent part, in Romy's future. Ostensibly,
I was saying the right thing: she must be free to decide. Yet,
embedded in that concern, there lurked another motive: I rejoiced
in Romy's hesitance. I needed her to continue to be a free

woman. So we use others to shore up the ramparts of dreams or faiths – just as elders of the tribe used generations of unready girls to shore up the ties and rituals of a closed community which gave religious sanction to male predominance. These girls were born to lose themselves before they found a future – or realized, even, that there might be a future to find.

Phillippa put this in a happier light. 'She would swoop down, catch you up in her wonderful freedom, and you felt you were, at those times, some other person.' Yet Phillippa had the grace to welcome Winston. As Eileen lay all day on the sofa with strength fading, Phillippa knew better then than any of us that life was fragile; that a chance to live must be grasped. From the start, she backed Winston.

Vryburg, where he grew up, south of the Bechuanaland [now Botswana] border, was settled mainly by English-speakers after the British took it in 1885. Before then, it had been Tswana territory, and briefly, from 1882 to 1885, part of an independent Boer republic, Stellaland, so called for its night sky: an incredible array of stars visible to the naked eye. Romy had slept outdoors one hot summer night in Vryburg under the full span of the Milky Way. Winston's father was a pharmacist; his mother, a driving force behind three sons. A daughter, Ingrid, on the other hand, was taught to sew, which she did imaginatively. The children liked to place pennies on the railway track and watch the wheels dent them as trains pulled out for Kimberley, five hours away. Winston went to school there, not the top school in the country but he respected his parents' efforts with a determination to make the best of what they could afford. When he broke his collar-bone at rugby, his mother chartered a two-seater plane, collected her son, and only when they were back in Vryburg contacted the headmaster to say: 'You may have noticed that I have taken Winston away.' He went to Cape Town to major in physics, followed by the one-year postgraduate honours course during which he mainly played hockey, playing eventually for South Africa. After he graduated, he wrote two letters: one to the

Metal Box Company who did not answer; the other to IBM who did. He has remained with IBM, fitting the executive mould, a man who allows his listener only a few words, which he is too intelligent not to hear, but which must give way before his own driving idea. Where Mark invited a listener to further expansion, Winston took you into his world, that of the avid collector. He might take you to an auction of Cape Dutch furniture – leading the way, saying (without turning his head for more than a moment): 'Come on, team.'

This was a far cry from the many-sidedness and endless palaver of academe. Yet though different in this way, Winston was also familiar: not only the sporting manner of my father, but certain similarities to Siamon – not looks or interests, but something more fundamental which may have had its source in rural origins. As Siamon had presented the image of a rock in his first letter, so Winston had his rocklike fidelity to his givens and choices. Self-contained, rather inexpressive, they guarded emotions that ran underground, a steady, undeflected course. When Romy threw herself at Winston she was not looking for responsibility but this was what she found. He was, she said, 'respect-worthy'. Such men dispensed help with the alacrity of ease, yet neither had manners in the European sense: their directness could be disconcerting, for nuance, though intelligible to them, was not their habit. What they had was what Siamon called 'steam' – go, energy, a readiness – the simple way of boys who were unspoilt by the diversions of the town and never jaded because, in those bare childhoods, they had learnt to depend on themselves.

Romy had met Winston through Marvin, Feige's son, who also worked at IBM.

'I know this terrific girl – you should get to know her,' Marvin had said to Winston, who had recently moved from Port Elizabeth.

They had met, two strangers, at the Killarney Sports Club. Romy, pining for Mark, was forcing herself through the ritual of 'meeting someone new'. She despised clubs, and had taken an immediate dislike to Winston. 'What am I doing here?' she had thought, crossing and re-crossing her legs as she made distant conversation. What was she doing with this hockey-player who didn't speak of films and feelings, but of 'dolls' and 'crap'?

'Did you perceive that she disliked you?' I asked Winston in Paris in 1990.

'That was part of the attraction,' he said. 'Nothing I could say was being received. I was young, attractive, Jewish – yet she wasn't falling all over me.' He laughed at his blatant self-confidence. 'I wasn't going to put up with this. After about an hour of this resistance, I took her hand – she was annoyed by the nerve. It was during a film – *Casablanca*. Afterwards, she discussed the film. She talked of "subtleties"; she liked to debate and intellectualize the morals and messages. I'd never had such a talk before, and knew that she would open avenues. I slept with her on the second date.'

'You saw at once that she was special?'

'I felt she would change me. No, not change exactly – she opened you up.'

'She restored to you a self you hardly knew existed.' I was speaking to myself as well as to Winston.

'What I brought to the relationship', Winston was on to the next point, 'was that I refused to get cowed. I overtook her physically and emotionally. She'd never been attacked without aggression. That's why she stayed with me.'

'She said that she'd thrown herself at you – that she hadn't given you much alternative.'

He laughed off the idea that she had taken the initiative. 'But it wasn't rape.'

'Romy was so impulsive,' I said. 'She had this idea that if she could get rid of her virginity in some passionless way, as a non-event, she could get over her horror of weddings.'

'Her motive may have been passionless,' Winston spoke with even emphasis, 'but she stayed with me because of that act. She struggled – hard – with the fact that she had done it. She couldn't believe that she had made this stupid mistake. Fed up with the men she had loved, she said to herself "I've had enough; I'll find a stranger" – then found herself committed to him. She was, in fact, surprised that losing virginity was *not* a "non-event" psychologically. It kept her attached to me, and this gave me time.' His voice deepened as he repeated: 'It gave me the time I needed.'

So it was that Romy tried to free herself of emotional ties, but found, in doing so, that she had tied herself in a new way – and to someone she hardly knew. Until then, Winston had 'steered clear of involvement'. But for him, no less than for Romy, what he had done came to feel irrevocable. In his own tenacious way, Winston, too, found himself attached by what had seemed, at the time, a casual act.

I thought over the mode of 'unaggressive attack' while I sipped, tentatively, Winston's tomato-juice concoction with lemon and pepper.

An attack would not allow much space for a woman's response – it would not invite her own forms of expression – but, at least, if unaggressive, might prove more compelling than hesitant sensibilities. Since Romy knew that ideal solutions did not exist, she had to make an impossible choice – and perhaps it was in part a relief, and in part disturbing, that Winston, so straightforwardly, made a choice for her. Unaggressive attack . . . I had dodged all the tests of culinary adventure the day before as we had strolled through the outdoor stalls of an antiques fair: I had shuddered at the sight of gigantic oysters with curly worms swimming in their juice, and left on my plate a fair portion of my spit-roast piglet in a strong mustard sauce. Winston judged people on their will to try. I thought of his mid-field position in hockey. 'You're there to keep the game on the move,' he had explained as he drove me to Paris from Charles de Gaulle Airport. He was, even now, resistant to the idea that Romy had been unmovable at that time, bound as she was to Mark.

'Since she was ready to give up her virginity, I thought she might as well get it over so as to get on to the rest. I awakened her,' he said positively. He was certain that subsequent times had been transforming. 'I'd had girls before, and when I fell for Romy, put them aside. Why couldn't she do the same?'

For him it was that simple. He was unable to see that she could come to love him and feel, at the same time, that part of her belonged to Mark. I wondered if her bond with Mark had something of the permanent ties of friendship which came first with Romy. When Ellie had quarrelled with Winston, he had been astonished to find that Romy was siding with her friend.

'We had our first fight over Ellie. When Ellie came to a conference in Jo'burg, the three of us went out to dinner. Ellie got drunk and picked a fight, and Romy blamed me.'

I could well see Ellie, vehement, not giving an inch of ground, unlike the 'dolls' of Winston's acquaintance; and Winston (who once nearly killed us by speeding up on a highway because we had shouted at him to slow down) wilful, increasingly pugnacious after a bottle or two of wine; and Romy between them, wishing they would stop, and wanting Ellie to like Winston.

'I was sore,' Winston went on. 'Though Romy criticized me, in her friends she saw no weakness whatever – only their strengths. I felt I was being differentiated, and all I wanted was equal treatment.'

Winston saw 'quirks' or 'edges' to Romy's nature. 'My objective was to smooth them off so that we could relate on a constant basis.' One main problem was her volatility which, it seemed to Winston, had its roots in her home. 'I don't know what created Reggie, but Reggie created the other two.'

'Reggie was his mother's favourite. David, the youngest and most vulnerable, was Reggie's victim,' I remembered. 'And Flora – Romy – had to protect David. She took the brunt of Reggie's rage. There was a lot of violence between brother and sister: they would try to hurl each other out of the window. Why didn't the Gevints stop it?'

'They were preoccupied with survival,' said Winston.

'Exactly. And they weren't sure how to communicate with

their rampant children whom they loved but who were, literally, foreigners. The Gevints could not re-establish the old ways; and their children were unaware of codes as such. At home they grabbed and shoved and howled like young savages. Neither Reggie nor Romy gained control of raw emotion – hate and need – until well into adulthood. You were patient, Winston; you seemed to be able to take calmly those storms that Mark couldn't, in the end, endure.'

'About three months after we met, we went to Cape Town. There, at a Christmas party, I danced (Romy thought) too close to this doll. She exploded, tore out of the party, and threw a scene at the gate.

'Accusations poured out. "How dare you . . .", et cetera, and "I'll never again . . .", et cetera.

'I said: "Shut up. I'm going to marry you."

'For once, she was speechless.

'But there were other scenes: crises of decision, reversals, more storms. I was always sure that, if I held on, we could work it out.'

He was referring, in particular, to an extended crisis of January–March 1969. Mr Gevint made an appointment to see me early that January. I was staying at Lanzerac outside Stellenbosch, an hour from Cape Town, and he drove all the way. I can see him, shoulders slightly bent and a grey, old world hat in his hand on that hot day, walking up the drive to say that Romy was ruining her chances, that she would kill her parents, and that I must, at once, intercede. I must say to her just two words: 'GET MARRIED.'

I refused. Mr Gevint did not speak to my involvement in the American social revolution of the late '60s, to its resolve to question the paternalistic authority that warped women's lives. And could one blame him? The racial issue was so insistent, and South Africa so cut off from the rest of the world, that what did filter through the media – the transient dramas of hippydom, hair, bra-burning, party drugs, and the licence to promiscuity inherent in the slogan 'make love not war' – did not take hold beyond the fashionable set which prided itself on keeping up with the latest styles and sexual mores. It was not until 1976, with the Soweto Uprising, that youth began to question authority, and then the issue remained race-related. The new questions about the position of women, which in America coexisted with resistance to the 'military–industrial complex', were not to reach South Africa for two more decades.

When I voiced liberation in the sunroom, Hubert let me go on at earnest length, then observed in his quietest measure: 'I have only one thing to say: I disagree – *totally*.'

Romy would never have tried Hubert in this way because relationships were more important to her than ideas. As she diverged from the anachronistic norm of womanly destiny, as it was still conceived in her milieu, she became diplomatic. An unmarked silence drew in her doubts beneath the breathy, open chatter that appeared as disarming as ever. Yet, from then on she rarely spoke of her own affairs and, if challenged, would evade questions with a bright-faced joke. Only her parents persisted: they hammered a way through her protective guard. There were reproachful scenes during which they demanded that she repay their love and all the years of hard work. They had done it, they said, for their children. Now, they said, she must repay them by doing what they told her was right and was certainly for her own good. She must stop the 'trouble' she caused them. She must marry, now, at once.

So the pressure went on. Mr Gevint said: 'If one Winston could solve England's problems, could another Winston not solve your mother's?'

Mrs Gevint was shamed repeatedly on the beachfront when cronies from the Old Country asked about Fruma. Mr Gevint, emerging from the peace of his books, said that he would not have his wife upset. She, too, he said, was brought to the verge of collapse. This was a standard tactic: induce guilt. Tell daughters what they owed to parents. Question their love. Though Romy recognized the tactic, she believed her parents could work up desperation to a point when the collapse of one or other might actually happen. She feared the power of her resistance. And then, too, there was her own need to move on. At the last minute before Winston left on business to the States, she agreed to marry. Jubilant, Winston used his few hours in Johannesburg to find a diamond, and sent the ring to Cape Town. Romy unpacked it uneasily.

'I'll never wear it,' she said.

We drove to Krafchik's to arrange the reception. When he saw Romy's hair, he raised his hands in a gesture of creative revelation. 'Copper!' he said. 'It will all be COPPER!' He planned a tented ceiling – yards and yards of muslin, a kosher *coq au vin*, and oodles of bliss. He promised, as usual, the wedding to outdo all weddings.

'I asked for a *plain* wedding,' I recalled as we drove back along the High Level Road. 'No fuss, I said. And then he produced this appalling surprise: a tinsel, life-size model of "a bicycle made for two", complete with lovers, and the band played "Daisy Daisy" as the bicycle pulled in a medley of desserts. All the guests said it was "the highlight of the wedding" – and Krafchik beamed: his show had triumphed after all.'

Swept up by Romy's continued dilemma, I hardly saw anyone else. She teetered on the edge of the engagement in a misery of indecision. Between storms, I went on with *Villette*, absorbing the between-states of the unmarried Lucy Snowe. It helped to see that Romy was not living capriciously, as her family thought, but following the overgrown and almost invisible paths of a buried self. Before our return to New York, she owned that she could not face the wedding.

I left, that time, more disturbed than usual by the artifice of exile, repeated in what was coming to be a pattern of willed departures. The plane rose above the beloved country, climbing to the blue mountains at the rim of the airport and, making a deep circle, turned north to Johannesburg, London, New York, to all those places where I did not want to be. I muttered my numbing routine, 'don't think', to allow the plane to take me away from a place that seemed, at those moments, the source of existence: the winter sun curling around Lion's Head and creeping down its ravines as I had walked its lower slope to Mrs De Korte's first school; the crash of the breakers at Rocklands; the everlasting sweep of the waves rolling steadily towards the sand, as Romy and I rolled in unison towards the shore of our shared lives. Now, strapped in the seat, I glanced at my husband, who was enclosed in *Die Burger* as he took the pulse of Afrikaner opinion. His course was clear: South Africa was a political disaster, to be left behind until it came to its senses. He was glad to go back to the international distinction of the New York laboratory and to the plays and music that awaited our return to what was, for him, civilization. Privately, I thought New York more corrupt than my own country – corrupt in its secret hollow-heartedness, an atrophy of the soul that would prove more tenacious, I believed, than present evil in South Africa.

As we passed through Johannesburg, Berjulie (from whose piercing queries no truth could hide) made a fair case for duty: 'What you have to give you can do in your own home. Perhaps it might console you to try to bear in mind how much it needs your giving.'

It happened that Winston's path crossed ours in the transit lounge at Heathrow Airport. He searched my face and saw, plainly, Romy's denial. For a few weeks the wedding appeared to go forward. A date was set, the guests invited, the presents began to arrive: the wedding gained its final momentum. A week before, Romy sought refuge at Willow Stream.

'Berjulie,' she took a deep breath, 'Berj, I'm so miserable. I just can't go through with it.'

'You can't do that to Krafchik,' said Berjulie, so firmly that Romy at once agreed: '. . . No, no, of *course*, I couldn't do that.'

Three days before the wedding, she and Winston returned to Cape Town. All was ready: Krafchik's copper bowls and autumn foliage, the menu, the wedding-dress. At the rehearsal, Winston said, 'You stand there, and I stand here.' Then, suddenly, the wedding was off: Romy had jaundice and would be ill for weeks. The presents went back.

Winston, whose 'whole world blew up', returned to Johannesburg, expecting his own jaundice. He watched his urine and, a week later, saw the disease. No one visited or saw him except Rosie Kunene, a Zulu who cooked and cleaned. For six weeks he read, including books like the *Alexandria Quartet* and *Crime and Punishment*, which had seemed too formidable in normal circumstances. He had not read in this way before, and it sustained him.

'Did you resent what Romy did?' I asked Winston that morning in Paris, many years later.

'Thank God she did what she did because if she'd gone through with the wedding, I wouldn't have been able to repair the damage.'

'What I find hard to understand is how you managed to combine your assertiveness with willingness to let her decide what she wanted in her own time.'

'I feel confident,' he admitted. 'I can do anything, practically. You have to see what is necessary, and try to provide it. The only time one demeans oneself is when one does things dishonestly.'

At first, Berjulie was inclined to excuse Romy on the grounds of illness. She wrote to me in March 1969:

Romy spent much time with me before she went to CT
and she told me of your devotion to her needs during
those traumatic weeks. I did my best from an older,
motherly point of view and the end of the story you
probably know – that she has gone down with jaundice! I
dare say that that is what was wrong with her as she was
just not feeling well at all and thought all her troubles were
emotional . . . Winston phoned me from CT and the
wedding will probably be in May.

May came and went, and nothing happened. 'Hubert and Berjulie weren't convinced that I would win this battle,' Winston recalled. 'Her parents thought I would stick it.' The Gevints were right. There seemed no bounds to his commitment.

'The past lived with her,' he said, meaning Mark. With patience and tenacity he built trust, again and again, as Romy would approach the prospect of marriage only to turn away.

In the course of his trial, she changed him: he learnt to talk in a new way, mastering a vocabulary of analysis and perception. She made him aware of feelings he had not known to exist. 'Locked up inside me were all sorts of capabilities which I had repressed because my peers saw these as irrelevant.'

'I'm changing you,' Romy observed, rather worriedly.

'You're releasing me.' She was, he said, 'a fantastic catalyst'.

In a sense she made him. The thinking Romy, whom Mark had developed, now worked on Winston in a chain of making. His love thrived on this release.

9

Futures: II

Soon after the broken wedding, I was called back to Cape Town: my father had Hodgkin's disease. Romy, too, came to Cape Town. I sat with my father, and she with Eileen, who was now very ill in Groote Schuur Hospital. My letters to Siamon from June to September record this time:

Sunday, 29 June 1969: My father came back from Groote Schuur yesterday afternoon. He is very, very thin, and a bit upset to have lost another few pounds. He coughs terribly. I still have no idea how long I shall stay.

Romy is here for the school vac. I've heard the whole traumatic story – somehow I think that she's further off from marriage than ever, in spite of the apparent calm of her and Winston's relations. She has her own flat now, though she says she can't bring herself to furnish it with things she should be buying for them both. One day she went to see Mark, on an impulse. He has another girlfriend, which she didn't resent, but she felt the distance of their long separation since the advent of Winston. It was, she said, a good thing: she no longer mythologizes Mark. Perhaps neither man was quite right. She feels for Winston, and respects his character but – it seems – not enough to set a wedding date. Berjulie, true to form, has been warning Romy that if she doesn't hurry up, Winston will start 'looking at younger girls'!

Saturday, 5 July 1969: My father remains fairly well – no temperature – but I'm shocked by his thinness, his coughing spells, and the slight change in his voice. There seems a radical blockage in his chest and, because of this, according to the doctor, he is prone to infection – the air in there can't circulate. He has been coughing now while I write . . .

Monday, 7 July 1969: I went for a walk on Signal Hill, and there was the bay spread below, the sharp smells of the bush, the old, familiar bird calls. I thought of you so hard I almost willed you beside me . . . The tension at home has lifted. My father's illness seems static, and can't help becoming commonplace. He is working at home every morning, walks a lot around the house. He does have terrible bouts of coughing. On Sunday I drove us all – the old family unit – along the sea to Clifton and up the mountain. My presence too has become commonplace: it's not exactly indispensable. Pip is the only one with whom I've had any conversation. He's worried by his inability to feel since his adolescence (Pip: 'Before puberty, I used to have pure feelings, pure love. Now the only emotion I experience is anger.').

I am rather lonely amongst my old friends here – Romy,

Phillippa, Ellie, Linn – for the old chords are overworked
and there are no new ones to strike, so it seems. Each
appears to be enclosed in her own severe world and there
seems little to say. This may be the result of prolonged
departure . . . I don't believe they are interested in the
expansion I've experienced since my illness – and almost
shield this side from them, whether for my sake or theirs, I
don't know. I want terribly to belong to these old friends,
in my love for them, and don't want them to perceive my
difference.

To-night, as I bathed Anna, she confided she was going
to marry a prince, 'a *little* prince', she qualified, 'who will
grow bigger'.

Thursday, 10 July 1969: Although my mother has not
complained, I can guess how hard it was for her when she
was alone here and my father very ill. He is having a
remission now, but no one can say how long it will last.
My mother has told me that the cancer has spread over his
body, and that there seems to be a separate tumour in the
lung. He sometimes has difficulty in speaking; his voice is
definitely changed; and he coughs most dreadfully. He
assures us that he feels 'normal' and even talks
optimistically of going overseas to officiate at the Maccabi
Games. Siamon, he's very changed though, even mentally.
His optimism is superficial – I think he's fearful really.
Phillippa's sister, Eileen, died two nights ago, and he said
he was 'shaken' to hear that she had the same disease. I
tried to brush it off, saying that Eileen has been ill for years
and years, as long as I can remember, but he's not a fool.
You might be right in your assessment of him as a realist,
above all, that his optimism is a social tactic and, of course,
a healthy one for his morale. I am worried if all that can
possibly be done has been done. He had only five treatments, and they didn't even tire him, except the first.

They've done wonders for him – but this isn't the radical treatment you envisaged. Perhaps the rationale is that it's too far gone?

I was with Phillippa yesterday while the funeral took place. We were laughing so much, she, Romy, and I – it was so *sane* really – though to an onlooker might have seemed macabre. Romy got into bed with her for comfort and later others came, Ellie and Sylvia, and we went on laughing. Phil had so much to lose in Eileen. I asked her today if I should go, if she wanted to be with her family – and she said wryly: 'No, stay, I've got no family.'

Sunday, 13 July 1969: Romy left on Friday night to start teaching and I expect, in an odd way, that will free me. She kept me hanging around a lot of the time because she never made final arrangements. She was a bit possessive, too, not explicitly, but in a way that made me feel awkward when I went outside the magic circle.

Last night Morgan and Linn took me for dinner to the Harbour Café. Morgan has been doing a crash course for three weeks at varsity and, it seems, has been stimulated. He said, to my surprise (and, I admit, confusion) that he wants Linn 'to get involved in some professional way again'. He is very kind to Linn. He stayed in the delivery room with her. For a businessman he is unusually self-critical.

I was pleased to read of your 'active self', the thrill of pitting yourself against uncertainty and imposing order upon it. I recognize your experience as a counterpart of my own when I am deep in a book, when it is so 'active' in me that I feel as though I am participating in its creation in my desire to 'complete' the work with some understanding. I can't exist without this sense of aliveness – and we are both lucky to have the opportunities to do the work we like. Morgan confessed last night that neither of

them had finished a book in a year, and that they had felt
flat for some time. I think only work, really, can save one
when life goes flat. Romy also confessed to flatness, and
for her, at the moment, marriage seems not only a remedy
but a necessity. She says that she has changed in the last few
months, from sheer panic at the idea of giving up her
freedom (you were right after all!) to an intense desire to
move on to the next stage in her life. She still hasn't
decided what that is to be, but I gave her a coffee-set we
chose together at Binnehuis, for her*self*. She gave me a
Gourmet cookbook in which she wrote: 'Remember this
afternoon, as I shall always.' I read it every night before I
go to sleep. There are some recipes I'd like to try out: one
for that nut bread we had at Nantucket.

I went up Table Mountain yesterday afternoon, and
then again this morning with my parents and Anna. The
yellow daisies are blooming on all the spiky bushes. Anna
collected great bunches of flowers and we strung some in
her curly locks. The day was breathlessly clear and widely
blue, and we could see across the Cape Flats to the criss-
crossing lines of the mountains beyond.

I hope climbing around was not too much for my
father. When we came home, he refused lunch, and has a
temperature of 100. Oh God, I hope it's not starting again.
He is due to leave this Tuesday for the Maccabi Games.
I've been cheerful about him for the last few days, but
sometimes succumb to nightmare thoughts in the dark. I
dreamt last night that I had Romy and then my father in
my arms, as they gave way to epileptic deaths. I was
grateful to Anna for waking me. . . .

Wednesday, 16 July 1969: I love this misty, foggy place, the
peaks looming through the morning haze, the tang of the
sea, and the foghorn – I want to *live* it, and yet, somehow,
can't get myself into the picture. I see from a point of non-

involvement – and it hurts to be so wilfully excluded! It is strange that New York, of all places, with which I feel no particular affinity, is so REAL. I am sad to have lost Cape Town, because it seems I am forced to leave my past behind. Perhaps, in part, this has to do with the shock of my father's illness – that the past has cracked quite suddenly, and can only be retained now separated from reality. In a similar way, perhaps, my father is now on the other side, no longer so dynamically in the arena. It hurts the most to have seen him handing over: the implications of this reversal. It's not that I can't accept the reins. The pain is that of having to take someone's place, not of taking up an unfamiliar role, but taking it *away* from someone you know. I am quite ready – only in the middle of the night, when Anna wakes me, there is that uncontained horror that made me so desperate once. As I lie in the dark, it comes close.

Sunday, 20 July 1969: My mother and I have drawn together more than at any time since our marriage. The religious question has subsided, some relaxation of her inner voice. For many years I puzzled over what she identified as 'a lovely girl'. My friends were never in this category. Finally, I realized what the 'lovelies' have in common. It is innocence. And where this appears to me deadly – this sitting on the grandstand and never getting down in the arena – to my mother is 'lovely'.

To-night my mother, Anna, and I are off to – guess – KLAWER. By puff-puff. I'm madly excited to be sleeping on a puffa train, and to see again the Real Africa. When my mother called Klawer Hotel she introduced herself, 'I was, you know, a Miss Press,' and she told me, quite proudly, 'Klawer's a VILLAGE now with SIX shops!' Last night (I was out with Phil and Robert), Phil said 'Goodbye, and enjoy *all* the restaurants in Klawer.'

9 a.m., Thursday, 31 July 1969: It was like a journey back
in time to wake in the morning and look out at the dark
body of the train curving in and out, and see miles upon
miles of thorn bush – like prehistoric earth, it seemed so
untrodden and vast, all outlines and shadows in the half-
light before dawn. The engine throbbed all night with the
smell of coal. We went to a farmhouse where we had
coffee and home-baked biscuits. I spoke Afrikaans, or tried
to. An inspector on the train asked where I came from,
and when I said New York, he was sceptical: '*Nee*,' he said,
shaking his head, 'you're built like a South African girl,'
looking from my breasts to my legs, 'strong and sunburnt'.
With the current Twiggy ideal of beauty, I'd rather be told
that I look tubercular.

Thursday, 7 August 1969: My father has come back – very
ill again. He was ill all the time he was away with temps up
to 103. I never realized how much I cared, and the pain of
seeing him so wretched is something new in experience. I
don't want to write about it – writing is analysing, and I
don't want to analyse pity and terror.

Friday, 8th: I hope you'll forgive me for taking so long
with this letter. My father's temp is still 103, and he looks
bad. I sat all morning in his room, and when he eventually
fell asleep, was relieved to get out of that foetid air. It's
awful to see my vigorous father so reduced, pathetic, and
even unpalatable. After the first 3 days at the Games, he
never got out of bed except once, to present the prizes. He
got an ovation, however, and perhaps it was worth it for
him. There has been a write-up about him in *Die Burger*
with a photo.

    Linn and Phillippa are away, but I see Ellie quite often.
With her I can expand. She reads seriously. Romy reads
the modish writers who are talked of at social gatherings.

On Tuesday, I am invited to Elizabeth's mother [the writer Anna Louw] for an evening of music.

Thursday, 21 August 1969: I've had some truly interesting and rapport-filled encounters with Anna Louw who is as 'twice-born' as my mother but agreeably unburdened by responsibility for my failures of faith. My mother thinks so much of God that it seems to exclude all else, while I long for experience in human contact as broad, as encompassing as the world and all knowledge!

There came a night in Groote Schuur, when I remained after the visitors, and saw my father sink back, drained. There was defeat in his eyes. It was at that moment that I realized there would be no further remission. Unable to speak, he stroked my arm as we looked at each other. Later, I stood outside the hospital, and death leaped out of the dark. I fled to Phillippa. It wasn't fair to her, but she would understand. She and Robert put their arms around me and allowed me to cry. Grief is the most private of all emotions, but that night they shared it.

Dryden said that to show 'the various movements of a soul combating betwixt two different passions' is the essence of tragedy. For three years after the broken wedding, Romy continued to love – in different ways – two men. With Winston she sustained a 'superficial equilibrium' that smoothed her 'quirks' and 'edges'; at the same time, she urged Mark to resume their wildly emotive bond.

In 1969–70 Mark was living in Hillbrow with Ghislaine, who was tiny, like a bird. She had emerged from a deprived childhood fragile and dependent. She cooked beautifully. She was, said Leonora, 'everything Romy wasn't'. One day, Mark's Aunt Gertie arrived to stay. Gertie offered to take them to dinner but Mark said that he was not quite up to it – he was not quite well. So Ghislaine and Gertie left, and Mark went to meet Romy at their usual

Italian restaurant. Then, into the restaurant, came Aunt Gertie, followed by Ghislaine – who was devastated.

'She was devastated by my lie,' Mark recalled, 'and didn't eat at all.' He was filled with remorse and pity. Romy, he said angrily, appeared unperturbed 'as though this would put paid to Ghislaine. She could handle confrontation – she thrived on drama. For me, it was harrowing to hurt Ghislaine. Romy came from a caring home; Ghislaine had a horrifying childhood and no home.' With Ghislaine, he could be the giver; Romy was 'stifling, overwhelming, possessive'. He thought she would do better 'with someone more contained, who retained self-command, who was not too convoluted and even a bit impervious'.

All the same, Mark was 'upset' when he came upon a photograph of Winston in an IBM advertisement showing the kind of personal representative who would bring its expertise to remote dorps and homelands, like Pofadder or QwaQwa or Klawer. The advertisement was based on IBM's ties with Twentieth Century Fox, and the caption read: 'How did James Bond get to QwaQwa?'

There was Mark, upset and guilty; Ghislaine wounded; Winston stoic and determined. Romy did not hide from him her meetings with Mark. And so it continued. No one was happy. So long as Romy could not move, four people remained in more or less constant agitation.

Her horror of weddings became a standing joke. She must be allowed, she said, 'a pet neurosis'. She defied her obligatory presence at Reggie's wedding – the unmarried sister of twenty-eight – by appearing in the tiniest of miniskirts in the most unbridal of glaring orange, set off by the long red mane.

One of her 'quirks' of this period, said Winston, was an attempt to disrupt the wedding of his sister. Ingrid was the last of the four siblings and the only girl. Their mother had set her heart on a wedding with all the trimmings. Since she was now widowed and could not afford it, Winston offered to pay for everything.

'It's not what I'd want myself, but a way of giving happiness to my mother,' he explained to Romy.

'Ingrid's too young to know what she wants, to know how *ghastly* it will be. She's *totally* in your mother's control, her victim if she only knew it. Why squander all that money on a *gross*, show-piece wedding that's over in a few hours?'

Winston said levelly: 'I'm going to do this, so you can shut up about your objections. It's my decision, and none of your business.'

And that was the end of it, though Romy continued to fume. They did often row, and Romy did attempt the dramatic exit, the earth-shaking finale of her scenes with Mark. But Winston never permitted a fight to the death. Tensions found a harmless focus in a set of Dali lithographs. At a South African Railways sale of lost property, in a lot that consisted mainly of discarded books and insignificant magazines, Winston had come across twenty-five lithographs of the *Aliyah*, tracing Jewish history from the Holocaust to the founding of the State of Israel. These had been lost, somehow, en route to Israel – presumably on South African Airways. Winston bought the Dali for R40 – about $50. Eventually they were valued at $15,000.

At the climax of a row, Romy would grab the lithographs and prepare to walk out.

'No, you can't,' Winston would say. 'They're *mine*.'

'We'll divide them.'

'Impossible: can't you see it's one sequence?'

They learnt quickly how to conduct the ritual exchange of the long-married.

And yet, of course, they had not married. In 1969 Winston had a flat in Berea; Romy in Killarney. Johannesburg was not New York: they could not be seen to live together. If Romy spent the night, she would slip away at dawn. At first, she tried to conceal this from Rosie Kunene, but after she vanished early one morning, Rosie said to Winston: 'Why she do this? Why she not stay with us, have a bath, have tea with us?' Then, Rosie recalled, 'they felt free. Then Romy became very, *very* good friend.'

Once she overslept. The phone rang at the bedside at 6 a.m. Romy divined it was her mother. She tore to Rosie's room and burst in. 'Please, *please*, Rosie,' she begged, 'say I'm not here.'

'Your mother will hate me,' Rosie protested, pulling on the blue beret she always wore. 'She know it's a lie.' She picked up the receiver.

Mrs Gevint was distraught. 'I phone her flat lots of times. I *must* talk. Call her. I *know* she's there.'

'No. No. She not here,' said Rosie with flat insistence.

'Winston's mother also get to hate me,' Rosie remembered, shaking her head. In 1969 Mrs Rosenberg left Vryburg and arrived to stay with Winston for five months. Though Romy tried to remove all trace of her presence, Mrs Rosenberg detected it at once. Rosie, cross-questioned, had to lie, yet again, when Mrs Rosenberg fell on a sweater which Romy, in characteristic haste, had overlooked.

'This is a girl's sweater,' she accused Rosie, looking her sternly in the eye.

'I say –', Rosie enacted the scene, shaking her head and giving her words an emphatic rhythm, 'I say, "uh uh – I don-know – whose clothes – is *that*." Then after, I say, "oh! I've re-*mem*ber! We had someone with a gel-friend here."'

A woman who could swoop down on her son's school in a plane was not to be beguiled. It could be none other than Romy, who had cancelled the wedding at the last, impossible moment, and instead went to bed with her son – obviously, this unprincipled girl, who couldn't appreciate what she had.

'Do you like Romy?' she asked Rosie Kunene. 'Does she look like a good girl? Or what?'

Rosie (staunchly): 'No, she's a *good* gel.'

Mrs Rosenberg: 'Does she come and help you in the kitchen?'

Rosie (regretfully): 'She doesn't.'

These five months were, in Rosie's word, 'heavy' for Winston, and no less for Rosie when Winston had to go away and she was left alone with Mrs Rosenberg. Romy stayed away, but would phone to say: 'How are you, Rosie? Never mind!'

While Winston was away, Romy's friendship with Rosie grew more intimate. 'One thing isn't going to please you, Rosie,' she confided. 'I don't want children. Children bring trouble. I see myself, what I've done to my mother.'

'My children fight at home – I see my boy hit his sister with an iron.'

'So you see, Rosie, when your children are small, their troubles are small; when they're big, the troubles get big. Take it from me and my parents.'

Rosie said, remembering: 'Oh! She was an open lady. After that, when she was free to me, she was my *dah*-ling, really my *dah*-ling. It was the first and last. I can't be so happy as I was with them.'

In 1970 Winston moved to Wilds Crest, closer to Killarney. The flat had one bedroom, a living-area, a kitchen, and bathroom. There was a garden attached to the flat, but no place for Rosie, who stayed at Willow Stream. She would arrive early to bring in the tea. One day, Romy said: 'I'm not happy this morning.'

'What's the matter?' asked Rosie, putting down the tray and pulling the curtains.

'Winston wasn't good to me in the night.'

Winston was incredulous. 'How can you tell Rosie?'

'I have to tell Rosie.'

Winston remained critical of what he perceived as immaturity in Romy: her resentment of his mother continued to annoy him. He thought her too self-centred to be a mother herself. This was not the view of her friends, whom she loved unsparingly and recreated in monumental form for one another. She put into practice (without knowing it) an ideal of friendship that Virginia Woolf set out in her masterpiece *The Waves*, where six friends of the same generation divine one another's characters and put them out to play in their imaginations. Her sense of character in action made her the performing counterpart of a novelist or biographer. Because she could 'see' who her pupils were, because she drew them out, she was a born teacher for teenagers who had little aptitude for maths. They felt affirmed in other ways; gifts of affection were more important, more wanted, than ticks and marks. She loved best pupils and friends in trouble because they offered the greatest scope for her blend of creativity and intense involvement which, for those of us drawn into it, was infinitely more effective than career advice or counselling. She was drawn, most, to women in distress. When Bonnie returned to Johannesburg in a state of chronic depression after two years in England, she did more for her than an array of therapists.

'Bonnie,' she said in the garden of Willow Stream, 'Bonnie, listen to me, you may think you're miserable, but *are* you miserable this very moment, talking here?'

'No, this is good.'

'So you must take each moment, savour it, remember it as making the day. *That* is living, and you *are* having what matters. To live is to recognize these moments.'

Bonnie was part of the jet-set of Jewish Jo'burg who played at sensuality: dancing with anyone but a husband at midnight, yet upholding (in tones of virtue) the 'Jewish values' of the stable home. 'It was all a game,' said Bonnie, 'sexual innuendoes, not intercourse; titillation, not passion. Key parties were the rage, but ours were sicker because it was imitation freedom. Romy warned me to get out of a set for whom wealth was the vital ingredient. "They'll deplete your soul," she said.'

It was typical of Romy that she could say that and, at the same time, take on the colouring of this set so as to enter it. She flew from school to Puzzi's to buy luxurious Italian clothes and, later that night, heavily eye-lined, cigarette in hand, exchanged banter with the foremost loverboy-husbands in town.

This was a Romy who vanished into chic night-clubs, salerooms, modish clothes, done-up houses, and the 'superficial equilibrium' of the day-to-day. She never met Rose again, but in those same years, in that same town, Rose too vanished into the set of incomprehensible photographs which she left behind: an unrecognizable Rose who had a new baby nose and whose hair was baby-pale, as though she were trying to obliterate her character. Did she enjoy, perhaps, the enigma of a baby-doll who was, at the same time, doing law and political science at Wits, and who earned an excellent salary in advertising? Photographs show Rose modelling a cocktail dress and beehive hat, kneeing the seat of a chair; Rose with a finger to her chin; Rose in the news at a first night of a new play or holding an artist's catalogue enquiringly to her face at the opening of an exhibition; Rose, again in the news as convenor of a medical ball, glamorous in her strapless dress; and, not least, Rose holding her babies. Nowhere was there any sign of continuity with the Rose who had bouts of 'hysteria' before a mixed party, who could not bring herself to arrive until she was two hours late, and who had played the vulnerable Dodo, sixteen, 'with a plain, pale, old face', in a university production of *Sport of My Mad Mother*. At her first entrance, Dodo looked startled and suspicious when she saw the audience, then decided that the best way to get round them was to try to amuse them. Tormented by an anarchic gang, led by the ruthless, fecund Greta, she held for a moment a gun to her chin, Dodo who had to 'try and bear the terror pressing in on your imagination . . . each moment as it passes is a moment won from the fear of being hurt', which Rose acted with the febrile playfulness of exposed innocence.

To ask which was the real Rose was, of course, the wrong question. For her triumph was a form of contrivance that would leave the essential behind: that Rose I had known, long ago, without make-up, who had dared to think at Good Hope and written essays of ambitious brilliance. When we met, once in '67 in an dark, empty coffee-bar one late afternoon in Johannesburg and once in '69 at her serene, baby-filled home, she was – serious. That is all: her masks and roles defeat the presumptions of the biographer.

There were years when I did not go back to South Africa: there were the Orals in April 1970 and a dissertation written between '70 and '72. Romy was bound up with Hazel Gordon, a fellow

teacher who was about to marry her brother David, and with
Bonnie who continued to need her. She once cornered Bonnie,
whose husband was still Mark's friend.

'Have you seen him?'

'Yes.'

'How is he?'

'All right.'

But, Bonnie, how *is* he? Tell me.' She needed to hear that
Mark suffered as she did.

Suddenly, she lashed out at Bonnie's divided loyalty. She would
not tolerate resistance to her emotional need.

A turning-point in Romy's life came in December 1970.
Ghislaine fell pregnant, and Mark married her. Romy was no
adulteress. This was the end.

Six months later, she fled to New York. She arrived without
warning.

Flinging herself on my bed, in June '71, she said in a voice of
stifled outrage: 'If you love a friend, a woman, it's for life. It's
impossible, this custom that if a man, who is part of you in the
same way, marries someone else, you are never to see him again.'

Romy came to America to try an alternative future. She was agitated, restless, even peremptory. She had in tow a thirty-year-old
predator called Moira, who had to be accommodated in our
crowded apartment: the two bedrooms were so dark and tiny that
we worked in the living-room. Romy slept in the living-room on
the divan, while Moira was on the floor of Anna's room on a mat-
tress that left no space for a child to play. It was expected that
Moira would remain all through the summer while Romy toured
the States. Moira's satin, peach-coloured underwear, too luxurious
for a washer, hung to dry all over the apartment. Her heavy scent
hung in the humid air. She spent hours painting her toe-claws.
Eventually, she made two ruined marriages but, at this stage, was
still tracking a life-story. Romy made no attempt to build up
Moira as more than a travel-partner, but to see Romy with her

had its pathos. At twenty-nine, she had fallen into the company of the hungry hunters. Time was running out.

Back in Africa, Winston waited. He was 'a rock', I said to him in 1990.

'Not always,' he corrected. 'There were fluctuations. For instance, that time when she went to the States. I hoped, but felt unsure. You can't be naïve.'

Romy, unsettled as ever, was searching – for what, she did not know: for some undertaking to which she could respond with total conviction. With us she met academics who had no trouble generating her enthusiasm for their disciplines – it might be American literature one day, anthropology the next – but as one excitement replaced another, none took hold. She was exercising her empathy, not catching fire – though to Americans, who did not know her, these scenes had their delirious drama.

She annoyed me by her facile enthusiasms; I annoyed her by indifference to glamour. She urged me to diet and dress in a bolder way. On shopping expeditions, she insisted on 'a proper bra'. She told me, with sisterly exasperation that I rather enjoyed, 'You're always changing your opinions'. Most of all, I annoyed her by persisting with work.

'The dissertation is a passport to the future,' is how I put it to her, knowing she would understand that better than the sheer compulsion of research. Romy's passport was her lovability which worked on everyone – except Mark.

In July, Romy joined us for ten days at the Trudeau Institute at Saranac Lake, up-state in the Adirondacks. She lay on the T-dock that floated in the sun while I wrestled with an abortive first chapter. I regret – how I regret – those days of not being with her in her time of need. I saw her as a temptation to idleness as I pursued that very work ethic I had once deplored.

For Romy's entertainment, we invited Gordon Antrem, a biochemist from Harvard. He came for the weekend: a bachelor with classical features and rather formal good manners. His colleagues regarded him as so irresistible to women that they would greet him in the morning: 'Have you heard? Three suicides last night in the Charles.' Romy remained cool: his politeness appeared to chill her. I was amazed to hear, after Gordon left, that she had obliged herself to sleep with him. It had been rather colourless, no more than a test: could someone else stir her? He could not. Poor Gordon: the tester tested. He would have agreed, with his unvarying, rather wooden politeness.

After that, Romy raced around the country: New Orleans, Las Vegas, LA, ending in August with Lynn Freed in San Francisco. She told Lynn this story: in Vegas she had gone to visit a certain very famous comedian, to whom she had an introduction. She found him sunbathing in the nude beside the pool. Suddenly, he got up and chased her. Round the pool they went, his penis flapping as he ran.

'I'm a virgin,' she shouted. He persisted after her. She tried again, still on the run and yelling louder through cupped hands:

'I'm *Jewish*.'

He stopped in his tracks. He wrapped her protectively in her towelling gown. He ushered her into his white Mercedes, and told the driver to see her safely to her hotel.

From Lynn's, she made frantic phone-calls to Africa in the middle of the night. Winston might tell her what to do: should she return? Or stay? In accordance with their agreement to free each other, Winston had found another woman. He told this woman honestly that, if Romy chose to return, the affair could have no future. Romy was now distraught with indecision. Back in New York, she tore about Columbia, trying to get a place at the last moment. All graduate programmes had long been filled, the secretaries said, but she swept past them into the offices of the heads of department: English one day, anthropology the next. Chairmen had only to meet her, to want her. A place – they would see to it personally – would just have to be made. She was winning, convincing, but in the end could not convince herself.

At this point, there came a phone call from Paris. It was

Winston. He was there on a visit to IBM's European centre. Would Romy care to join him?

France . . . for Romy it had the tug of the past, the Bardot aspirations of her teens and the sophisticated civilization that was Mark. Winston said he could wait a while until she decided. This new possibility raised the fever of indecision. Paris offered the temptation to live for the moment; New York offered the long-term promise of an alternative future. The fevered days passed. I no longer worked. Once again, I was wholly absorbed in the urgency of Romy's drama. Which would it be? Our days debated the question, though she was loyal to Winston and I had no idea of the possibilities or drawbacks of that side of the scale. All I could do was describe the demands and rewards of the kind of study that would lead to a career. She wished to engage with this possibility, but had to reckon with her nature: she had certain necessary qualities – brains, flair, memory – but not staying-power. As an undergraduate she had worked quickly – and effectively – under pressure, but she had not that doggedness which intelligence tests do not measure but is vital to all forms of public achievement.

'Perseverance,' I said, and Romy tasted the word.

It did not, admittedly, strike sparks.

I thought of the endurance of Tess of the D'Urbervilles as she dug swedes from the unyielding ground, crawling like a fly over the horizon of Flintcomb-Ash. Though Romy did 'suffer' – it was a word she often used – she did not hold with suffering. She was made for laughter, engagement, passion – a celebrant, not a victim of life.

And still Winston waited.

And still Romy could not decide. It was now the last possible day but one that Winston could hang on in Paris.

Suddenly, she booked a flight. Within two hours she was gone, her forehead creased as I waved at the taxi. She was under some extreme pressure – time, was it, and guilt for the patience that Winston had shown? Would she ruin another relationship as she had ruined hers with Mark?

We parted on that unhappy note. I had not helped her in the way she had once helped me. I had not surrendered to her crisis, but adopted the crass value of work first. And I had allowed myself to become impatient with her vacillations. At nearly thirty, it was time to take an effective role in a 'communal enterprise', which is how I dreamt of teaching in a remote, pastoral place, far from New York.

Romy, too, was impatient to assume her future, but could not bring herself to believe in any future that presented itself. She was like a restless sleeper, tapped on the shoulder by new dreams, but no dream on offer from the world of men – neither marriage nor professionalism – was commensurate with her specialness. It was not a matter of finding a compatible mate. She said repeatedly that she was 'happy' with Winston. She wanted something more from life than the wedding-bell plot – but what it was, she could not define. 'We want – we want – but don't know what we want': was there to be no escape from that silly, vague chant of girls of fifteen, perched on the ledge outside Flora's room on the High Level Road?

Mark had occasioned the despair of a dream almost realized: a rare man who could tune into a woman's dreaming self, that shifting space of prolonged suspense and indefinable becoming. He had left in his wake a destructive fever of unrealized possibility. After his marriage, Romy made an effort to recover her zest for possibility. But it was gone. She had lost her dreaming.

If we had ever been settled in New York, by the start of '72 we were settled no longer. Offers for Siamon came from Oxford, Farmington, Indiana, and Harvard. We drove round Central Park at night, looking up at the dazzle of lights, round and round again, deciding what to do. Every weekend we dashed to Boston, looked at houses, and wondered if we had the strength to take on, once again, the bright indifference of an American city. Every college in the Boston area rejected my applications. They all sent their 'regular' rejection letter: a routine discourse of regret. The parrot-faced Nobel Prize-winner who wished to employ my husband shook his multiple chins at me in his Beacon Hill drawing room, graced by his young Italian wife.

'You'll come [shrug], and eventually you'll find something,' he said with marked lack of interest. A wife's pretensions to a future should not interfere with arrangements.

It was a pleasant distraction to run discussions on Modern novels for a group of women in their early thirties who called themselves 'Banking Wives'. They were all married to executives of First National Citibank, and were members of the exclusive Junior League. We met every Friday morning at the Smith Club near Madison Avenue. Reading *Howards End*, the women showed a keen concern for the position of Margaret Schlegel, wife of the businessman who cannot connect 'the prose with the passion'. I was therefore curious about the bland way these Banking Wives appeared to accept their own position. For in those days, twenty years ago, the bank could still count on the unpaid service of the employee's wife, serving starry dishes in the background while men put their heads together over the important affairs of the world. A wife could be expected to move at a moment's notice to Hong Kong, and there devote her time to entertaining the bank's clients. One of the smartest of the wives, Martha, used to take clients on two-day tours into mainland China. I ventured to ask Martha the question that hung about snippets of their lives.

'What if you rebelled?'

'It's . . . not possible,' said Martha reluctantly. 'It would reflect on my hubby. The barracudas would think: if that guy can't deal with his wife, how can he deal with our clients? At Citibank, a guy's either a barracuda or a guppy.'

I decided it was time to act. If there was no job in the States, I would do what I had always wanted: return to South Africa.

'Exile', I argued, 'is not the only way. It's the less courageous alternative. Through teaching American literature, I could be making a case for freedom and human rights.'

'You don't belong in South Africa.' Siamon's point never failed to confound me. 'You are a peripheral member of an irrelevant white group. The Afrikaners will appoint their own. And the blacks won't want you – it's their struggle.'

'I don't belong here, either. Nor, for that matter, did I belong in Israel.'

'Not belonging is a condition of being Jewish. To be a wanderer.'

'I don't want to resign myself unless it is unavoidable; I want to do something.'

'You will. Be patient. Your time will come.'

'I've hung on too long. Rachel's left, and Faith, and Lynn. At the core of the buzz of New York is a heartless void. It's time to leave.'

I wrote to the English Department at the University of Cape Town, and soon received a favourable reply. In the tide of American rejections, it washed up like a message in a bottle: a job, a civil letter in good English, written to a person. In July 1972, I went to Cape Town, partly for an interview, partly to try out a return. I took a house for the winter in Diep River – a poorer, less picturesque area that was outside the perimeters of my group. There I wrote on Eliot's ordeals, his arrival in England and his first marriage, while little Anna drew beside me at the table. We took walks on the wet sand at Muizenberg. My neighbour, a widower, sat heavy with loneliness across from me in the evenings. I struggled to put my loathing for apartheid into Afrikaans. There were long pauses as he thought it over, then he would shake his head saying, '*Ag, nee wat*' ['You can't be serious']. I knitted a dress in pink stripes for Anna's birthday, and we had a cake in the shape of a seven. Mothers who brought their children from Clifton and Constantia said in candid asides: 'I couldn't live here.' Only Lizzie saw the mountain in the distance where the sun rose.

It was bracing to be alone for that short time: there was the adrenalin of venture. I went to the interview in a sailor dress and drank tea in a friendly Department. Professor Gillham intimated that the job would be mine. But, too, there is no denying that I was lonely in Diep River and missed Siamon very badly. He wrote that for him 'marriage came first': he was prepared to contemplate a trial post in Cape Town, but had hopes, still, of a future overseas. I should be patient: something would turn up. He was, as it proved, right, but it took a long time. In the end, the strength gained in Diep River enabled me to return to New York, to more rejections and another year of hesitation.

Passing through Johannesburg, I spent the last troubled night on the sofa at Wilds Crest. It seemed reckless to give up that solitary job. It was now Romy's turn to be irritated.

'You're naïve,' she said pointedly. 'You don't know South Africa as it is now, banning orders, censorship, state-organized disinformation, and all of us under the vigilance of the Special Branch. Preaching freedom! You wouldn't last a minute.'

The departure on the nineteen-hour flight via Rio was almost as fraught as Romy's departure from New York a year before – tugged in reverse directions by unbreakable bonds. Winston drove his fastest, beating time to the airport. I kissed Romy, the last touch with home. She gave me an encouraging push, but my nerve failed to see the safari crowd. Back to the democratic cant that guards the grasping riches and secret snobberies of New York. Back to hanging about the mailroom on Riverside Drive, hoping for 'a message from heaven' that would open the future.

The early '70s seemed to have no end: hanging about on the brink of being. It appeared incidental that Romy and Winston got married one morning. Mr and Mrs Gevint were not invited, nor Hu and Berj, nor Leonora nor Bonnie, nor anyone but David, Romy's younger brother, and his wife, 'Hazie'.

The decision was Romy's. From the time of the broken wedding, Winston had resolved never to mention marriage again. He tried now to dissuade her. But this time, she said, she was ready.

Romy notified her parents the night before, taking the pulse of their reaction. Would they be overjoyed?

'Just do it. Get it over,' said Mr Gevint impatiently, in a tone that implied he was worn out.

So Romy – finally – did it, in a purple dress, before breakfast. Little old men at their quiet, customary morning prayers were astonished to find themselves participants in, of all things, a wedding. But it was not as other weddings, for the pair, abjuring the parts and pomp of bride and groom, spoke to each other throughout the service. All show, all distraction, was pared away. There were no guests, no speeches, no caterers – only breakfast at home with eggs and toast, as usual, and the addition of champagne. For once, IBM had to wait till the afternoon. Winston had the first dance with Rosie Kunene in her blue beret. The Kwela blared.

'What's going on?' demanded a neighbour of a 'garden boy'.

'Weeding, Madam,' he said. She went away, baffled.

Such a wedding appeared to be a deliberate non-event. I did not bother with congratulations. Later, Romy reproached me for oblivion to her move. As far as I was concerned, we still awaited a defining future.

10

Moves

To wait for a letter from heaven would seem to invite disappointment. Yet such a letter did come, for me in April 1973, and for Romy in April 1974. These letters sent us to other countries with a decisiveness that seemed to take us once and for all out of that country of the past in which we had both – for different reasons – lingered for so long.

By the beginning of 1973, a pattern of rejection had been established. An interviewer for the University of California told me that I was the first of fifty, all of whom he expected to run through in one day. He was proud of this democratic gesture, since the job, he confessed with the same beaming frankness, was 'almost sewn up'. It was the shortest interview I ever had. Jacques Barzun, one of the examiners of my dissertation on Eliot's early years, suggested that I might submit the typescript to Farrar, Straus & Giroux. It was returned with their rejection slip.

Princeton University Press also rejected the book, with a reader's report that grumbled over its deviations from the standard line.

There was one rejection of this time that was not discouraging. The English Department at Princeton gave me a proper interview, a mark of favour from its chairman, A Walton Litz. He was then bringing out *Eliot in His Time* and interested in my dating of the fragments of *The Waste Land* manuscript, which had made it possible to attempt an account of the evolution of the poem over seven and a half years. There were better candidates for that job, and I did not expect to get it, but it was stimulating to talk about Eliot with a knowledgeable scholar. Walt Litz encouraged discoveries and liked to share them. Soon after, I began to get letters from Eliot scholars like Helen Gardner and Hugh Kenner, advancing their own theories about the evolution of the poem.

One day in March, I happened to glance at a small notice tucked amongst many on the vast English board in Philosophy Hall. It announced a Rhodes Fellowship at St Hilda's College, Oxford. This was before Rhodes Scholarships were opened to women. To change Rhodes' will, a bill had to pass through Parliament which was expected to take some years. In the interim, the Rhodes Trust had resolved to do something for women, with the result that five fellowships were offered to what were still the five original women's colleges in Oxford. I applied, but it seemed so remote a possibility that I dismissed it from my mind. Then in April came the letter, inviting me to fly to Oxford for an interview. I would stay in college and have 'privileges of the Senior Common Room'. Even more amazing was another letter that followed it closely.

The second letter was from Helen Gardner. She said: 'I shall be coming to viva you.' Until then, I had not been aware of her long connection with St Hilda's. She also invited me to lunch at her home in Eynsham, where she would show me photocopies of the manuscripts of *Four Quartets* which she had started to put in order. This was thrilling: I boarded the plane for England thinking whatever fool I made of myself at this 'viva', there were the manuscripts to look forward to and Dame Helen herself. And I thought of English gardens and twisty streets.

In London, the trees seemed to fountain up in Eaton Square, where I stayed two nights with my flamboyant aunt, Victoria de Luria Press. Starting out as a designer in New York, she had married one of my mother's brothers and spent twenty-five years hating Johannesburg. Quickly, Victoria had perceived that she had only two alternatives: to allow my family to devour her entirely or to cut herself off. She chose the latter course, and her seven children grew up in the seclusion of the gardens at Inanda House. Their self-sufficient lives, walled off from obnoxious South Africa, reminded me of a movie called *The Garden of the Finzi-Continis* about a Jewish family walled off in Mussolini's Italy. Part of the beauty of such a life is its impossibility – its evanescence. Victoria was then in the process of moving to England: every year she stayed a bit longer at her flat in Eaton Square and placed more of her children in English schools. She thought England the only civilized place on earth. She advised me in her drawling, gravelly voice: 'Wear dowdy things, and *don't* look impressed. Now, gimme a cigarette.'

The next day, I took a waste land walk in the City.

'Billingsgate fish-market,' I said to the taxi-driver. 'Could you please take me there?'

'It's almost noon, luv,' he said, shaking his head. 'Not open at this time of day.'

'But noon is what I want.' He looked uncomprehending. I explained: 'It's in a poem: "Where fishmen lounge at noon".'

'Oh, *I* see.' He was very polite.

And there they were in Lower Thames Street, as Eliot had seen them in 1921, two or three fishermen still lounging against a rather dingy wall that edged the great old river.

Further along Lower Thames Street was St Magnus Martyr, the very High Anglican church which Eliot had entered during lunch-hours when he had worked as a clerk in the basement of Lloyds Bank. Alone in that retreat from City streets, I took out a minute box of paints and, inadequately, tried to set down the 'Inexplicable splendour of Ionian white and gold'.

Phillippa was then living in London (while Robert prepared for a specialist examination). She drove me to Oxford through rays of sunshine that played across the hills of the Thames valley. St Hilda's was on the bank of the river. It was not like an institution, more like a hospitable country house. Across the river, schoolboys were playing cricket on a wide stretch of lawn. It looked like the story-book England that colonials imagine: I had not expected it to be true.

That evening the Principal, Mary Bennett, gave me her 'red settee treatment'. This was a welcoming chat on one of two facing settees in the Senior Common Room. Nothing could have been more humorous (as she enquired about Diana Trilling, who had not enjoyed her dining rights at St Hilda's) or less like an interview, but it was, in fact, an interview of sorts: that idle chat, indigenous to Oxford and the basis of its tutorial system, casual, understated, yet eliciting a fair amount to be discerned.

'Dame Helen is coming tomorrow to tell us all what to do,' was Mrs Bennett's parting remark, rather nuanced in tone, as though the forthcoming scene might be found to be rather more amusing than not.

The interview was formal. The Fellows of the College, grouped on one side of a long table, their heads close together, appeared as in a medieval picture. I sat alone on the other side of the table, across from Dame Helen, a brisk, handsome woman in her mid-sixties.

I was taken aback by her opening question. It had nothing to do with scholarship.

'If you came to Oxford, what would happen to your husband?'

'He's on a grant from the American Leukaemia Society which he can take to any reasonable place.'

Dame Helen drew herself up. 'Why, thank you for considering Oxford reasonable.'

The dons chuckled while I looked at the table.

'Why do you want to come to Oxford?'

There were the old buildings, of course, but it seemed appropriate to say something academic. I couldn't think of anything.

'I should think you'd like to meet people,' prompted Dame Helen after a long pause. She meant herself.

'Yes, of course.'

It wasn't exactly a promising interview but Dame Helen had me elected. Afterwards, she told me frankly that I owed this entirely to her. We were driving to Eynsham, a few miles west of Oxford.

'Tell me, is the University of Cape Town a *correspondence* university?' She drew out the word 'correspondence', enunciating every letter of this put-down. From the vantage point of Oxford, I was an ignoramus from the back of beyond. It was accurate enough. I felt only thankful for the new story that had opened up as I sat, incredulous, in Mrs Bennett's office and saw through her window the spires of Oxford.

Now, over lunch, we would talk about work. I took a deep breath as Mrs Gordon, the housekeeper, served the roast. 'Eliot . . .'.

'And what do you think of my home-grown carrots?' interposed Dame Helen proudly. She was making it clear that conversation took precedence over shop. I also learned the curious fact that, however deprecating the English manner, this is no bar to boasting about vegetables.

'Do you know what you're eating?' she asked over dessert. It was some sort of fool, rather whitish-grey, but tasty.

'Um . . . no.'

'Gooseberries, also home-grown. But, of course, you would know only the Cape gooseberry which is different.'

The last of these inauspicious scenes took place in Harrods. I was buying gifts when my cheap, straw suitcase burst open in the Food Halls, scattering ski-underwear on the immaculate floor. Titters sounded behind me. I kept my head down as I stuffed the leggings back and banged the lid. There was no way to explain what I was doing with ski-underwear in May. The truth was that my idea of a women's college had come from Virginia Woolf's account of privation at Girton in *A Room of One's Own*. I had imagined freezing corridors and cold baths, but had found, instead, a heated Hall and the golden days of England's May.

Siamon was not able to join Anna and me for the Michaelmas term of 1973. It was lonely at first, but it had the interest of mystification. There were words and conventions that were new to me. The Fellows were scrupulously polite, so much so that I had no way of knowing what they thought. But it was exciting to join a community of scholars who lived as well as worked together, and with a consideration for one another that was all the more impressive for its matter-of-factness. Coming from New York, I was charmed by the peace, the garden that edged the river, and most of all by the idea of a women's community.

In November, Ellie came. We walked across Magdalen Bridge in the mist, discussing the problems of women.

'Will you fit in here?' asked Ellie.

'I can't say yet. In New York, I could – just – accommodate through a rule of silence. At Columbia you could be a mistress, a mother, or a freak – but not a colleague. Professor Groper said, "Women are cats". I pushed off – I think one should save words for better things. Others would say "fight him", and I am thankful, naturally, for the benefits their fights achieve. But, in my view, Groper is unredeemable. We're not going to convert men with that kind of misogyny; I mean to live as though they don't exist, as though their time is past.'

'Are men different here?'

'Too soon to say, but I'd guess misogyny is here all right. The men's colleges which will go mixed are not going to rush to appoint women. But they'll turn them down with smooth, tactful words. They'll say how very much they really do want women only, alas, there's no one *quite* suitable at this moment. And then, they'll employ a few in lowly, ill-paid positions – and allow them to do a lot of work. I would be prepared to do that work, under the circumstances, because I do want to teach and continue to learn. You learn, really, from your pupils – and hope lies in the new generation. Ours will carry the marks of struggle.'

'At least you're here, with people who govern by law. You can't imagine what it's like in South Africa: black people have begun to strike for higher wages and improved working-conditions, but of course black unions are illegal and their leaders take mortal risks. You have only to think to be detained without trial, and the horrors go on beyond the cut-off points so that the mass of whites needn't know: tortures hidden away in prisons and murders sanctioned from the top. And the educated leaving all the time: civilization departs; mental life atrophies. You can't wall off, and it seems irrelevant to think about, say, the purer problems of psychology. I'm planning to move out of academe into industrial psychology.'

'What I do appreciate in this society is the custom of consideration for others. The Old Testament calls it loving-kindness; the New Testament calls it charity: "Charity suffereth long and is kind." Yes, there is kindness. They may not feel it in their deepest hearts, but they do it. They have their code – one might call it manners. They are prepared to lend themselves to what others think – this is part of the tutorial system: thinking together, which seems to me a preferable mode of education, especially for women, to that of showmen.'

We paused to look through the mist at the slow-moving river. I thought: I've become a listener to women and am learning something about their lives. There was character in the single women who still formed the majority of the fellowship in 1973. It intrigued me that these women, in a community that had continued since 1893, had managed not to surrender some distinctive deposit, which men did and still scorn (sniggering uneasily about 'formidable' women), but which seemed to me a precious portent of the future. My silence was no longer a protective wall; it was attention to what I could not understand but should like to know better. What was it that Jane Mellanby had said, plumping down comfortably on the red settee after a meeting of scientists? 'I've been very tiresome,' she had said blithely from a ground of her own. Here, one could be a person; here, one could shape thoughts to utterance. After Trilling's airs and Ahab's pain in his balls, here was elderly Miss Nunn bending over a plant in the rockery. After Groper's fancy buttons, and Syracuse with his urgent clutchings and self-pitying cries, here was decorum, duty, and a standard of conduct. To New Yorkers it might sound dull, but after nine years in that metropolis, the plainer virtues had a kindly aspect. Absolute virtue had not occurred to me, brought up in a Jewish tradition, which takes a realistic view of human limitation, surrounding it with a thicket of laws, but absolute virtue did exist in the self-effacing figure of an English tutor. I thought: I shall always be grateful to St Hilda's for taking me in – Dame Helen's words, recalling her acceptance by the College in 1926. It was gratitude for the acceptance that invites one to develop. I shall do this for my pupils, I vowed on the bridge.

'You don't feel a stranger?' Ellie broke in.

'Oh, I am. I can never be anything but a South African, how-ever shameful that may be. Yet to be classed as a foreigner is not a bad position. One floats free from other labels – not bad for a woman at this time. They can't know one.'

In December, Romy came while Winston took a course in Amsterdam. Anna, aged eight, had mumps. We entertained her with ridiculous duets: a wild charleston and our solemn school song: 'Between the mountain and the sea,/Our alma mater stands . . ./*Constantia et virtute.*'

A letter to my mother, written after Romy's departure, shows some resistance to her disruptive energies. It was as though she burst in from another life:

Romy was here this week – fun, but I had the nagging
idea that each day of the vac was needed for Eliot. I
MUST revise, now and quickly, but find it terribly hard to
begin. With Romy here my thoughts, which had been

turning to the *imitatio Christi* and to Vivienne's diaries in
the Bodleian Library, refocussed on the old Good Hope
issue: *does* one have a man or doesn't one? Isn't it the most
important experience in life? I wondered if I gloss over this
with scholarly preoccupations. Romy left me rather
disrupted – out of touch with my mind. But we had fun-
filled excursions to Blenheim Palace, Minster Lovell, and,
of course, boutiques.

She said nothing, really, of her present life. Later, I heard that she
was involved with the Black Sash, the women's organization
which had devised a way of embarrassing apartheid politicians.
Wearing white dresses with black sashes, they stood silently with
heads bowed at the entrance to Parliament or wherever politicians
were due to pass. The Black Sash also gave legal advice to blacks
who struggled against apartheid laws.

Romy said nothing, also, of marriage. Though we had questioned the institution of marriage, its actuality was inviolate – and
private. Neither of us mentioned Mark. She talked lightly of a
recent vacation in Cape Town when they had taken a flat at
Clifton. At last, after years of waiting, Mrs Gevint could look
forward to the daily phone call from her Married Daughter. Their
conversation, as Romy recalled it, went as follows:

'Hullo Mommy.'

'So, what are you doing, Frum?'

'Lying in bed.'

'But – shouldn't you be cleaning the flat?'

'Winston's doing that, Mommy.'

Mrs Gevint puts down the receiver, shaking her head.

Over the last year, Mrs Gevint had become thinner. She was
tired, and there were days when she did not go to the shop. Soon
after Romy's return from Amsterdam, she had a mild stroke. Romy
took her mother to Wilds Crest, and while she nursed her there
came the letter that was to change her life. It came, of all places,
from France: the centre of Romy's fantasies from adolescence to

Mark. Ironically, it was the practical Winston who was to carry the dream to realization:

> Wilds Crest.
> Tuesday, 2 April 1974
>
> My dear David [she wrote to her brother],
>   I wanted you to know that there is a strong possibility that Winston is going to be sent to Paris for a minimum of two years to act as a link between IBM Europe & IBM SA. We will know by the middle of May. We are not telling anyone here because we could not bear it if it did not materialize so please, David, don't breathe a word. Like mommy says, you don't accept that 2 people are engaged until you see it in the newspaper.
>   Look after yourself.
>   Your loving sister R.

In May, she helped her parents move from the house on the High Level Road to a more convenient flat:

> Winston helped me clean up the top part of the house but had to leave Cape Town after 5 days [she wrote again to David]. Then the grind really began – sorting through crockery and clothes and junk that had accumulated since we moved in 1957. I felt terribly anxious all the time because I felt that I would never cope.
>   I sent mommy to the shop every day prior to the move, and even the day of the move, because I knew exactly how she felt. She had been moaning about the house for so long but when it came to it, they were both unhappy to leave. In fact although 237 High Level Road ceased to exist for me once I locked that front door on that fateful Wednesday, it was still very real to them.
>   Although in retrospect I see that I should have involved mommy more, she appeared so frail to me and so incapable

of making decisions & so happy that I had come to Cape Town, that I thought it better to try to make all the decisions myself.

I found it very difficult trying to buy carpets & curtains that would be a reflection of mommy and daddy, and not of myself.

I found it extraordinarily difficult to part with them this time. It is possible that my feelings are coloured by the knowledge that we shall probably be moving to Paris in July. But when I delve even deeper I know that despite myself I am deeply involved with them, I care terribly about them and find the bonds very hard to bear.

I have lived in Johannesburg for over 10 years now, have married in Johannesburg, have my own flat which is a reflection of me and not of anyone else but, strangely enough, I still think of Cape Town as HOME because (I suppose) of mommy and daddy.

I am excited about the Paris trip because I think of it as an adventure. It will be wonderful to experience another culture and acquire a new language. But as the time approaches, suddenly the conflicts emerge – leaving mommy and daddy, all my close friends who mean so much to me . . .

In mid-July, a phone call came from Paris. It was Romy to say that she and Winston had been sent there briefly to find accommodation for their return at the start of August. 'We've inspected seventeen apartments between 2 p.m. on Wednesday and 4.30 p.m. on Friday. The estate agents are peroxided ladies who breathe intimately down our necks that this particular apartment is "*très calme*" when earmuffs would be a necessity.'

Three days later, she phoned again to report that they had seen forty apartments: 'The housing department at IBM has been fantastic while I've made their lives a misery. Of course, I collapsed – and you know how well I can collapse. I wanted an apartment to face south, on the top floor, on the Left Bank, not too big, not too small, near the action, away from the noise, good view and good vibes.' By now she was laughing with me as she raced over the top: 'Winston in desperation was planning to move a particular apartment, brick by brick, from the Right to the Left Bank and stick it in the top of Notre-Dame. But at last we've found a place in a courtyard at the very top of a cul-de-sac called passage de la Visitation. It's charming, you'll see. Close to Saint-Germain-des-Prés but wonderfully quiet – protected by green doors. This is bye for now. We'll be back in two or so weeks to begin *living* in Paris which has become *necessary* for both of us.'

So began the space in paradise. In Paris, Romy was to find herself in a way she had never found herself in any other place. Her initial alienation was brief:

> 11 Bis passage de la Visitation,
> Paris 75007,
> France.
> 5 August 1974

My dear, dear friend [she wrote to Bonnie],

    We moved into our apartment on Monday and until the weekend I felt listless, apathetic and self-absorbed. Wilds Crest is no longer our home. Jbg is no longer my town. The transition from one world to the other was so quick that there had been insufficient time to think too deeply about what was happening. And on Monday there we were – for better or for worse there we were. Winston and I simply looked at each other uncomprehendingly.

    To give me a framework, I enrolled immediately at the Alliance Française. I go for 4 hours per day, Monday to Friday. In fact I cannot wait to learn the French equivalent of 'fuck off' so that I can casually say it to our concierge one day in her own taal. I hate her. I despise the French lower classes. They are uncouth, uncivil and pigs.

Winston is rapidly adjusting to our new life. The new milieu at work is exciting for him and he is, as you know, always positive. (Sometimes it gets me down.)

I miss being able to pick up the telephone and to hear your voice. I have no desire at the moment to contact anyone. It will take me a long time to get over the loss of my friends. With new acquaintances there is too much explaining to do. I am looking at the world through the wrong end of a telescope – but am sure that it is temporary . . .

One day she walked home alone from IBM. 'I stopped for tea and croissants in the Tuileries Gardens, under some magnificent chestnut trees,' she wrote to Phillippa. 'All of a sudden I became aware of the fact that the emotion threatening to split my body in two was pure & unadulterated happiness. I shall cherish that morning and that experience for as long as I live. Winston is special (even I realize this) & if it is at all possible our relationship has deepened since we arrived in Paris.'

At the end of the first month she wrote to Bonnie: 'Winston is leaving for Holland and Belgium next Tuesday & although I would like to go with him I don't think that I should break the continuity of my studies at the moment. The challenge to master this most beautiful language is too strong for the time being. Yesterday I went to meet W. on the Right Bank because he had seen a lamp, which we eventually bought. The shops are so exquisite, the people are so attractive to me that I felt quite transported. Every corner seems to have a flower stall so that the sudden blaze of colour is quite startling.'

It was this transported Romy who made us welcome that August on our first visit to Paris. Their apartment was on the fourth floor, reached in an open, creaking lift. The living-room and bedroom were furnished with Cape Dutch yellow-wood, with a kist at the foot of the brass bed, and there were a few of the Dali lithographs on the walls. The French doors opened on the courtyard below and the vista of mellow roofs. It was this vista, Romy now knew for certain, she had waited all her life to find. She made Paris her own as we walked arm in arm, in that summer of content, towards the Seine and across a bridge to Notre-Dame.

'It's another way of living,' she said. 'You savour each impression, you become alert to every pleasure like sitting, with all this about you, and sipping espresso in the sun.' I looked up as she pointed at the graceful lines of the buildings along the *quais*, as academe paled rapidly into relative unimportance.

'Paris transformed her,' Winston recalled in 1990. 'She had the opportunity to range on her own, find things – find herself. In Paris, too, she looked at me with different eyes: I was performing in the city of her dreams.'

She found herself, he said. But what, I wondered, did she find? Was it what she had always moved towards: being, not doing, not that absurd busy-ness that protects the rest of us from confronting our void? Was it Lewis Carroll who said that the achievement of living is the formation of character? If so, Romy and other unknowns had their achievements that are not measurable in public terms.

And Rose? Had she, too, her achievement? By 1974 there were three girls: Deborah, Lisa, and Julia, born between 1968 and 1972. She had taken a second degree in politics, and worked for two advertising firms, earning a great deal. Twenty weeks into her third pregnancy, she was featured as 'Today's Woman' in *Fair Lady* magazine. 'A complete tip-to-toe make-over was one of the highlights for our Today's Woman on her fairytale trip to Paris,' was the headline. There followed a step-by-step series of photographs as Rose was transformed. Charlette Maucourant 'found Rosabelle's make-up too heavy' and, encouraging her to play up her freckles, proceeded to apply the following layers: creamy-beige Hale de Mai Tent Naturel, Pink Sand Translucent Powder 'fluffed on lavishly with cotton wool, with Chestnut and Tiger's Eye powder-shadow 'rainbowed right around the eye'. To finish, 'lashes were laced with three light coats of black block mascara

Dior and cheekbones pinked with Paprika Blush Powder for a dash of excitement . . . Charlette's work of art was complete.'

But where was Rose?

She had moved on to the Parisian hairdresser, Alexandre, 'who said "what pretty hair, my favourite colour," as he studied Rosabelle's bright red tresses at his elegant salon in the Faubourg Saint-Honoré.' He chose his 'Guy Laroche creation' for this head of hair. 'Outsize rollers are essential', he told Rose, 'for naturally curly hair like this to get a smooth, sleek line.'

In June 1973, Rose became Public Relations Officer for the Johannesburg Chamber of Commerce. Her husband, Ronnie, said that she had enjoyed writing a newsletter once a week.

'But Rose could have written creatively,' I said to Phillippa in 1990. We were walking amidst the vineyards of the Constantia valley. 'Did someone discourage her at some stage in her youth? Some local editor who turned a story down? Discouragement would not have been difficult. Rose was tentative, vulnerable. Her jittering vivacity hid her nervousness. But why commerce, why advertising? Was this her father in her? Why set her sights so low?'

'She rated her gifts too lightly,' said Phillippa.

'She wanted so badly to succeed as a "woman". She was serious, but would spend hours on her appearance.'

'She was always late, remember? Not late in the ordinary way, but an hour, even two hours late. She was never satisfied that she was ready. It was the sort of behaviour that ended relationships.'

'I can't make her out,' I said irritably. 'She was inconsistent: fluffy and serious. She would read Conrad and then study, with equal and earnest attention, a woman's magazine.'

'She was consistent in her inconsistency,' said Phillippa with tolerant affection.

Late at night, on 31 October 1974, Romy phoned from Paris. 'You won't believe this: Rose died.'

'*Died*?'

'Yesterday. Acute leukaemia. She was ill for a week.'

Her husband said, in 1990, that to Rose leukaemia had been romantic: 'Leukaemia has replaced TB as the romantic disease. *Love Story* [a best-seller on this theme] came out a few months before Rose died. She read the book a week before the illness began. When she fell ill one Sunday morning, I took her to a doctor who felt an enlarged spleen. "It's leukaemia," said Rose calmly. She knew right away – she had read the novel. At that stage, doctors hadn't yet done marrow transplants, though it was beginning at Barts in London. I thought of taking her, but she quickly became too ill to travel.'

'Was it hard for her to die young?'

'Rose said to me: "I've had a good life."'

'Rose was an actress. She could carry off anything. Is it conceivable that she was acting a *Love Story* role: the good dying wife?'

'She was not acting.' Ronnie spoke firmly. 'It was from the soul.'

I thought of a woodcut in my copy of *Wuthering Heights*, whose jacket was wrinkled because, at fifteen, I had dropped it while reading in the bath. It was a picture of Heathcliff and Catherine, cheek to wild cheek, clutched in each other's arms, frantic at the prospect of death's separation. Rose, on the contrary, had been calm and rational. She had faced the fact of death without a murmur. She had said the graceful words to her husband who was a sensible, skilled obstetrician of the kind whose mind is on the job rather than on the bedside manner. He was not the person for affecting scenes, and still less Rose's father, that market-man with shrewd eyes. Neither was made for the emotional demands of a galloping death. So Rose, I imagine, was alone.

During that last week, she called for a lawyer to make a will. The terms she dictated with careful exactness: her leavings would go to her girls. She had to secure their futures against the likelihood that Ronnie would marry again. There was a life of Churchill at her bedside. Her face was made up. Deborah, the

daughter over whom Rose had hummed, remembered the silver
eye-shadow in a poem she wrote at seventeen:

> Orange-red gel
> Its sticky scent
> recalls
> six-year-old lips
> tiny and poised,
> tightly pursed
> to be exotically adorned
> by mommy's
> lip gloss.
> the vivid pink transparent
> memory
>   overlaps
> the dull tangerine
> reality.
>
> The sickly sweet smell
> under the shiny
> silver lid. 'Christian Dior'
> conjures up the
> soft-textured hair
> and the green-checked shirt,
> and the freckles
> on the pale eyelids
> of the mother
> who died.*

It could be said that Rose's death was her achievement. She died
with her mask in place, calm – and invisible to the end.

*

---

*Published in a student magazine, *Omphalos*, in 1988.

A month later, early in December 1974, Mrs Gevint had a second stroke. Romy flew overnight to Cape Town. For three days her mother lay in a coma, her china-blue eyes open, but fixed. Romy sat beside her, talking, convinced her mother was listening, even if she could not respond. Then it was over. Back in Paris, she saw an 'old face' in the mirror, with a stale look that repelled her, as she wrote to Bonnie who had seen her on the return journey through Johannesburg:

> Paris.
> Sunday, 5 January 1975
>
> . . . Bonnie, you will never quite understand what those few hours with you meant to me. And as I am well aware of the danger that, sometimes, in verbalizing feelings, one only succeeds in minimizing them, I shall say no more. You must know that in spite of our differences I accept you totally. I suppose that's what love is. It's the way I feel about my father, David my brother, Winston, and a very few of my friends. It's the way I felt about my mother.
>
> At the moment, I am still wavering between reality & fantasy because from such a vast distance it is very hard for me to accept that my mother's illness, her suffering and then her death was not simply a ghastly nightmare, similar to the nightmares of my adolescence – but still only a nightmare. At times I resort to waking Winston to reinforce this feeling but he can't help me. For me she is still alive. I cannot describe to you the horror of the moment when I managed to put through a call to my father and I spoke only to him.
>
> It would appear to me that I truly did love my mother with a passion, and I cannot perceive that there will be no more funny stories to tell, no more Yiddish songs to listen to, and no more unconditional love.
>
> . . . I had decided very recently that I needed a drastic change in my appearance. I couldn't endure any longer the

sight of that sad, old face staring back at me every time I looked in a mirror (an unhappy person tailing me constantly); so, prompted by your letter, I went to CARITA yesterday afternoon where I had all my hair shorn off. I paid much money to look as I tried not to, at the age of 15. When I returned home W. fainted, and still stares at me with an infuriatingly bewildered look . . .

I did not contact anyone for quite a long time after my return. For some reason I did not feel like seeing anyone who was not part of my life prior to August. Berjulie Press has been in Paris and of course it was a treat for both of us to see her. I am only sorry that at that stage I was still suffering from delayed shock which had left me feeling numb.

Another letter to David veers between the consolations of Paris and the 'inwardness' of recent shock:

Paris is, well, it is difficult to describe to you how much we get out of living here. It's the visual aspect of the city which appeals to us the most. Of course I am isolated because of the language but I feel rather inward so people really are an intrusion . . . I must admit that I have postponed telephoning Daddy because in some strange way the fact the Mommy can't speak to me gets through to me in a most incredible way. But enough of that.

Grief matures slowly. This phase, more painful in its way, began in February as Romy studied. She was due to sit an examination for UNISA in Private Law after a course which she had carried through in her offhand way.

Paris.
20 February 1975

Dearest David,
    . . . This period has been a very disturbing one because

of the memories it evoked. Whenever I opened a book to
study I would smell Cape Town, summer, mommy, 237
High Level Road.

These feelings I can only share with you, because
Winston has never known or been part of that era. No
matter how understanding he is or tries to be, it's not the
same. When I used to be moaning & groaning & generally
feeling sorry for myself I knew that mommy would hear
me and come up to my room. And sure enough, with
monotonous regularity, I would hear the bed creak and
then her footsteps up the stairs. It was very comforting.
She was honest enough to tell me when I was studying in
Johannesburg in '72 that 'Tanks God' I was in
Johannesburg and not in Cape Town.

. . . Please, please write soon. I really do need to hear
from you.

   <u>Romy</u>

For some reason, Romy disapproved of the further study that
she and Winston had undertaken. Perhaps it was the subject, the
form of Roman-Dutch law practised in South Africa. She may
have thought they should never return. After the examination
she wrote to Bonnie:

Paris.

16 March 1975

Beloved friend,

I am ashamed to have to admit to you that Winston *and
I* both wrote UNISA examinations at the SA Embassy
towards the end of February.

Although I had no intention of doing so, somehow,
on 21st of February I found myself opening the
enormous dark green doors of our courtyard, sauntering
down passage de la Visitation with my law file under one
arm and catching the 63 bus which rolls along boulevard

Saint-Germain and into Quai d'Orsay.

Mr Botha, one of those smooth Afrikaners with an affected English accent, informed me that the key to the library had been lost and I would just have to wait.

The Embassy is a modern monstrosity which cost millions to construct and as I didn't feel like inspecting it I told him that he had to do something. Eventually the door was broken down. An hour after I began, surrounded by home-made chocolates and éclairs from my favourite patisserie, the lights fused.

Mevrou Marais, my blonde '*tzutzka*' [Yiddish for superfluous decorative object] invigilator, who 'yates Paris laike poison', said 'shame' so many times that at one point I was ready to ram my fist down her throat.

It's been snowing for the last 3 days. On Tuesday morning very early Winston shook me awake to see the fairy-tale picture from our window . . .

. . . We know many people now and socially we are quite active but really I am not interested in forming personal relationships. I miss you & am happy that you are corresponding with me. You & Berjulie are the only 2 of my South African friends who have bothered to write. It is important, Bonnie. I realize now that it is necessary to share experiences even if the only available medium is via letters. Somehow my other friends seem to be very remote at the moment – and it's a pity!

   Your loving friend,
      Romy.

Towards the end of the Easter vacation, we visited Paris for the second time. In six months, Romy had integrated. She took us to a party where we were the only foreigners. The chic hosts were gracious, but we were bores. We couldn't speak French and looked dull in our English woollies. I felt that Romy had to put up with me for old-time's sake, and that it was bad of me to be sleepy at 9.30 and ask to be returned to passage de la Visitation, while Romy dashed off to hear the latest songster – I didn't bother to hear the name.

'I don't know why I like you,' she said rather crossly as she accompanied me along the rue de l'Université to find where Eliot had lived in 1911.

That spring, Romy and Winston began to tour France in their second-hand car. 'In April', she wrote to Bonnie,

a French colleague of Winston's insisted that we stay with a friend of his in the Loire Valley. When we arrived and saw a chateau, we knew we had made a mistake and W. asked to use the telephone. In fact, it *was* the place and for the first time, Bonnie, I wished that I had sewn up the gaping holes in the armpits of my coat, instead of always being so lackadaisical. In addition to us, the Marquis had invited 3 young Parisians with whom we have become very friendly. He told us that in 1946, when Elizabeth & Philip were planning to visit La France, the police, for reasons of security, arrested the representative of the Haganah in Paris and found the name of the Marquis in his jacket. They raided the chateau and discovered 25 sub-machine-guns in his cellar. He spent the following 11 months in prison. We slept in a room which was one entire turret of the castle. Magnificent tapestries and Old Masters dripped from the walls. In the evenings, we dined in the main dining-room through which the tourists traipsed during the day & had coffee in the room in which Louis XII at the age of 68 had first set eyes on Anne of England (17 years) and tried to seduce her.

In May we visited the South of France & the Côte d'Azure. Everything we saw was extraordinarily beautiful except the Côte d'Azure. It's highly commercialized and the beaches are simply odious compared to Clifton.

Using the Michelin Guide we managed to find

charming auberges with 1 or 2 star cuisine where we
would spend a few nights at a time. Part of the pleasure of
that trip were the taste sensations. We have been to one or
2 top-class restaurants in Paris, but nothing here compares
to the cuisine in the Campagne.

I have become friendly with an Indian model who
works for Pierre Cardin & shall be going to the next show
at her invitation. We all have the same problems. Her
mother is having a nervous breakdown because she isn't
married.

Later that summer, Mr Gevint visited Romy in Paris.
She wrote to David that she found it hard to believe that
he was almost seventy because 'to me, daddy had always
personified eternity. I was so moved when I saw his
Chaplinesque figure that I crashed through the customs
barrier to hug him (pursued by the inevitable customs
official) and was greeted by "Why is your hair so
funny?" . . . He left after 4 days because W. & I bored him.
I felt so rejected that I resorted to infantile behaviour
altho' I had vowed not to – but he wouldn't respond.'

Mark, too, arrived in Paris but, in Romy's phrase,
'declined gracefully' to see her. She and Winston reassured
each other that they could have met Mark 'now that our
relationship is so stable'. Romy wished to see him 'because
I like him' and Winston because he had 'a healthy
curiosity to meet the person who had had such a profound
influence over my life and emotions. But I suppose it is
never to be.'

While Winston was in Denmark, she caught a train,
alone, to Versailles. After watching the sunset, she listened
to a chamber group, with a young flautist, playing Bach in
the marble courtyard beneath the bedroom windows of
Louis XIV. As the candles fluttered and the music soared,
she thought she would 'simply burst from both joy and
pain and disintegrate into little pieces'.

In August 1975, we left Oxford and returned to New York, Siamon to a post at Rockefeller, I to one at Columbia. To see, again, steamy streets, heaps of garbage, and the crazed homeless, was like return-ing to prison. In Bloomingdales on a Saturday afternoon, I had a surreal impression of over-dressed, glassy-eyed matrons, locked into a glittering front of chokers, bracelets, and great hooped earrings. They advanced on their buys in a kind of phalanx.

'It was like a nightmare – I ran out of the store,' I confided to Professor Syracuse.

'Look, it's great – you have to see that New York is just a great show,' said Professor Syracuse, gesticulating with widened eyes and parted hands. 'It's a wunnerful carnival.'

Columbia's lack of communication made it clear that I was now a faceless functionary whose services had been bought for a price. On landing from England, I paged curiously through the Bulletin to discover what classes I was to teach in a week or two when the students arrived.

'You mustn't care,' was the advice of other junior members of the faculty. 'You're a gonner if you care. There's no justice in this game. Play it cool.'

In December, Siamon and Anna went ahead to Cape Town while I flew via Paris. On waking, Romy opened the long win-dows, and we looked out together at the pearly shades of a winter dawn, the vast, sleeping city with buildings in perfect proportion to the human scale, and an expanse of sky which freed the senses from the shafts of Manhattan. We drank pungent coffee in the kitchen at the back of the apartment. There was an old tree at the window, and I gazed through its bare branches at the slanting roofs as we caught up on the last few months: my initiation into an embattled department where half the faculty did not speak to the other half; Romy's 'bursting' moment at Versailles.

Next day, as the plane crept down the map of Africa, the sky grew ever wider and bluer: this was my sky, and as I saw again the great mountains and valleys of the Cape, I said a prayer of thanks for having survived to see this once more.

Unexpectedly, Romy and Winston came to Cape Town two weeks later, in January. She was with her father, and I saw little of her. Once, amongst a bevy of visitors in my mother's garden, I caught a look of impatience. She was pale that day, even a little gaunt under a wide silk scarf binding her head. I did not know that she was pregnant.

When the time came to return to New York, she came with Phillippa to say goodbye. It was mid-morning, and as we looked out of the windows at the ripening fruit of the bent fig tree, turning its large, flat leaves to the sun as it climbed strongly above Signal Hill, the years meant nothing. We shed layers of accreted event. It was as though the trials of our twenties – Romy's loves, Phillippa's deaths, my exile – fell away as we dreamed of meeting on the coast of Brittany. Then they left, and I never saw Romy again.

She spent the last days of the holiday in Johannesburg with Berjulie and Rosie Kunene. There was a stopover on the tropical island of Mauritius in the Indian Ocean en route to Paris. Almost at once Phillippa arrived from London to join Romy in Paris, 'talking, talking over cups of coffee in cafés which had witnessed intensity of friendships', firing Romy's 'gift for reaching one's soul'. So, Phillippa set the scene. On the Friday, Romy didn't feel too well. Not ill, really – on Saturday night Winston took them for a drive along the Seine – but on Monday she went into the American hospital. A precaution, the doctor said. Then it was pneumonia. When this did not yield to the usual treatment, she was moved to a hospital for respiratory disease, the best in France. There she died. She was ill, in all, three days.

On the day of Romy's death, Mark phoned Leonora. He was 'demented with grief. He couldn't talk. His wife had been immobilized since 1971 with postpartum depression. Her mother and sister took possession of the child, and she felt a mere vehicle. In Mark there was this rage at the cruelty of life.'

*

Beatrice, who worked for Berjulie, phoned Rosie Kunene. Rosie
fainted. 'When I wake up, Mrs Basson took me to Mrs Press. And
I couldn't talk,' she said shaking her head, with lips pressed: '– m, –
m, – mmmm.'

Winston has built Rosie a house. When he returns to South
Africa, he visits her, and when he comes, she cries. In '89, he
phoned in advance to beg her: 'Please, Rosie, don't cry this time.'

Rosie said: 'I can't – when I see him, I remember Romy and
her jokes.'

'I cry for Romy', Phillippa wrote. 'I cry for Winston and I self-
ishly cry for myself and my loss. At first when it happened, I
hated Paris. But you can't hate Paris. I thought of all the joy it had
given Romy and I am consoled by the fact that Romy got so
much out of life. That she always did all she wanted to do. And
she never compromised.'

A few months later, that same year, 1976, two hundred and
twenty-one American Legionnaires met at a convention in
Philadelphia, and with shocking speed thirty-four died. When
Legionnaire's disease, as it came to be called, was identified,
Siamon said, 'the bacteria lurk in stagnant water in unclean air-
conditioners. There would have been air-conditioners in the hotel
where Romy stayed in Mauritius. It's a possibility, you know, that
she caught Legionnaire's disease and brought it back with her to
Paris. It would explain why she died so fast.'

'Would it have helped had the doctors known?'

'Yes. The right antibiotic, erythromycin, taken in time, could
have saved her.'

In 1990, I sat with Winston on a Sunday morning in his apartment on the outskirts of Paris, in Neuilly-sur-Seine. He said:
'There were tough years. We were working towards a solution. I
was convinced that it would work – I could get her, get something
back. She was convinced – too much – that all was well. She

wanted to have a child, but we weren't ready – Romy wasn't ready to be a mother. When she got ill, the pregnancy had been confirmed only a couple of weeks. Her death was – a catastrophe. We had spent so many years trying so hard to achieve something, thought we'd achieved it, and it went out like a fucking candle.'

11

Memories

It was a Friday in February, and a pallid sun had emerged for the afternoon. The Humanities course had reached the end of the Middle Ages with *Sir Gawain and the Green Knight*, and next week would begin the sixteenth century with Montaigne and Shakespeare. To celebrate the end of the week, I bought, as usual, cheese at Mama Joy's and flowers at the fruit store on 110th and Broadway, and was carrying a great bunch of daffodils when Siamon met me at the door of our apartment, in the Rockefeller faculty block, on York Avenue and 63rd. From the silent way he led me towards a seat, I knew something had happened. I don't remember the blow of Romy's death, only incomprehension, a blank refusal to believe this, as I lay back against the brown corduroy chair in the featureless apartment-box suspended on the twenty-third floor, while the traffic went on blasting round the corner onto the Franklin Delano Roosevelt Drive.

As February turned into March, the disbelief that had been fortified by distance began to crumble before the daily awakening to the fact of death. I began to scribble the odd scrap as a form of relief:

March 1976: I lie awake in the early hours, remembering one detail of the past after another and feeling that a part of those of us who shared our youth with Romy will die with her. Life will not be the same again, ever, now she is gone. It is not so much the shock of the death of someone so piercingly alive that is so devastating as the days and weeks that follow, as one is gradually forced to accept it. It is still breaking and breaking on my mind which at first could not take it in.

In that month following Romy's death I had a recurrent dream. It lingered, so live and active, that I wrote it down:

March 1976: In my dream, Phillippa and I are going up a flight of stairs with Romy, to have a last cup of coffee before she is buried. On the way up these stairs, she asks me, half-joking, if I cannot find some way to stave off her burial, and there is the most frightful sense of helplessness. Then she lies with her head in my lap. The light coming through the trees outside the windows plays on her face. She desperately doesn't want to die, but at the last moment – this is just before I wake – we suddenly relax, despite it all, into a familiar state of rapport.

Couldn't I make Romy live again by writing about her in some way?

Those early mornings with Romy – bobbing in the wavelets; lying on the burning ledge on the High Level Road, daring to shout to the sky 'we want, we want . . .'; Mad Friday, with Romy's red hair jerking above the mike to the screams of the girls; bopping at the El Morocco when Romy kept her bargain with

God; the saviour arriving in New York in her miniskirt and white
bonnet; Romy saying that she could not go through with the
wedding, and her dismay to hear that 'you can't do that to
Krafchik' – brought back the intense reality of the past in contrast
with the unreality of the present: the dinning in my ear of words
like 'star' and 'fame'. 'Fame is the spur,' said Professor Syracuse
solemnly when I asked why he put himself through agonies of
ambition when his publications had been justly admired.

Two days after Romy's death, I went to Columbia for an early-
evening lecture on Edith Wharton. It was given by Wanda Getty,
who posed as liberated but ignored women in the department.
Fixated on the top males, she swam up to them along the corridor on the fourth floor of Hamilton Hall, lifting her eyelids in
helpless appeal. With them, she practised old-fashioned promis-
cuity. Her writing, on the other hand, vented the latest platitudes
of women's power. These contradictions confused men, and perhaps herself. As one teacher put it, with the punch of New York,
'I'm never sure if she's gonna stroke my prick or cud't off.' Her
mobile mouth poured out words and rounded them with lavish
gesture. Her eyes widened and sparkled with energetic animation.
But the torrent of words had nothing to say. There was nobody
behind those open gestures and wide blue eyes. To the audience
this did not matter. Since she took care to press modish critical
buttons – 'freedom . . . feminism . . . Freud . . . the anxiety of
influence' – the ovation was automatic.

Going home, I shared a cab with Professor Syracuse. As we
entered Central Park, he gave a loud groan.

'What is it?'

'I am dying, Egypt, dying.'

I laughed.

He gave me a long, hurt look. It occurred to me that he might
expect to be seduced – a consolation for falling greatness.
According to this scenario, I should initiate the action and – it
came in a flash – take the blame. The drama was fraught with subtleties beyond my experience. There was a plea for compassion

and an unstated reminder of what I owed to this man who had backed my work with generosity. But why this need? He had an attractive and selfless wife with exceptional gifts of understanding. As though on cue, he explained.

'By nature, I'm polygamous.' He said this proudly, as a fact of manliness.

I said to him silently (but he was too wrapped up in himself to hear): 'I admire you as an academic, but as a man you are a disappointment, for at this moment almost any available woman would do.' Aloud, I said: 'There's Adrienne Rich reading at the Y. Would you like to go?'

He gave me a you-can't-be-serious look. 'No, I *wouldn't* like to go.'

'I'll go on my own, then.'

There was an uncomfortable silence. I felt a moment's compunction as the cab swung out of the Park at 67th: I was not indifferent to him.

'Can you tell me what's bothering you?' I asked gently.

He put his head in his hands and groaned again. 'I don't know.'

I had an idea. 'Can it be the Celestial City?'

'That's it, I guess.' He looked at me in soulful reproach. 'No one is *ever* going to help. Nothing I do will *ever* be enough.'

With that, he dropped me at the Y. The cab turned round and plunged down the Avenue, and was soon lost in the dazzle of the mid-town lights, bearing him on his path to adultery. I had no doubt that he would find a Wanda, and find her quick. For a man of such consuming sorrows, any boost would do.

Professor Syracuse nursed a coterie of devotees who were bowled over by the scale of his emotions. Others called him 'the Hamlet of Riverdale' – Riverdale being the bland suburb where his forgiving wife typed his packed, bravura prose, while she awaited his erratic returns.

With Romy's death came a new sense of time:

I am at the age, thirty-four, when one notices that the

friends who, a few years ago, were lingering on campuses as
devotees of the ageing Hamlets who were our professors, are
themselves ageing: the lines about the eyes, the realization
that one may not bear another child; and then, if someone,
a father, a schoolfriend, dies, the crystal of childhood
detaches from the continuum and assumes the shape of time
past. Death releases the past. When Romy died this year,
Romy who was so exuberant and funny, the '50s and '60s
seemed to seal off with her life.

Now that Romy was no more, there were days when her head-
long existence came at me with an immense, an overwhelming
force. I taught my classes on Montaigne, *Hamlet* and *Lear*, living in
the past with Romy as well as in the past of literature, and it happened that the two began to merge. What I read brought out
Romy; Montaigne's essay 'Of Experience' gave what she said,
and what she lived more than said, a new lustre. It was as though
she went on speaking through the challenge of Montaigne: 'What,
have you not lived?' It was Romy's question. It was this challenge
that had driven her existence, like the force that through the green
fuse drives the flower. It was this question that she had conveyed
at Saranac Lake in the summer of '71 when I shut off to write; and
again, in the outdoor cafés of Paris, with intent talk and lovers
kissing in the late summer of '74. And, carelessly, not listening
very hard, I had returned to Oxford to another academic year. But
now, Romy gone, there lay before me, as before the freshmen of
Columbia College, the full challenge of her alternative: 'What,
have you not lived? That is not only the fundamental but most
illustrious of your occupations . . . To compose our character is
our duty, not to compose books . . . Our great and glorious masterpiece is to live appropriately.'

What was it to 'live'? Professor Syracuse who taught with
arresting vitality claimed to be 'dying . . . dying'. It was not altogether a ploy. For are we not all dying? From the moment of our
conception we are on course for death. Life is what we do with

the time that beats this course. We might measure out our lives with coffee spoons or, as Wanda the Wide-Eyed WASP, a succession of one-night stands. Romy, at least, had her moments – her rhythmic laughter ringing louder than the school bell, her scream at Mark nine thousand miles away, the span of stars at Vryburg when she slept with Winston, and her closeness to Phillippa on the balcony, with the salt of the sea in the sharp Cape air, before Robert called for his cricket togs.

But how to convey that 'life'? Dr Johnson could be relied on to warn the foolhardy who attempt the impossible: a pulsating vein of living moments in place of the plod from pedigree to grave: '. . . The incidents which give excellence to biography are of a volatile and evanescent kind, such as soon escape the memory . . .' Thus Dr Johnson, in the *Rambler* on 13 October 1750. As memories rose in the wake of my dream, they seemed random and too insignificant to share. The public life leaves behind its purpose in the form of poems, sheets of music, journeys, battles won or lost. The private life secretes a point of its own. 'I have often thought', Dr Johnson said, 'that there has rarely passed a life of which a judicious and faithful narrative would not be useful.' But how to find a use in the lives of the obscure; how to observe through memory alone what Wordsworth called with enviable ease 'the ties/That bind the perishable hours of life/Each to the other . . .' so that Romy's life might be sustained?

That year, I began to read Virginia Woolf's papers in the Berg Collection. It was safer to study writers' lives, with their public achievements and tangible records. Meanwhile, Siamon was elected to a Readership at the Sir William Dunn School of Pathology in Oxford. We returned to England in September 1976.

It was a year of divides: an end with Columbia, the departure from America and, brooding over this, the divide of death. Because it was usual to be apart from Romy, full awareness of that divide had yet to come. To forestall it by writing of her seemed, at this stage, impossible in so far as she had been part of a South Africa I could no longer presume to know. That country of the past had never seemed so distant, so abhorrent, as police opened fire on schoolchildren who were resisting the regime in Soweto. To point guns at black children seemed to point towards a future in which racial divides would widen to an irreconcilable and anarchic end: black power that might prove as uncompromising and brutal as the white power it now opposed. Even more damaging could be the purposelessness and mental debasement that must be the fruit, in the next generations, of Verwoerd's policy of minimal education for blacks in his Bantu Education Act of 1953.

Back in England, at a gaudy at St Hilda's, I met a poet, Jenny Joseph. After leaving the College in the mid-'50s, she had taught at the Central Indian High School in Johannesburg, and worked for *Drum*, the popular magazine for black readers. In 1959 she was deported. During her futile efforts to discover the basis of her expulsion, she became aware of a fog of suspicion, rumour, and aspersion – 'an acquaintance had always suspected that one of my acquaintance was a police informer: had I considered the possibility of . . . and perhaps I had better look into . . .'. She resolved not to give way, she said, to 'that network of fearful minds on which a corrupt police state depends and that is more sickening really than the laws and methods that bring it into being. This aspect of the situation in South Africa has always interested me – the great damage people do to themselves because of what is done to them. This is the inevitable result of bad laws: they make bad men.'

'Have you read "Africa Emergent",' I asked, 'the last of Nadine Gordimer's *Selected Stories*? She explores with extraordinary acumen this fog of suspicion amongst blacks and whites who defy apartheid – she sees that subtler tragedy that you experienced: the warping of defiance as it becomes infected with the very thinking it defies.'

Jenny showed me her poem about a friend, an Englishwoman, who fell in love with a black man and despaired less of the law that forbade their tie than of the man himself. He did not treat her well. 'To a Friend, Dead in Africa' spoke to the guilt I felt as an expatriate for the paltriness of this distant existence, and the widening of a divide that words could not cross:

> . . . I see deserted shores round Africa
> White and too hot to touch, and from this softness
> I pray to God that you have found your peace.
> . . . We live here with the decencies of an age
> That mute the words for praise and other passions
> Along with crudity, or I would try
> To shout a sonorous dirge for you . . .*

In January 1977 I made a brief visit to my mother, who complained that, thirteen years after my departure, my belongings still cluttered the drawers of the 'top' room, which had been occupied, intermittently, by my grandmother and which, as a child, I had shared with her. I could remember the warmth of her fragrant body in the double bed that had been her marriage bed, the snip-snap as she undid her corsets at night, and her copy of *Katherine* by Anya Seton, containing scenes which she judged unsuitable for a girl of twelve. She used to lock it at the top of her tall wardrobe, unaware of a duplicate key that I used in her absence. Now, in '77, I unlocked the wardrobe and went through its drawers again: sum-books from King's Road Junior School, diaries from Good Hope, outgrown bathing costumes, limp and faded sun-hats, an almost empty jar of 'Metamorphosa' freckle-cream, and batches of letters – Romy's letters in 1959. Opening their careless folds, smoothing creases, I read them slowly. It was nearly twenty years ago: Romy's first year at varsity; Cowboy at Hout Bay; Rose and Linn at Herman's twenty-first; Johan in the rose-garden; Ben at the drive-in. The letters had the breath of the past upon them. Virginia Woolf spoke of letters as 'the unpublished works of

---

*Jenny Joseph, *Rose in the Afternoon and Other Poems* (London: Dent, 1974), p. 66.

women'. Here was part of Romy's unpublished life – could I find and imagine the rest?

With the discovery of possible records, however tenuous and minimal, I scribbled more scraps. Since Rose figured in the diaries, it occurred to me that she belonged in the story. 'Romy and Rose' I headed the next scrap, undated, but probably written at the beginning of '77:

> Neither, perhaps, should have married – there *were* no men in our closed group who could have brought out whatever did not reflect the requirements of male pride. Yet as products of the '50s, an unmarried life was unimaginable. They were instinctively free, yet conformist to a degree that astonished me. Both were painstaking about their society, took care not to offend its norms, in fact reinforced them. I must write about their school-days when they were – with me, I believe – most themselves. I shall 'possess' them, I suppose.

'Men here have very high standards,' Pip said one evening as the family sat in my mother's garden. Discussion had turned to a certain young cousin, and her inability to attract the appropriate husband.

'If you mean appearance, I think she's lovely,' I said.

Uncle Louis shook his head. 'She has to lose at least ten pounds and throw away her favourite sun-dress with gathers around the hips.' He spoke with a leisurely assurance which evoked that woman-making ground that Rose and Romy contrived to cross. They crossed it with a generation of women who took decades to recover their old selves. Before their eyes, dinning in their ears, were a set of definitions of womanliness which they adopted, using their flair for surrender as mere adaptability. Rose had awareness, Romy 'empathy', but these they dissipated, too often, on the requisite image that turned Fruma into Romy, Rosie into Rosabelle, her satiric streak painted out by layers of Moonglow foundation with 'Tiger-stripe highlights' about the eyes:

January 1977: Flora and Rosie were obscure growths of post-colonial South Africa. As such, I was part of them, they of me, and I want to claim that part. I am the divided relic of these friends, and feel the footsteps of their lives in mine.

February 1977: Romy did things abruptly, and that was how she died. There was no preparation – her sudden marriage; her sudden arrivals or departures from New York. Without due notice, one's responses were not aligned. She could move with dramatic swiftness into place – others went more slowly, so that the unreality, common in death, has persisted. Even now (a year later) her death is simply not true. I still expect a sudden appearance, a call, and the sound of her breathy laugh.

February 1977: 'Pointless.' She turned with quickening interest. Quickness was her gift: she seized a whole way of thinking from a murmur, heard the unspoken, and sometimes in her eagerness tore through the veils of silence.

September 1977: Did I support my Romy too long? Longer than she wished to be that Romy? Vicariously, from the comforts of marriage, I partook in her freedom, and ignored its price. When, in the end, she did marry, I neglected to write. She died soon after. But our friendship was only flickering, for the Romy I'd known seemed to have disappeared – as girls of the '50s disappeared into marriage. (Marriage, that is, as the closed commitment we took it to be.) Her husband would no doubt tell a different story. Mine is about independence. My Romy is the 11-year-old with corkscrew hair who bounced up amongst the cowed girls on the first day of school and demanded to know – in her unashamed accent – who we were.

Seven years passed. We had a second child, Olivia. From 1977 to

1984 I tutored here and there, mostly at Jesus College. The prospect of a permanent post grew dim: I was never short-listed. Dame Helen disapproved of these applications – and if she thought I did not have the learning to be an academic, she was right. She had another objection. Trapped in a car from London to Oxford, I had to sit through a dressing-down about feminism, which she disliked. It was personally so abrasive that I stared out of the window, unable to speak. After that, we did not meet for some years. Then, in November 1984, she telephoned immediately after I had participated in a 'Bookmark' programme on Virginia Woolf.

'I don't care for Virginia Woolf,' said the forthright voice, without preamble, 'but would you come for tea next Sunday? You might help me to sort my books.'

Sunday, when it came, proved too sunny to be indoors. Dame Helen decided that I might do better to prune her rose-bushes. She had no wish to hear that I had no idea what to do. While Olivia, aged six, raced a wheelbarrow up and down the path, Dame Helen leant on her stick, watching closely where I cut; then she tapped the stick impatiently, saying in exasperated tones: 'No, NO! Lower down!'

By 1984, I was back at St Hilda's, which had given me what, in my forties, I no longer expected: a proper post. By then St Hilda's was one of two remaining colleges in Oxford which reserved its posts for women. Overall, the number of these had shrunk by the early '80s. The colleges which 'went mixed' had appointed, as expected, a succession of men. In the Senior Common Room of a college which had been mixed for ten years but, in all this time, had appointed only one woman to a fellowship, I overheard in 1983: 'Undergraduate women seem to perform as well as men but, of course, when you get to the top of the tree, men are best.' It had the mild sound of long agreement.

In the course of many tutorials, it happened, again, that Romy emerged from certain texts. She empathized with 'moments of being' in Virginia Woolf. She retreated before the absurd, relentless pressure of Mrs Bennet with her five unmarried daughters, or lent the resonance of her scream to the stifled one of Marianne Dashwood, who could not integrate the demands of passion with those of decorum. 'And what the dead had no speech for, when living, /They can tell you, being dead.' She had this continued presence. I heard her footsteps as I stopped to look over Magdalen Bridge, leaning my bicycle against the wall, or as I lifted my head in the middle of a tutorial to look through the window, or presented women for degrees in the Sheldonian: '*insignissime vice-cancellarie, vosque egregii procuratores, praesento vobis has meas scholares in facultate artium ut admittantur ad gradum baccalaurei in artibus.*' Bowing to the Vice-Chancellor and the Proctors, I saw Miss Hulston in the still, heavy heat, and felt the dreaming languor of girls of sixteen in the Good Hope classroom of 1958. Yes, I was getting to know Romy better than in the course of her life. She came closer as old lines swerved from their context. Tennyson, keeping faith with Hallam, showed how to hold to the dead as they pass through the frames of those who live on:

> Whatever way my days decline
>   I felt and feel, though left alone,
>   His being working in my own,
> The footsteps of his life in mine.

Could any act of reciprocity give back to Romy what she did for me? She invented her friends, made us up, endowed us with qualities that were congenial to her. This was the source of her attraction. She gave to each what each most needed. Since I was plain and freckled, she gave me, at sixteen, a charge of confidence. Since Phillippa, at twenty-eight, was blighted by death, she infused a continued surge of life. When Bonnie thought of suicide, she taught her to dwell in the moment of being. When Ellie got lonely and drank, despairing of a succession of feeble men who sapped her vehemence, Romy restored her to clarity. In Winston, the Springbok, she awakened a depth he did not realize he possessed. All of us she urged to play our parts in character. But could we do this for her? Could we find her in that elusive 'between' in which women of our generation lived? How do we divine the language of the sigh or the scream or that state of pure happiness that we called, delightedly, 'hysteria'? There will be, I thought, no path to follow. There will be no easy truth. It will be an imaginary meeting of divided halves: the biographer and the subject, the living and the dead. There is no essential truth and no end to truth. Biographic objectivity is an illusion: that voluminous 'Definitive Life' favoured by publishers is but a shell. For the only approach to a living truth is, on the basis of fact, to imagine the life – which is to take it to the border of fiction.

In 1984 I sketched a sequence of chapters for a memoir of Romy and Rose, and tried out a version of the school scene in Chapter One. Then I put it away, and went on with the kind of biography I knew how to do. Three years later, as I completed a last chapter, I broke off to walk to the lake at Saranac. It was the summer of 1987, but I was back in the '50s and '60s. The memories were irresistible – Granny asking 'Why didn't you marry him?', Mad Friday, and communal cheating. I launched into Chapter One – nine pages. 'Why is friendship not more definite?' I wrote in a scrappy aside. 'Why doesn't it leave something more tangible than Romy's coffee-grinder on a shelf in the kitchen and a cook-book with an inscription – "Remember this afternoon as I shall, always"? How little relationships matter unless we compose them. Then the past expands and Romy becomes complete as she could never be in the present. I see her substance in her absence. If I let Romy take shape in my mind, will she go on existing in some form? Can memory take the more durable form of biography? But it is all so tenuous – I let go, and she dissipates like sands blown by the tearing south-easter.'

The phone rang. There was the rush of distance, then Ellie's voice. It was June 1984. Intercontinental calls were not our practice – I knew before she spoke that something was wrong.

'Ellie?'

'Lyndall . . .' she sighed.

'Ellie! What is it?'

'I'm . . . sick. Metastases.'

'What's that?' My heart was pounding.

'I found a lump when I examined my breast. It was small. I had a test at once and . . . it was malignant. My doctor said I had caught it early – he was hopeful. I had radical surgery. But now, oh God, there are secondaries – at the base of the skull. When I went to Groote Schuur for new tests, the technician – who had been encouraging the first time – said, "Not you, Ellie, not you". She didn't pretend, and that's how I want it. No barrier of false hope. I don't want this to distort my relationships with you or anyone. So, I'm telling you straight. And I'm saying, straight, that I want to live; I'll do anything to live. Now, I'm coming to London. There's a specialist, Mr Mayhew, a world authority in this field, and my father has offered to pay. It may be useless, but I can't afford not to take every chance.'

'Ellie, I'll go with you – will you let me go with you?'

'That's what I want. I can't go alone. Be with me when he tells me – whatever he has to tell me.'

In July we sat holding hands in the taxi as it rocked through London, then out through miles of suburbs – half an hour, three-quarters – the journey seemed to go on and on. Ellie was clear and composed. I thought her tremendously brave as she walked unsteadily but resolutely from test to test. I held her coat. They were busy with her; there was no time for talking. Then we were in the last room waiting, with others, for the opinion of the great man. Almost at once, they called her and, as she got carefully to her feet, she gave my hand a trembling squeeze. I waited: now, now, she was hearing the sentence – 'life or death, life or death, life or death,' my heart beat. How could she bear it?

She came out smiling. He had offered a reprieve: this new treatment they were trying at the Royal Marsden. It would take weeks, it would be nasty – it would attack the female hormones that, in theory, promoted the cancer – but worth a try. The waiting taxi rocked back to the Green Park Hotel where Ellie had her thimble room. The flowers sprang up in Hyde Park; the boats on the Serpentine bobbed happily in thin English light. To celebrate, we went to a Tandoori restaurant, near the hotel, with Ellie stopping every few paces to rest.

She did not appear ill, except when she walked. Her light eyes were brilliant, her creamy-brown skin smooth as ever. She was beautiful, with her pointed chin and silky brown hair cut in a straight fringe across her eyes.

'Have you washed your hair?' I asked idly.

'It's a wig. The chemotherapy affected my own hair – a lot fell out. Then Mr Hugo, my hairdresser, made this wig in my style and I go each week as usual – to have it combed.'

She looked coolly elegant in her well-cut suit and Italian shoes. Her touches of make-up were discreet.

'No one seeing you now would guess what you've been through,' I said.

Ellie smiled a little wanly. 'Last night, when I had a drink before dinner, a businessman chatted me up. He was pleasant. He wanted to sleep with me. What would he have said if I'd told the truth: "I can't make love because I may be dying."'

'Ellie . . .'

'Forget it. Let's drink to the future. I'm refurnishing my consulting-room: white chairs and a furry white rug. It should be calm, comfortable, and not too clinical.'

'Do you find it hard to end a session? I find it difficult to bring a tutorial to an end. The hour often ends at the very point when discussion is getting somewhere.'

As Ellie warmed to her favourite subject – psychology – I wondered why she went on alone. As long as I had known her, she'd had a man – worldly men who travelled abroad and knew their wines. There had been lovers: she spoke of men, now and then, not with the urgency of Romy, nor the flippancy of Rose, but matter-of-factly, as a psychologist might survey some necessity for complete well-being. There had been men who wished to marry her but though she wanted marriage in the abstract, she resisted it in practice. We used to assure each other that work was crucial. It was obvious that her patients absorbed her attention. Yet, according to Bonnie and Phillippa, Ellie's sexual ties damaged her.

'You don't know Ellie,' Phillippa said later on her white balcony. 'You came so seldom. With you she could be perfect – the Ellie who was intelligent and compassionate, not the Ellie who got involved with hopeless men. While she was a student there was James, the first and best: a businessman who admired her academic side and encouraged her materialistic side: the need for ten imported pairs of shoes. That it ended was her father's fault. She had an almost obsessive attachment to Mr Ben-Ari, who rated his brainy Elisheva at her true value. He thought a businessman not good enough for his daughter. When James asked Ellie to go with him to England, Mr Ben-Ari said she must refuse. In England, Ellie's brother spotted James with another woman; it probably meant nothing at all, but was presented to Ellie as a sign she should never see James again. So began the years alone. I've found a letter that Romy wrote me from Johannesburg in 1966 – in it she compares herself with Ellie . . . here it is . . . page 3:

> . . . The difference between us is that by making a life for myself I have achieved a measure of independence – so that to be married is not the be-all & end-all. Ellie is waiting around at home for marriage. She wants it so badly that she clutches onto relationships and becomes so intense that they inevitably turn sour.
>
> You say that Ellie's wants are so simple, a husband, a little house, children. But, Phillippa, this is the trouble – the need has become exaggerated out of proportion – a man's become the means to this end.

'In the late '60s, you remember, there was Jos. He was a good sort, kind to Ellie . . .'

'But rather dull,' I interposed, 'a pleasant companion for gourmet dinners. Sweet, of course.'

'No, he was clever,' said Phillippa, 'but he didn't present well.'

'He had this slow, plodding manner.'

'Yes,' Phillippa admitted. '"Point one . . . point two . . . point
three . . ." Do you know, he told me it was impossible to find his
ideal woman.'

'And all those years, he dined out with Ellie,' I said, 'and all that
time, lived safely with his mother.'

'Afterwards, in the mid-'70s, she went to Jo'burg where she
took up industrial psychology,' Phillippa went on. 'This is the
part you don't know: she began to be crazy in her thirties. She
went out with the left-overs, honestly – the dregs – and she'd put
up with them, and make much of them, and let them destroy her.
Then she would drink, and there would be scenes. She became
impossible.'

'Then, she would call for help,' said Bonnie.

'One night, she phoned at 2 a.m.,' said Peter. 'Bonnie and I
were asleep. Down the line, Ellie was crying. A man was pointing
a gun at her. "He's going to kill me," she cried. "Come *quickly*." I
flung out of our house in Parktown, hunted down the obscure
address, and knocked at the door. No one came, and I knocked
again. I could hear Ellie's cries and I thought, "As he opens the
door, he's going to kill me." But the door remained locked. Ellie's
cries grew louder. Then I turned and ran for the police: they said
their car was there already. I returned to the place to find the door
wide open, went in, and there, quiet now, Ellie sat chatting with
a man. "It was all a misunderstanding," Ellie explained and, dazed,
still shaken, I went back home.'

This, then, was the other side of not marrying at twenty-one.
The exhilarating side was Romy in her early twenties; on the
other side, a loneliness which work could not fill. I said: 'She did
race in her little car to and fro across the mountain, round Signal
Hill, round Lion's Head, to Clifton, to Hout Bay – to fill up the
spaces. She couldn't bear her loneliness – but who could bear it?

You'd have to be a saint. Ellie was made for talk, for contact, for communion.'

Yet in the long weeks of treatment in London, Ellie stood up to being alone in the most trying of circumstances: alone in a foreign country, alone with a dangerous illness, alone with fear and pain. Not once did her resolve flag. I was away for a week on a family holiday in the Outer Hebrides and, from the Isle of Harris, used to speak to Ellie on a pay phone that pipped every minute. The treatment was terrible, but she was determined to go through with it. Oh, she was brave in her thimble room.

The great specialist put Ellie through tortures of useless treatment, yet she wanted it. He was grandly unreachable when she was in agony at night, but she accepted it. She could not afford to waste energy on resentment. All her strength – and whatever crazy things she had done, her illness called out a pure strength – went into the will to live.

On my return, I found Ellie walking with more uncertainty. She leaned on my arm as she climbed, step by step, to the basement of Dillon's bookshop to look at psychology books. Ellie meant to go on with her practice. Of this, she spoke with confidence. But her voice wavered at the prospect of a return to Conan, a divorcee in his fifties, by all accounts a wailing baby who had succeeded in draining Ellie's reserves of professional understanding. He was given to jealous fantasies. If she went to a conference, there were scenes: moans, threats, and cunning questions. It would have been ridiculous had Ellie been less considerately attentive, had she not allowed herself to become entangled with this damaging creature. I had never seen Ellie upset before. She expressed more torment over Conan than cancer. And the two, it occurred to me, might not be unconnected.

In February 1985 I heard that Ellie was confined to bed and drugged. Conan had disappeared. Without her knowing it, Ellie's friends tried to reach him. They were going to beg him to relieve her, for the time that was left, of the additional stress of his

withdrawal. He was not to be found. His secretary said he had left
town 'for an indefinite period'.

I wrote to Ellie that I would come at the end of term. It was
mid-March when I opened the gate of her father's house in
Melrose Avenue, high on the pine slopes of Oranjezicht.
Although I was prepared for a change, it was a shock to see
Ellie without her wig. Her head was grey. She half-lay across the
bed, emaciated and clearly dying. In the days that followed, she
was sometimes dressed in her wheelchair, with wig in place and
elegant shoes on her feet; but often too drugged to talk. Katrina,
the nurse, made signs from behind Ellie's back, whirling her
index finger round her ear to indicate that Ellie had lost her wits.
Katrina had a relish for the minuter details of deterioration: she
spoke of these in triumphant whispers behind her hand at the
front door and all the way down the long, dark corridor to
Ellie's room, as though her triumph was to look at the ugliest
facts with a directness that anguished visitors could not muster.
Ellie herself treated Katrina with a grateful and almost effusive
politeness. A private nurse was hard to find, and Ellie, determined to stay at home, with her father, was exerting herself to
make the best of it.

She told a friend of a dream about Romy. They were at a
party, and everyone, including Romy, looked as usual – only,
Romy had sparkles between her lashes. She said, 'I came to tell
you that it's alright.'

I talked to Ellie of her work and, sometimes, she surfaced to
answer. The vigour convinced me that, behind the screen of
drugs, she took in everything – in fact, it often appeared that she
was studying it with almost professional detachment.

I said to her, on impulse: 'Ellie, are you writing a book – in
your head – about this experience?'

She nodded, emphatically. She held my hand with awareness as
though she was pleased that I knew. Her last words to me made it
explicit what the 'book' was about.

It was April 1985. I had brought her some soup and fed her

teaspoon by teaspoon. She was lucid, that evening, though very weak.

'You don't have to speak,' I said. 'If you go to sleep, I have a book to read.'

She lay very quiet, looking at me. Then she said: 'I have to face mortality.'

I shall not forget the calm tone of those words, nor my cowardice. She asked for honesty, but I could not meet her as she wished. I muttered some comforting lie, and changed the subject.

'Dying is creation . . .' says an explorer in a novel by Patrick White. At the last clear moment, Ellie wished to share her exploration of the mind as her body died. She was alert and interested, not – as I – unnerved, backing away, unable to face death. When my own time comes, I shall have nothing to say. 'I have to face mortality': those unshared words will always haunt me.

Long before, in the late '70s, I had told Ellie of my wish to write Romy's life. As we strolled between the oaks of the Avenue through the Gardens, we had not proceeded to speak of Romy. Phillippa, too, and Romy's brothers knew of the plan. But none of us spoke of Romy. And the years passed, and then Ellie was gone, and still we could not speak. It was as though we held back from an impossible mystery. They had mattered too much and died too soon, with gestures in mid-air and conversations unfinished. As I lived with the mystery of Romy, Rose, and Ellie, so others lived with these dead – but they were not necessarily the same dead. I began to wonder how far the Romy of my reading-life diverged from the Romy of Leonora with grown children on her distant farm in the Free State; the Romy of Berj and Hu still at Willow Stream; the Romy of Phillippa, who was putting cuisine to one side to devise 'street food' for a mixed populace in need of nutrition; and not least, the Romy of the men who had loved her: Ben with dry, evenly closed lips in his factory in London; Mark with a sad face in Johannesburg; and Winston in Paris.

The first outside information of this kind came from David Gevint, who arrived in Oxford in August 1985 with a batch of letters. We talked in the garden, between the rose creeper and tubs of geraniums, while Olivia swung under the apple tree. After he left, I wrote:

Oxford.
9 August 1985.

Dear David,

It was good to see you and, through you, to reach back and renew my friendship with Romy. You look like her, laugh like her, and tell stories in the same way – your Gevint-temper story of Romy's pestering you to carry her suitcase downstairs when you were still asleep at 6 in the morning until, suddenly, the full suitcase went flying out of the fourth-storey window of her Paris apartment, and a chastened you and Romy having to face the furious owner of the car on which the case had landed. And then the story of Ellie's eloquence at your house which led Feige to place her as a lesson to women who were 'too clever' for their own good. Siamon thought it was like a scene from Jane Austen who said that 'a woman, especially if she have the misfortune of knowing anything, should conceal it as far as she can'.

I shall treasure the letters that you brought: no gift could have meant more. I read them immediately after you left, and they brought her close – the humour and also the generosity when you were going through the divorce and she wrote that you were your mother's favourite child. How she loved you, David!

If you remember other Romy stories, I'd be grateful if you'd write them down. One idea, if I ever do this memoir, is to bring out her comic sense.

In 1988 I visited Paris and met Winston:

Paris, 7 April 1988: S. and I are here in the Hôtel de l'Abbaye, in the rue Cassette, on our 25th anniversary. Tentatively, after 12 years, we phoned Winston. The last time we spoke was when I phoned him from New York after Romy's death, and his sobs came so violently down the line that I thought for a moment he was laughing – it sounded like R's excited, gasping laugh. There was a reserve after these years of non-contact, compounded by my guilt for supporting R's resistance to marriage. I must ask Winston if he ever understood R's hatred of weddings. I think our rebellions did issue from the conformities of our S African Jewish roots: certain inflexible assumptions about women's roles in relation to men that were inseparable from their place in that most shuttered of communities. Remember Berjulie's injunction to R. and me: 'If you're not with us, you're against us.'

'But we love you,' Romy said, pleading, 'and you *do* love us.'

'Couldn't we compromise: have friends inside *and* outside the community?' I asked.

Berjulie was adamant. 'If you aren't heart and soul in the community, you won't belong.'

Personal feeling was overruled by group identification. When I pleaded on personal grounds for a relative who planned to marry out of the faith, my mother said, 'I have to think of history'.

'You will cast yourself out,' my mother told the girl.

'Only if you cast me out,' said the girl. It was the right answer, but it carried no weight.

The fixity of our group derived from the Covenant, and in another way from the Holocaust, but may have gained a measure of reinforcement from group obsessions in South Africa, at their elaborate height in the '50s and '60s. Taboos against intermarriage always had a rational basis; now, the more superfluous customs which, theoretically, should have been adjustable – say, the show wedding that Romy refused – became signs of obedience to the group. To Romy, forms that did not fit her feelings would have seemed coercive.

Winston looked much the same, still ruddy, vigorous, matter-of-fact, and assured. A man of sense; rather controlling. As we walked towards the restaurant through the Paris streets with the shadow of green hovering about the trees, it seemed artificial to avoid R.'s name.

We were talking of mothers.

Winston said, unexpectedly: 'My mother didn't like Romy.'

'Why?'

'It was Romy's attitude. She made that fuss when I offered to pay for Ingrid's wedding.'

'She had, of course, a thing about weddings.'

'Don't I know it,' he said with a flash of a smile. 'Remember our meeting at the airport? Your face told me there would be trouble.'

'What a feat to get hepatitis – the perfect excuse for calling off a wedding at the last moment.'

'It came, to be exact, two days after the cancellation. But that,' he went on, 'was another reason for my mother's dislike of Romy.'

'That she let you down?'

'Yes. And the fact that, for years, she couldn't bring herself to marry me.'

Paris. Last day: Sunday, 10 April 1988: Last night Winston brought Madeleine to meet us. She is tall, with a shapely Parisian haircut, and a dimple. She wore a silver top with a purple shawl, a silver necklace and earrings. Though seven or eight years younger than Romy, she is more mature. Her poise is not a mode of sophistication; it comes from a responsible nature. She revealed that her English father had

abandoned his family and that, by the age of 21, she was a
financial support – a harder school than Romy's. I gathered
that she saw her younger brother and sister through their
educations before she 'felt free to leave'. She dreamt, like all
S. Africans, of Europe, but unusually (since we had no
French at school) she chose to live in Paris. That brought her
to IBM at the end of '76, where she met Winston. She told
me this as we walked back from the bistro, across the place-
de-Saint-Sulpice. The trees were just coming into leaf; the
shutters visible behind the barish branches. Along a cobbled
side street, Winston staggered (rather drunk) with Olivia on
his back. He was playing around, exaggerating his stagger,
when I saw O. in slow motion slide head forward toward the
stones. Siamon made a dive to catch her, stumbled, and
landed on his face. Winston managed to break O's fall –
bending low – and she was unhurt. But Siamon's knee was
bleeding, and stiffened as we went along, so Madeleine's
story was cut short by our goodbyes.

Olivia called Winston 'Mr Er . . .' because she could not
remember his name. She had a computer game which they
bent over during the meal. He has a way with children and
should have been a father. I thought of Winston's child who
would have been 2 years older than O., a talking, sportive
child. O. has the power, bounce, and opinion that his child
would have had in its unfolded genes. Phillippa says that he
will never be a father because he can't replace Romy. There
is life-long sorrow and, what I did not expect, anger: not
only a dull rage that R. shouldn't be with him always, but
the more ordinary crossness of a husband whose wife is exas-
perating and unwilling to change. The anger is hot and still
unresolved. He smokes and drinks heavily; gets aggressive
when he's had too much. He told us comic stories of his
hairbreadth dashes to catch planes, says 'I don't like to wait,'
but enjoys, I think, the sheer sport of beating a record. How
strangely, after 12 years, the memories stir. He brings Romy

back when he tells a story and sinks back laughing. She used to laugh in that way, with a kind of helpless and tolerant mirth at her own follies. We'd tell each other stories, making the past, giving it shape and point. Romy is the collaborator in her biography. I simply relay her oral performance. She rarely wrote; there are too few letters. She was a speaker – utterly uninhibited – a speaker lying on beds and sofas with other women who would all be crowing with laughter; a speaker on the telephone (with my father, pacing in annoyance as he waited, saying, 'telephones are for messages').

Oxford. Monday, 18 April 1988: Handed in the revises to OUP this morning, and can now, at last, think of that day with Winston and Madeleine: Sunday a week ago. Driving to an outdoor market, Winston mentioned a crash they had two years ago, while racing to catch a plane. Madeleine's leg was injured; the car irretrievable.

'Is your leg healed?' I asked.

'Not really,' she said, but so casually that it only occurred to me afterwards how selfless she is. It must be hard to be the comfort of a broken-hearted man – for he is still that, as I learnt later that day.

'I like Madeleine,' I said, as Winston and I strolled ahead at the flea market.

'She's good to me,' Winston said. 'I'm difficult.'

'You are?'

'Yes. Difficult.'

There are times when his manner changes – he is self-willed, even reckless. Madeleine's calm was, then, an achievement. She accepts him with his dangerous edge – a surrender that is unquestioning not out of weakness but out of complete sympathy. If she appears uncritical, she is not without her dignity. She would not lower the relationship in her own or our eyes. During lunch, W. was tickling Olivia who sat next to him.

'Do you like tickling?' he asked.

'No!' shouted Olivia.

'Madeleine does,' he teased her across the table. 'She likes it very much.'

She made a slight movement of reserve. This was not the basis for her, however much he chose to cast her as his physical comfort, along with the whole bottle of red wine which he was, at that moment, consuming. I came to Paris to find Winston and discovered Madeleine. It was Madeleine who lifted Olivia from her fall; and who said quietly, 'it's not Olivia's fault' when Winston nearly crashed the car as he leaned over to play with the excited child, and Siamon, trapped in the back, became angry.

Our last outing was to the flea market. W. and M. bought two seals for their collection with much debate and delay while S. wished to start for the airport. Suddenly, Winston walked me away, put his arm around me and said, stroking my cheek, 'It's been so long.' Then he was weeping, silently, for Romy. 'Life's a shit,' he said, meaning that he had tried to win her for so long and she had died too soon after they had begun to be happy. He returned to our meeting at Heathrow Airport in January 1969 – not a memory I enjoy: I felt a worm.

Monday, 6 June 1988: I saw Romy again last night, for the first time in many years. Winston was there too and, in my dream, he kissed me as he did at Orly Airport – for her. Romy was 'Flora' in my dream: blooming, restored, looking again like a very young Brigitte Bardot. Her hair was done in intricate plaits which ended in two bunches, tied with neat, small bows on either side of her face: that ripe-schoolgirl look of the '50s. Then I felt she had withdrawn in a way that was confirmed by the elaborateness of her hair-do (withdrawn as Ellie was, once, wrapped in her turban, when we went to the Round House for dinner) – and yet, neither of us could forget the bond of school-days when there was complete trust and the abandon of shared thoughts.

Did Romy appear last night because Anthony Sheil [the literary agent] asked me to come to London and see him about 'a publisher's suggestion'? It will be another biography. Did Romy come to call me back to what I really want to do?

I began this book during the long vacation of 1988 at the Trudeau Institute in the Adirondacks. Never had I written so freely as I drew on Romy's words. Her sharing came to me now, not as a private knack, but as a triumph of women's tradition and portent of women to be. No sooner had I touched on this than it was interrupted by a series of phone-calls from a 'researcher' at *Time* magazine. She was bent on getting information on T S Eliot for a piece on his centenary. She posed a set of controversial issues to occupy my mind between calls, and intermittently, over two days, her tearing questions raced through Eliot's life. The effect was to ransack years of real research. In the piece that appeared, the careful structure of truth had been reduced to a set of biographical clichés, translated into hypercute jargon. When I protested to the Editor-in-Chief, he had various women reply that such was their 'policy'. I could see them in the '80s uniform of women's power, manikins in rigid suits with padded shoulders, mouthing the language of 'policy' on the model of the boss. Eventually, the 'researcher' wrote to disown responsibility for what she, too, termed 'policy'. I wondered if there could be such a thing as telephone rape, conducted by a member of my own sex? The tangle with *Time* left a smirch beyond its apparent triviality. I put notions of sharing aside, and wrote a set of lectures for the following term. Then, after a while, Romy and her promise returned.

In September 1988 I went to speak on 'The American Eliot' at Princeton. On the plane to Newark, New Jersey, I talked to 'Romy' rather than 'Flora', a person of my own age, who could look back from the same point at the life she had helped to shape:

But for you, Romy, I would not have been a candidate for the mated existence; I would have been, for a long time, a subject of family conclaves (which they would have enjoyed) about improving my appearance and manner, along the lines of Press advice, when I was 14, to be less of a prude. I should have been, according to family prediction, a Miss Prim of a nursery teacher, waiting around, after friends had married, for some second-rate husband who would have me. That goes back 30 years: at 17 the private life gave way – and all the more irresistibly because it was so unlikely – to the shared existence: one in which a man declared at the outset that there were standards to be met. I was to work, not be a housewife; and to write: biography, he decided, would suit me. His effect was like that of Night-Sister at the John Radcliffe when Olivia was born who marched in to review the case of another, rather sleepy new-born who was too lazy to eat. 'We *expect* things of you,' she told the baby in bracing tones.

So I worked; S. was in his element as adviser: exacting, severe, encouraging. He wants me to write serious biography, not this indulgence about you of whom he disapproved. He makes me cut descriptions of Phil's food which you, I know, would have appreciated. But I give in when he says, 'You don't want to write a Good Food Guide to Grief.' Sometimes, he does laugh and say: 'Go on. It's not true, but it makes a story.'

Cape Town. Friday, 16 December 1988: We came yesterday. When I opened the *Cape Times*, I saw that Mr Gevint died on 14 December and had been buried that very day. I went to Reggie and Daphne's house for prayers; later in the evening, we sat on the stoep. Their elder daughter, Jeanette, aged 16, sat with us. With her bright hair tumbled up and pointed little nose, she was like Flora.

'I love poetry,' she confided shyly. She had read 'Do not

go gentle into that good-night' to her grandfather when he was ailing.

Reggie said: 'When the doctors told him it was imposs-ible, he still went to the business for two or three hours every day, and he died there, as he would have wanted, amongst his customers. That was life to him.'

Jeanette said that she had poured out herself in a school essay. 'I thought it was the best essay I'd ever done, but my teacher said it was rubbish.' Shades of Flora and Miss Tyfield in 1958.

Oxford. February 1989: I wrote to David [in Israel] after Mr Gevint's death, and on 29 January he wrote back about his last two weeks with his father: 'His mind was sharp but his body wasn't functioning. As he put it, "I'm like an old crock and there are no more spare parts." He verbalized things about his relationship with me that I had always wanted to hear. Romy & he had a special relationship. She gave him love and he reciprocated. I remember 6 months after her death, he complained of not feeling well. I took him to the doctor who put a hand on Dad's shoulder and said, "Itzhak, what's the matter?" Suddenly, for the first time, I saw my father cry. Sobs wracked him as he cried out: "How could it be that my daughter had to go before me?"'

I wrote back: '. . . I still think of her a lot, and have started writing down some memories of our school-days which I'd like to show you when next we meet.'

I went to South Africa one more time, in December 1989. There followed some unexpected encounters. The increasing closeness to Romy, as I wrote of her, freed me to speak with Phillippa on her balcony, with Reggie in the sunroom, with Leonora, Rosie Kunene, and Mark in Johannesburg, and with Hu and Berj at Willow Stream. It was a voicing summer. Together, we broke the wall of silence that was first breached by Winston in Paris. All, it appeared, had come to need this as much as I. And some surprising and rather adverse views did, in turn, break into my own.

It was Saturday, 23 December, and we had arrived in Cape Town the night before. Phillippa, Robert, Peter Keating, Bonnie and I sat outside Phil's white house, overlooking the sea. I shall refrain from describing Phillippa's apricot tart with almonds. She and Bonnie wore white shirts tied up in front over white skirts with spotless white sand-shoes. I felt wrong in my English clothes: a green brocade waistcoat with Granny's cream blouse. Phillippa was talking of her daughter, an artist:

'Jann and her friends don't care about overseas any more. Our local scene is their material – they're proud of our vigour, our colours. They find England tired.'

I thought of the last Degree Day in the Sheldonian. I was seated next to Basil Shepstone, an ex-South African who was Dean of Degrees for Wolfson College. During the procession of university dignitaries, he said in an undertone:

'I went to the South African Embassy this week and – you won't believe this – there was a poster saying "The Dismemberment of Apartheid".'

'Propaganda,' I dismissed it beneath the slow pomp of the organ.

'Even so, such a poster would have been unthinkable before the election of De Klerk. Last month, leaders of the Broederbond itself met the ANC here in Britain.'

Could a lifetime's assumptions be overturned? Could apartheid possibly come to a peaceful end? I turned again to Basil: 'Shall we go back?' It was a joke, for were we not here, in place, in our English *sub fusc* – cap, gown, and hood – in Wren's great domed hall where we had planted ourselves (we had thought) for life? And yet – it was not a joke, for had we not always longed to go back? Weren't the mountains and valleys part of us, and the live-hot, vehement people – Rosie Kunene, and Romy, and Rolf of the *vetkersmense* – more part of us than twenty-six years of civilized people and famous places . . .?

'. . . Romy changed my life,' Bonnie was saying. 'It was more than influence. But she was possessive of her friends.'

'Possessive isn't the word,' said Phillippa loyally. 'She brought friends together. She wanted us to enjoy one another when she wasn't there.'

Bonnie said thoughtfully: 'It's because of her, isn't it, that we're here together? Still, with men she couldn't let go. It's my belief Mark never got over her – and perhaps (Winston wouldn't like me to say this) she never entirely got over him.'

'But she was happy, entirely happy with Winston,' I interrupted. 'She said so often.'

'Yes, but that doesn't preclude the other.'

I recalled her outrage after Mark married, when she realized they would never see each other again.

'I saw her dancing, once, in Johannesburg,' said Bonnie. 'She was what men would call "all woman" – the most sensual woman I've ever seen.'

'Yet she said to me', I recalled, 'only three men had really attracted her. She was not promiscuous, despite her manner; she was highly selective, and with both sexes. You felt chosen and, if so, compelled to surrender wholly to her. When Robert called you, Phil, she said that she felt nothing less than fury. She resented the wifely duty that took you even momentarily away from her. I think she feared this herself: to be tethered; the spirit chained and changed by the obligations of wedlock.'

Phillippa mused under the white shade: 'She made you feel special because *she* was special. If she chose you, you – who thought yourself ordinary – had to be special too. She would phone ahead and say, "I want to see you so badly that I *must* see you alone." She would "charge in" and sweep you away from families who were irrelevant to those special times together.'

'She was so *possessive*,' burst out Bonnie. 'She wanted everyone to *herself*. Mark still suffers from those battles against his family, her determination to have him entirely to herself.'

*

'Do you have dreams?' Reggie asked, a few days later.

In his dreams he continued to play out the fights with his sister. He shook his slightly greying red head, and sat with the bowed shoulders; then laughed over the pressure of Feige, working through their mother, on all the family.

'I, too, couldn't bring myself to get married – I don't know why. Here I was, thirty, and I didn't want to lose Daphne, but I couldn't go through with it. Feige's children did what she wanted – except for the only son, Marvin, who never married. Like him, like Romy, I just – couldn't face – a wedding. And I think, also, we were spoilt – it took us too long to grow up. In the end, I said to Daphne, "I'll do it if you leave me out of everything and get it over in three weeks." She did. That's when Romy shocked Feige and shamed her parents by that flaming dress that showed her thighs.'

In January, I went with Phillippa to a wine farm at Constantia, one of the first to be established. 'Buitenverwachting' was built in 1695 by Simon van der Stel. We had our drinks on the back stoep, overlooking the rising slopes of the vineyards below the peaks that looked down on the leafy lanes and white gables of the old Dutch farmsteads of the Constantia Valley.

'Mark phoned this week,' I said. 'He agreed to meet. I hadn't expected him to reply to my letter. It would have been understandable if he didn't wish to go back to the past.'

'No, it's good to talk; especially if we talk of the little, funny things. It's as though she's with us again.'

'When I asked Reggie if it was too hard, he said that he did want to talk of her. Yet, though words came, he seemed on the point of tears. Is there, do you think, a certain piety in keeping silent about the dead?'

'In *War and Peace*, when Prince Andrei has died, Natasha says: "Do you know, I am often afraid that by not speaking of him for fear of desecrating our feelings, we forget him." And then his sister asks, "Is it possible to forget?" Do you remember,' Phillippa asked, 'you gave me that book?'

I nodded. 'Natasha and Princess Maria felt that what they had lived through could not be expressed in words and that any reference to Prince Andrei profaned "the mystery that had been accomplished before their eyes". So they would, as it were, halt at the barriers that fenced off what might not be spoken about. This preserved the purity of their grief.'

'Now and then,' Phillippa went on, 'I say to some stranger, "I had a sister who died. She was twenty-one." Then they say, "how terrible," and then they forget it and talk of something else. I don't blame them. Yet I feel bad – as though I had given her away, as though I had used her for mere conversation. Do you understand? There's no way to convey what it meant to me.'

'Then we shouldn't speak. I shouldn't be doing this to Romy.'

'Oh, but you *should*. It makes me sad that I can't share Eileen. My children were too small, and there's no one else. The other day, I found a folder that she gave me and in it were recipes I'd written at that time, some of our mother's, and a letter to Eileen from Romy – it was good to go back to that . . .'

'Exactly how I felt this year, reading her letters. It was right to have waited: before this, I wasn't ready or able to speak. None of us could have spoken in this way until now.'

I flew to Johannesburg on Friday, 12 January. At the airport, Berjulie waited with the chauffeur, a huge basket of flowers, and three kinds of home-baked biscuits – her special gestures of welcome for members of family. She still looked amazingly young with the brisk swing of her dark hair, her sparkling blue eyes, and quick directions as we retrieved the baggage. Then, at Willow Stream, there was Hubert's thoughtful face between the candles. After prayers and dinner, we sat on the stoep with the moths dashing against the lamps and, below us, the sweep of the lawn towards the willows that clustered over the falling stream. Faintly, through the growing darkness, came the murmur of its wandering course.

'From 1964 to 1974, Romy lived here,' I said. 'Was it her hectic decade?'

Hubert spoke with characteristic measure. His thoughts, as ever, were formed and final. 'Romy was seeking in regard to life, and seeking, too, the right husband: these were her seeking years. After her marriage, she went to Paris to seek further. This search made her exciting: her impressions, her redhead impetuosity. If I were you, I should say that those whom the gods love die young.'

He watched me draw back, and tried again.

'Had she lived, there would have been no story. Winston lived with her during the years of love, and then lost her. It was unnatural – and wonderful. He can never forget this: for him, a lifetime, because he has lived with her memory, her *young* memory. For the greatest enemy of love is time.'

He spoke his elegy in soft, slow tones. His was a romantic Romy, yet one bent on 'finding a man who would be the best she could do'.

Had Romy manufactured an image that left men stirred with the romance of youth? Leonora, next morning, took a more critical view of Romy's insistent allure: 'Attention-getting, the traditional substitute for honest sex,' she said, black eyes snapping. Where Bonnie pointed to Romy's possessiveness, Leo saw an insatiable hunger for reassurance. And she deplored, as Winston had done, Romy's indifference, even resistance, to the claims of mothers.

Rosie Kunene had been a reluctant conspirator against the mothers. Thoughtlessly, Romy had not scrupled to force upon Rosie certain partisan actions. Given Winston's loyalty to his mother, it had been unfair to Rosie as a Zulu, dependent on Winston for her pass. And yet Rosie spoke of her time with Romy as 'the first and last'.

On 13 January, she sat waiting near the entrance to the Rosebank Hotel, with its piped muzak, waiters, and whites lounging about the pool, around which the glassed lobby circled: she sat patient in a black blouse and blue wool beret. South Africa was uproarious with 'the post-apartheid society' – it was two weeks before the release of Nelson Mandela and the unbanning of the

ANC – yet the presence of apartheid was palpable as we passed through that lobby. A group of blacks was having drinks there, but they sat separate, as whites sat separate. As we settled together outside, at the pool, we were conscious of eyes. Rosie was sceptical of current optimism; to her it was facile, living as she did amongst whites who objected to the sight of her grandchild playing on their premises. What appeared to me insufferable, she regarded with the steady resignation – 'what can you do?' – of the woman who is inured to prejudice. Rosie alerted me to the prejudice of gender as well as race: the exploitation of the black woman by the black man, which is unpublicized by the reductive alignments of the international press but remains, as ever, pervasive in Africa. Rosie typified the black woman who brings up her children on her own because her husband is not to be found when it comes to support. Neither tribal law nor white men's law attends to her problems.

What the state had offered her children was an education which designed them for servility: where R2,508 was spent on a white child, R476 was spent on hers. What the state had offered her since 1956 were the Pass Laws that would deport her to KwaZulu if she lost her job, and 'Job Reservation', the law that reserved good jobs for whites, preferably Afrikaners. Women like Rosie were forced to be servants. These were often required to 'live in' with the result that mothers were compelled to separate from the children they worked to support. It was customary for servants to be on duty from early in the morning until after dinner, with Thursday afternoon off, and alternate Sundays after they had cleared up the long midday meal. Since the Group Areas Act kept the children in locations at a distance from town, and since transport was slow – the crowded buses passing the woman waiting and waiting at the stop – it was often impossible for such a woman to visit her children in the time allowed. Even liberals paid wages that were below subsistence level ('seeing that she takes [food] for herself') and housed her in an outdoor room which was tiny and airless, a fraction of the size of the garage which housed their cars. 'They have different needs,' liberals reassured one another.

It is rare for an abandoned wife to return to her parental home. In traditional society, a prospective husband paid a bride-price, *lobola*, in the form of cattle. If a wife returned home, the wealth she had brought her father would still be there. More recently, *lobola* takes the form of money – about R3,000 for an educated woman. This is usually gone by the time a marriage ends. A woman returning with children would present new mouths to feed. Without a remaining sign of her contribution to the household, they would appear a liability. 'The manifold problems of women in black societies have barely begun to emerge, and for the present there is no doing away with *lobola*,' said Sandra Burman, a South African lawyer who has written on the problems of black women. 'What is needed is a drastic reform of *lobola*, turning it into an insurance scheme for the woman entering marriage.'

With Romy's resistance in mind, I asked Rosie about the Zulu wedding.

'When a Zulu girl leaves her parents' house, there's crying but you have to go.'

'Would it be possible to refuse?'

Rosie laughed: 'How? How can you refuse? You can't.'

As we talked it was still bright at 5 o'clock on that summer afternoon. Rosie sat calmly, rooted in herself and her people – the only black who was a guest, not a servant, amidst the whites who languished over the glamour of imported fictions as they dangled their feet in the pool. Rosie still cooked and cleaned for a member of the Black Sash, Mrs Basson, to whom she had passed when Romy left South Africa in 1974. The centre of Rosie's life was now her epileptic grandson of ten who lived with her in order to attend a special school. She was passionately grateful to Mrs Basson for getting the child into this white-run school, and for allowing him to share her three-quarter bed in one of the rooms for live-in servants that were attached to the block of flats. Other whites, as I said, complained to the manager: it lowered the

standing of the flats for a black child to be seen in the grounds —
as though black people were residents. The manager therefore
asked Rosie to keep the child indoors. So there they lived, in the
narrow passage of airless space (hot in summer, chill in winter)
between the bed along the one wall and the single wardrobe and
small cupboard along the other. There, Rosie cooked on her
primus on her days off when she was not to use the kitchen.

Yet Rosie, like Mandela, Sisulu, Mbeki, and Sobukwe, did not
appear to be embittered. As Benjamin Pogrund put it in a biography of Sobukwe: 'The patience of blacks, and for so long their
non-violence, has been a South African miracle.' It surprised me,
the absence of hate. It was as though Rosie, who had summoned
the vigour to support her children on her own, had the life that
had gone out of protected women who lay limp from perpetual
sun around the pool. Rosie's wide smile broke over her face at the
thought of Romy who had her own core of life and never thought
to distance herself from any person.

'Romy was the first somebody to let my friends enjoy
together in the kitchen — to set table and use dishes.' It was
common for servants to use the discarded and chipped plates.
'Winston, he collected the cracked plates, broke them, and
threw them in the bin. Usually friends must stay at the back.
Sometimes, I stand at the door with friends, and Romy she say:
"What's wrong with you? Here are chairs. Why don't you come
in?" Then she sit down, talk, laugh, join the tea or offer drinks.'
Winston, too, did not behave in the usual way. 'He is a quiet
somebody. He never shout. If he gets cross, you never see he gets
cross. When he make some change, he pat my shoulder. He
notice my face. He say:

'"Why do you look like that? Are you all right?"

'"Yes," I say.

'"You don't sound like it's all right. You must tell us." They
show me you must never hide yourself from them. They notice
me very good.'

She still had the communicativeness that Romy valued. She still had her vitality and her wide smile, but she was certain that a special part of her life was over – her rapport with Romy.

To be in Johannesburg was to discover the way Romy had surrounded herself with talkers. An abundance of memories presented the problem of synthesis. In the different case of Rose, the mystery only deepened. Her eldest daughter wrote from Jerusalem:

                                                    23 January 1990

Dear Lyndall,

   I received your address from my father who told me about your connection with my mother, Rose, and who suggested that I write to you.

   As you know from my poem, the loss of my mother affected me greatly. I really don't know anything about your connection with her, but I would appreciate it if you could write to me and perhaps fill me in about what she was like. I must say that I don't know much about her, except certain things that I remember and what a few people have mentioned in passing . . .

   Best wishes,

      Yours sincerely,

         Deborah Klein

When I had written to people I had hoped to see in Johannesburg, Ronnie Klein was quick to reply with a long-distance phone-call from his consulting-room. He came to the Rosebank Hotel, with its tinny, unrelenting muzak, on a Sunday afternoon, 14 January, bringing his two younger daughters. As I came out of the lift, I saw a young woman with a rounder face than Rose, and her darker hair fashionably rumpled, yet it was Rose's round eyes that met mine. This was the second daughter, Lisa. Next to her sat Julia, with a waterfall of brown tress to one side of her neck. She had been two years old when her mother

had died. She was quiet, and it seemed to me that she was waiting
to be told – something, that in fact they all had come for something that was not in my power to give.

Ronnie was proud of 'the girls' he had brought up on his own.
Lisa argued against 'girls'. When did 'girls' stop being an objective
term and become condescension? Was there a cut-off point when
girls became 'women'? Ronnie enjoyed sparring with the politi-
cized Lisa. Though slightly greying, he had the casual manner of
the young: blue jeans and chewing-gum. The gum gave a shy man
something to do. He spoke in a strong South African accent with
ready, rather challenging opinions – the daughters had to spar if
they were not to be meek. Lisa held her own with a quick retort,
puffing a cigarette and running her fingers through her chopped
hair. Julia gave sweet, deprecating smiles of disbelief at Ronnie's
darts.

Ronnie, still a leading obstetrician, criticized natural childbirth. He thought fathers unsuited to be present. A friend, he
conceded, might provide more support. I said it had been 'a comfort' to have Siamon with me.

'No. No!' said Ronnie, waving him mentally away.

He was thin, determined, and the sparring guarded – whether
he wished this or not – his privacy. I could not but respect it. He
had brought a packet of memorabilia, mostly photographs, and
dwelt on two events. The first was the visit to France to celebrate
Rose as Today's Woman. His role as escort had been that of 'a
spare wheel', he said rather proudly. Then he outlined, with
remarkable directness, the more curious aspects of Rose's dying:
the romance of leukaemia; the dying words. Like Ellie, she had
faced mortality. At the age of thirty-three, leaving three small
children, she had been able to assure her husband in a way that
came 'from the soul' that hers had been 'a good life'.

But when I pressed Ronnie about her wish to write, I drew a
blank. Had this vanished? Had she contrived to hide, from her
husband, or even from herself, this need?

I had left Rose suspended and about to vanish into marriage, into the magazine image of Today's Woman, and then into death. I knew by the end of this visit that I would have to let her go.

On the day of departure, 16 January, I met Mark. I had not seen him for twenty-three years. He came to breakfast: a professor now, and attractive as ever with sensitive lines around his mouth and the used-looking face of a man who has employed his mind not merely for study but for awareness. We didn't waste words; we leapt to exploratory talk. Was Romy too demanding? Mark had found her 'overpowering':

'She put unfair pressure on me to throw up work and jump on a plane to New York.' His active exasperation was oddly like Winston's.

'Perhaps I've idealized her,' I said. 'I saw her as free, listening to her own rhythms, doing what she wanted.'

'But *was* she doing what she wanted?' Mark put it rhetorically.

'She could be single-minded.'

'I'm not sure that she did know what she wanted,' he insisted.

'She wanted to be open to possibilities – this struck us as tremendously daring.'

'It was.' He nodded. 'And she retained that.'

There was no need to make conversation or think up questions or put him at ease. We talked together as two who had been possessed by the same person who had disappeared and left us with her impact on our lives, conscious that whatever we were or had become, she had – to some large extent – made us. Over our meeting she presided, having brought us there, to that corner table, with the pink napkins and the marmalade. We were adepts at Romy-talk.

'I haven't talked like this in years,' Mark said. Her shade directed the familiar issues: should she, *could* she have married him? Had he done right to seek another tie in which he could be the giver, not the consumed?

'Winston', Mark thought, 'provided an anchor.' He recalled that, in Romy's early days with Winston, she 'would knock IBM.

Winston was stronger than I: he could stand that and still want Romy, see beyond that.'

Mark went on: 'I was haunted by her. I am unable to accept her death – Romy's death – which I . . . which I . . . there was a certain unfinished business. In our good moments, we'd talked of living in Paris; we'd have children there, at the American Hospital. Hemingway and Fitzgerald went there, and it features in their works. That dream of Paris caught hold of her.'

'*Why* did she die?' I asked suddenly. 'She was always well.'

I thought of her getting jaundice so conveniently when she could not face a wedding in 1969. Could the final illness have been a result of stress of some kind, perhaps the unreadiness for motherhood that Winston foresaw? Little is known, as yet, about the links of illness with states of mind. Winston had satisfied Romy with physical love, had given her a rock-like strength, and devotion, and the child she wanted, and yet, Bonnie claimed, she never really got over Mark – Mark who arrived in Paris six months before her death and said that he could not bear to see her. Romy herself declared her stability. For this commitment, she and Winston had struggled for eight years. But I wondered at the tenacity of dreams.

Imaginative versus physical love: which was stronger in its effects? Had Romy kept imaginative love alive by refusing to sleep with Mark, by not marrying for so many years, and then – irrevocably – by dying young? Could it have been like Joyce's story, 'The Dead': the persistent, overpowering memory of lost love in the mind of the contained wife, Gretta, despite her good husband?

And then I remembered, too, that before Romy, Mark had an affair with a married woman, a woman of nearly fifty, whose marriage had broken up and who had committed suicide. Her death, Romy's, and his depressed wife: why was this man surrounded by pain? Did he draw women by a promise of understanding, without the power to carry this through? And had the promise of Mark been more painful to Romy than the mass of men who offered no promise at all?

Mark was saying: '... The first time I went back to Cape Town – it was December '76 – we were in Bonnie's bungalow at Clifton – it was a nightmare. Cars would glide about, and I couldn't believe that Romy was dead. All her friends, Ellie especially, were always driving to one another – two, three, four times over the hill and round the mountain – always leaving to go elsewhere, that constant network across the mountain, to see, to talk ... There was an intensity in Ellie's driving that didn't seem to have a *basis*. Romy's activity had been real.' It was an astute distinction: Ellie was filling the empty spaces; Romy renewing her network of contact.

When he left, we exchanged addresses – we would continue. In Cape Town and Johannesburg, Romy's old network sprang to life at a touch. This was no ordinary biographical research; it was the renewing of bonds which was, to Romy, the essential act of life.

12

Words

What began in dreams and acts of memory has become, in its final stage, collaborative. What was written after breaking the silence in South Africa at the beginning of 1990 has been an attempt to fuse the words of others with my own biased hoard. We exchanged our stories of Romy, Rose, and Ellie, a continuation, a recovery it seemed to me, of the vital part of friendship: we had circled a passing phase of life, had recognized in what we called 'stories' the muddle of our indeterminate existence – trying to *see* in the Conrad way that Rose discovered at sixteen – and had drawn closer as we spoke.

Different speakers have challenged a version of the past that tugged Romy towards my own life. 'Partners' was shaped by Leonora; 'Futures' by Winston and Rosie Kunene; 'Moves' by David Gevint and Bonnie Keating. And 'Memories' could not have been written without the advancing dead, their words nearer, louder, the resounding echo of the past.

Two events, in 1990, affected this stage: first, the events in South Africa, beginning on 11 February with the release of Mandela after twenty-seven years in prison, setting off an inexorable process of political change. This has barely begun. What will happen to white rulers who for more than three centuries practised what J M Coetzee has called 'blindness to the colour black'? What will happen to blacks who now murder one another in battles for future power? Over nine thousand blacks have been killed by other blacks since 1984, and hundreds of thousands made homeless. The townships and squatter camps have become, in the words of Sisulu, 'the killing fields'. Can they defy their history in order to share power, as Afrikaners – speaking, now, not as '*muishonde*' [skunks] but from their 'higher ground' – make their astonishing, belated offer to share the country? Afrikaners recover the soul of their nation, in place of the debasing effects of power, through their capacity for conversion. For they may do what no other ruling power has ever done: voluntarily share power, suspecting absolute power to be unworkable as well as evil. If the Great Trek was their emergence as a nation, and the Boer war their trial by fire, this is their dark night of the soul. They are attempting to purge forty-two years of an evil regime by casting themselves in the wilderness en route to a new land.

After twenty-five years, Siamon went to work in South Africa. Early in March, he left to teach in Cape Town and to present work with an Indian Rhodes Scholar, Satish Keshav, at a meeting in Pretoria. There, he joined his ex-pupil Taole Mokoena, a Sotho surgeon who had done a further doctorate at the Sir William Dunn School of Pathology in Oxford.

Siamon's first letter spoke of renewed contact with Afrikaners, whose language had once been his own. He wrote from Pretoria:

I have been catapulted into the past and future simultaneously. Easy conversations with friendly, open

hearted Afrikaner doctors of the platteland with their
stories of country practice and distant calls-out at night to
all kinds of home and farm, and the striking elegance of
black women (a few GPs and nurses are here because
there is a combined programme with rheumatologists).
There is a great deal of open discussion of hopes, perhaps
not as naïvely optimistic as in England, exploring fears
and prejudice with a frank directness. It is almost as if
people are discovering for the first time that they inhabit
the same country and share a common fate. A bit
disturbing is not only the large-scale violence, perhaps a
sign of social disease, but a recrudescence of overt anti-
Semitism from extreme right-wing whites. The English
here go their imperturbable way, showing slides of
beautiful flowers, interspersed with sound but dull clinical
research.

Satish and I gave a combined 2-talk session which was
well received. Taole appeared with an Indian student in
tow, shy at first, but then quite pleased to share the 'glory'
of the lab-descent. We've chatted quite freely about
everything – last night, as we drove through the streets of
Pretoria, he suddenly said: 'Last time I was here was in the
Central Prison, for 6 months, as a final-year medical
student.' So behind all the talk & wishful thinking, lies a
core of reality – or is it a dream? Strange how little hate
there is, although Taole says I should see the black
commuters returning home by train after a hard day. De
Klerk is the new African hero – a good Boer. The Boer is
admired for his directness – you know where you are with
him, even if for so long he expected you to know your
place: '*kaffer in sy plek*'.

. . . I am more outgoing than usual with these strange-
familiars, but do also miss home. There are always
moments of aloneness, but not the isolation one can feel in
other countries. Yet I am still pleased to live and work in a

civilized society where the values are creativity and merit
rather than material . . .

While he was away, I went to Somerville College on 21 March
to hear a professor from Lesotho, Njabulo Ndebele, author of
Fools and Other Stories (1984).

'The South African stage, at this moment, is full of actors with
many competing scripts,' he began. 'We are witnessing a frantic
entrance of new actors . . . What is in the scripts now? This is the
foremost question of the times.' He went on to say that 'the new'
must remain for a long time undefined. The new is 'a process of
becoming' which would be true also in art. South African writers,
he suggested, had difficulty with conclusions. It was hard to hear
his soft voice from the back of the hall, but I thought he implied
by this that conclusions must remain difficult. There was, he
declared, the need for new forms of art that would take in the
'process of becoming': plays, poems, novels ('and biography', I
added in my notes, 'to see the shape of the past not from the
polarized angle of protest but in view of the change of 1990').

At the end of the talk, a woman in the audience asked his
opinion of the idea of culture as a 'weapon', which Albie Sachs
had recanted in a paper to the ANC in Lusaka in 1989, published
in the *Cape Times* on 15 February 1990. Break free, Sachs urged,
from 'the solemn formulas of commitment that people (like
myself) have tried to impose', to find a new 'cultural vision' that
corresponds to 'the new country and new people that is struggling
to give birth to itself'. Rejecting a language obsessed by the
oppressors and the trauma they imposed, he asked for one that
'bypasses, overwhelms, ignores apartheid, establishing its own
space'.

Ndebele replied along the same lines: 'We need to respond in
more complex ways to South Africa and to a depoliticizing of
experience, without sacrificing political vision. To do this we
should not be using literature as a weapon but as a way of life; we
should not use literature as a form of destruction – this is sterile.

We want to be as inclusive as possible . . . In Soweto, on the day that Mandela was released, there was at a certain point a thin line between celebration and lawlessness. People had cars commandeered by jubilant crowds on the edge of violence – these shades are present all the time. We must talk in a manner that will humanize, in a speech which is a struggle for meaning.'*

I cycled home up the Woodstock Road, between English trees in early blossom, wondering how to bring this book to conclusion, and obscurely comforted by Ndebele's comments on the inconclusiveness of process. Dare I consider myself, still, a South African? Was I ever one? Did that country of the past not belong to its indigenous inhabitants – its animals, its flora, and the extinct Khoisan people, yellow with large bottoms, who had spoken a clicked language with a hundred synonyms for cattle and no word for thanks: those San hunters and Khoikhoi herdsmen who had roamed the spaces of Namaqualand before blacks came from the north and whites from the south? As I passed the entrance to St Anne's College and approached that of St Antony's, I asked myself other unanswerable questions: about the future sharing of South Africa. What, for instance, would be the future for black women whose status in traditional tribal society, as well as in the ANC (except as sycophants of the leadership), has been abysmal?

Lily Becker, a lecturer in social work at the University of Cape Town, said that in 1989 black male students had demanded that women students cook for them as part of the ancestral obligation of one sex to serve the other. There was a furore when the women refused. 'As yet,' said Lily, 'there is no teaching of women's issues as a distinct social problem because the racial problem has been so commanding.' Sandra Burman said that in the squatter camp she visited, it frequently happens that women and children may not have their evening meal until their men return. 'Often, they'd

---

*The speech was on 'Liberation and the Crisis of Culture'. A slightly revised version, without the responses to questions, was printed in the *Southern African Review of Books* (Feb/May 1990), pp. 22–23.

return so late that the children would have fallen asleep. Here we have a particular form of starvation, induced not by lack of food in many cases but by reluctance to waste fuel in cooking twice, and above all by the strong ethic of sharing – no woman must be seen to put her own child first. If an ailing child is taken to a clinic and given vital food, its mother will have to share that food with a large extended family: the ailing child might get only a minute portion.'

Sandra's current work was on illegitimacy. She said that until the '60s girls in some townships were still regularly checked for virginity by older women. 'No one knows why this broke down. It was not the effect of the permissive society but, probably, an increasing move into urban areas. Here, girls often lose their virginity at about fourteen. About seventy per cent of babies born are illegitimate by any system of law. The girls compete for men, who don't permit contraception, partly because they regard fathering as an affirmation of masculinity.'

Of all the oppressed, black women have, arguably, suffered most. Enfranchisement of blacks was refused in 1910, and British women refused to include their black sisters in the Women's Enfranchisement League. Tactfully, Woman's Hour (on the BBC) cut this disagreeable fact which I brought up in the course of an interview on Olive Schreiner, who had made the case for black women. Now, a Xhosa contemporary, Sindiwe Magona, was telling the dauntless story of her emergence. *To My Children's Children* (1990) placed itself in the tradition of Xhosa grandmothers of untold generations who related ancestral stories to stir sleepy children before the fire. Reading this spirited life, I wondered what might be the place of women's stories in Njabulo Ndebele's new culture – would their lives and oral records continue to have the insignificance of 'women's talk' in the outback of literary forms?

Siamon brought back a new biography of Olive Schreiner, in Afrikaans, and he had written his inscription in that language – the unused and almost forgotten language of his childhood. It originated as the kitchen Dutch spoken by slaves and indigenous peoples of the Western Cape; then it was the language of resistance to British imperialism; and then it became the language of the law and the *baas*, a focal point for new resistance. Going back, Siamon wrote: '*My geliefde vrou*' – the words were still there – '*op ons 27ste huweliksdag*.' It was an anniversary present for 7 April.

Soon after, I went to Paris. In December, I had written to Winston about this memoir, and to ask if it were possible to see him. For two months there was no reply. Then, one Sunday night in February, he phoned Oxford from his apartment in Neuilly-sur-Seine. Cool and decisive, he said I might come.

'I've feared that you don't want this,' I said.

'That remains to be seen.'

It seemed a frightful intrusion. I resolved to leave all talk to him – a needless resolve, for it was immediately apparent I was to put myself in his control. Whether he said anything at all would be his decision.

I excused myself at 11 p.m. on the Saturday night after a long day that began with inspecting a possible house for Winston and Madeleine on the outskirts of Paris, followed by minute investigations of an outdoor antiques fair, the national fair of *brocante et jambon* at Chatou. It was a cold, grey day and my toes froze in light shoes. Winston was gentler when I crawled off to bed, damp and coughing.

We talked early the next morning, while Madeleine slept. It lasted no more than half an hour, a set time it seemed, cordoned off from the rest of a social weekend. Winston was candid and exceptionally succinct, with a crisp turn of phrase. He knew exactly what he wished to say.

'What does Madeleine think of the reason for my visit?' I asked at the end.

'I haven't told her,' was the laconic reply. This was the only time that I felt uncomfortable: it seemed deceptive to stay there in the guise of a guest.

When Madeleine woke, we shopped for dinner at the Place-de-Marché at Neuilly and afterwards Winston drove to a scientist in rue de Monsieur to collect antiserum for Siamon's laboratory. Along the Champs-Elysées, the vista opened up of the Arc de Triomphe and, rising beyond it, la Grande Arche, and I thought of Romy's need for vistas which Paris had given her.

Suddenly, Winston parked, and sat back in silence. Where were we? What was happening? Then, slowly, it broke on me that it was the cul-de-sac, passage de la Visitation. I had not recognized it because, in the '70s, the doors to the courtyard at the end of the street had been open. They were closed, now, for security. Here was the familiar, short *passage* and its slice of sky, but the *appartement* itself was hidden, like a shut memory, behind the high wall. Winston had performed this gesture for my sake. He sat still and self-contained in the car. Madeleine was putting up with this, I supposed. It was hard to look and linger.

We unfroze as we drove away from this impossible place. None of us could muster emotions appropriate to the occasion – Winston, in self-protection, had sealed off; Madeleine was left rather unkindly to herself; and I felt nothing but dismay at being unable to feel.

It was a relief to do the ordinary thing, to drink espresso at an outdoor café near Saint-Germain-des-Prés; to walk in the Ile de la Cité; and to return to a dinner of salmon, cooked in wine by Winston, at their home.

'Come on, team,' Winston would say as we left, and 'hullo, home' as we returned. It is a lovely home: much time and energy has gone into polishing old brass and copper, into flooring and tiling. Winston has found some red stained-glass for the bathroom window, and made lamps with left-over pieces. Their apartment is full of *objets* from fairs and sales. Eight of the twenty-five Dali lithographs, newly framed since Romy's time, hang in sequence on the wall. There is a musical doll whose hands move to her tune; a wooden horn gramophone; a seal collection, mounted in a type-tray, on the wall of Winston's study; and

Madeleine's collection of unusual frames with photographs of her English family: her Scottish grandfather in the uniform of the first world war; herself and her sister, little girls in bathing-costumes, leaning forward on their elbows to gaze into the camera. All this blends unobtrusively with the Italian sofa, the green and pink floral cushions, and the flourishing plants. Madeleine has a way with plants; there is not a sick leaf in sight. On the small balcony, she grows rosemary and geraniums.

Madeleine has lived with Winston for thirteen years. She has celebrated her fortieth birthday and continued at IBM, rising from secretary to a position in International Marketing with a secretary of her own. For amusement, she acts Molière in an amateur drama group in which she is the only foreigner. Her French is perfect. She is a keen photographer, and thinks of taking leave to photograph hidden places of Paris. She would like to share her finds with select tourists.

With Winston, she is rather English in her manner, considerate, amused, eyeing him with an indulgent twinkle of mock exasperation when he gets too forceful. He has learnt to laugh at his dominance. 'How dare you make such good fruit salad without consulting me?' he shot at Madeleine during dinner. I gathered that he annoyed her sister by insisting, when they stayed there, on his own regimen. He led our walk in the Ile Saint-Louis on Sunday afternoon, and I had the image of Chauntecleer with the obedient hens – though neither Madeleine nor I am obedient. But we have learnt not to waste steam on trivia. I was obstinate only twice.

The first occasion was when we came upon the seventeenth-century home of Camille Claudel, along the Seine. She had worked there from 1899 to 1913, which date ended her brief career as artist and began the long burial in the asylum – '*la longue nuit de l'internement*', it said on the plaque. Letting Winston go, I lingered over the words of a letter that she had written to her lover, Rodin, in 1886: '*Il y a toujours quelque chose d'absent qui me tourmente.*' Could this, I wondered, speak for Romy and women like her, who cannot accommodate to the given lot: 'There is always something missing which torments me.'

As we crossed the Pont Saint-Louis a street musician was playing the clarinet. A speaker filled in the orchestral parts of Mozart's Clarinet Concerto – blaring too loud, then too soft – and the player fiddled with it anxiously between the solos. It didn't matter: the vivacity of the Seine more than compensated, the neo-classic grace of buildings *sur les quais*, and a serene sky. Winston had said of Romy: 'Paris was her delight. Paris transformed her – there she found herself. There, also, she looked at me with different eyes. I was no longer an emigrant from Vryburg; I was performing in the city of her dreams. In Paris, too, she escaped your group.'

As I met this Romy, who had been distant in her last years, I let Winston press on, again, towards Notre-Dame. I stood on the bridge, and the music swelled and carried her forward, buoyant in the mild sun, her reckless past – the scream, the virginal frenzy, the broken wedding – contained by the graces of Paris. The speaker dimmed, swelled again, and – suddenly – she came close, hiccuping with laughter, laughing wildly as she did at school, shaking back her red curls. It was for this that I came to Paris, without knowing it, not to speak to Winston, nor to visit her home or grave, but to meet her on this bridge in the city of her dreams.

To the beat, she advanced and, beyond her, the round face of Lion's Head, the sun-stroked verges of the Good Hope grounds, and the waves as we bobbed to the shore in 1954; and Rose at the Little Theatre in 1961, putting a gun to her chin in *Sport of My Mad Mother*; and Ellie listening intently in 1966 as I raved in her car. I heard their voices in the roll of the sea, in the wild southeaster, in the street cries of Cape Town, in the light and shadow of Lion's Head, in the rustle of the oak-lined Avenue which we paced from school to town. I range with them over those remembered places. Have people, apart from those faraway people, ever existed for me?

Voices rise, words come, from the country of the past.

MARY WOLLSTONECRAFT
A NEW GENUS

Lyndall Gordon

Author of *The Vindication of the Rights of Women*, campaigner, wife and mother, Mary Wollstonecraft (1759–97) was the first of a new kind of being, 'a new genus'.

In this exciting new biography, Lyndall Gordon proposes that at each stage of this extraordinary life – as teacher, writer, traveller, – Mary Wollstonecraft was an original. She had advanced ideas on education and her attitudes to single motherhood, family responsibilities, working life, domestic affections, the importance of friendship and sexual relationships now look astonishingly modern. She tested the new ways man and woman might live together. 'Imagination must lead the senses, not the senses the imagination', she told her lover, Gilbert Imlay, and repeated to her husband, William Godwin.

And though she died young, her new genus lived on in the lives of her daughters and immediate heirs, Mary Shelley, Frank Imlay, Claire Clairmont, and Margaret Mount Cashell, and later again in women writers such as George Eliot and Virginia Woolf.

Yet from the time of her death in 1797 until now she has acquired a reputation as unstable and loose, a wild woman doomed to extinction. Lyndall Gordon's biography, the first to enter into the full scope of her brave and exhilarating experiment, probes these myths and vindicates her life in accord with Wollstonecraft's own values.

This account covers her period as a governess to the aristocracy in Ireland; as self-supporting writer in London; as on-the-scene observer of the French Revolution; and as a daring traveller to Scandinavia on the trail of an unsolved crime: the disappearance of a cargo of Bourbon silver. Like a detective story, the biography follows a newly clarified trail leading from Norway to Hamburg, when Mary Wollstonecraft uncovered the mystery of missing treasure, the true nature of Gilbert Imlay, and her own delight in travel.

From a biographer of brilliant repute, this is the remarkable story of Mary Wollstonecraft and her particular genius.

Now you can order superb titles directly from Virago

☐   Mary Wollstonecraft   Lyndall Gordon   £25.00

The prices shown above are correct at time of going to press. However, the publishers reserve the right to increase prices on covers from those previously advertised, without further notice.

Virago

Please allow for postage and packing: **Free UK delivery.**
Europe: add 25% of retail price; Rest of World: 45% of retail price.

To order any of the above or any other Virago titles, please call our credit card orderline or fill in this coupon and send/fax it to:

Virago, PO Box 121, Kettering, Northants NN14 4ZQ
Fax: 01832 733076   Tel: 01832 737526
Email: aspenhouse@FSBDial.co.uk

☐   I enclose a UK bank cheque made payable to Virago for £ . . . .
☐   Please charge £ . . . . . . to my Visa/Access/Mastercard/Eurocard

Expiry Date ☐☐☐☐   Switch Issue No. ☐☐

NAME (BLOCK LETTERS please) . . . .
ADDRESS . . . .

. . . .

. . . .

Postcode . . . . Telephone . . . .
Signature . . . .

Please allow 28 days for delivery within the UK. Offer subject to price and availability.

Please do not send any further mailings from companies carefully selected by Virago ☐